D1123236

The Mind of Bill James

The Mind of Bill James

How a Complete Outsider Changed Baseball

Scott Gray

DOUBLEDAY
New York London Toronto Sydney Auckland

PUBLISHED BY DOUBLEDAY
a division of Random House, Inc.

DOUBLEDAY and the portrayal of an anchor with a dolphin are registered trademarks
of Random House, Inc.

Excerpts from *The Bill James Baseball Abstracts* 1982, 1987, and 1988 by Bill James,
copyright © 1982, 1987, and 1988 by Bill James. Used by permission of Ballantine
Books, a division of Random House, Inc.

Copyright © 2006 by Scott Gray

Cataloging-in-Publication Data is on file with the Library of Congress.

ISBN 0-385-51464-6

Book design by Chris Welch

All Rights Reserved

PRINTED IN THE UNITED STATES OF AMERICA

1 3 5 7 9 10 8 6 4 2

First Edition

Subject: Red Sox Jubilation

Dear Bill,
thankyouthankyouthankyouthankyouthankyou.

Scott,
yourewelcomeanequalnumberoftimes. Iwillpasson-
thethankyoustothosewhodeservethem.
Bill

Take nothing on its looks; take everything on evidence. There's no better rule.

—Charles Dickens, *Great Expectations*

When you have grasped its meaning with your will,
then tenderly your eyes will let it go . . .

—Rainer Maria Rilke

Sabermetrics: from SABR (Society for American Baseball Research). Coined c. 1980 by Bill James, sabermetrician. The search for new knowledge about baseball; the systematic study of baseball questions. ("What I do isn't 'running a computer' or 'checking stats' any more than what a scout does is just driving a car and scoring games." —*Bill James*)

Contents

Preface

We shouldn't be too confident about the things we think we
know. —Bill James, *The Baseball Book* 1992

Bill James first influenced my thinking in 1983, when I read
his *Baseball Abstract,* but my favorite piece of Jamesian wisdom
comes at the end of Ben McGrath's 2003 *New Yorker* profile. Trying to
explain the connection between his obsession with crime stories and
baseball, Bill wrote in an e-mail, "I feel a need to be reminded, day in
and day out, how easy it is for a fantasy to grab hold of your foot like a
rope, and dangle your life upside down while brigands go through
your pockets. The essential message of crime books is: Deal with the
life you've got. Solve the problems you have, rather than fantasizing
about a life without them."

My first Red Sox memories are from October 2, 1978, when the
Yankees beat Boston in a one-game division playoff. My love of the
Sox was innocent until that afternoon, but the shock of Bucky Dent's
game-deciding home run introduced me to the fact that life isn't
a fantasy and baseball is complicated. My response to heartbreak
remains, as Bill phrases it, the horrible compulsion to understand
what happened.

Bill grew up rooting for the hapless Kansas City A's. In 1977, following college and a stretch in the army during Vietnam, he started
self-publishing books of baseball analysis. At first his ideas were as
popular with the baseball establishment as a drunken garbage worker
at a sorority mixer. But recently the ideas have taken hold in a handful
of baseball front offices. With the Red Sox winning the World Series
two years after hiring Bill as a consultant, a study of his life, work, and
influence seems in order.

Bill points out that people like simple explanations, and *love* simple explanations that are actually partially true. There's nothing too simple about the mind of Bill James, but by sifting through his books, talking to his friends and family, and urging him to discuss things like the diversity of lemurs in Madagascar compared to the homogeneity of baseball teams under antitrust exemption, patterns emerge.

This book is about baseball, of course, but it's also about psychology, politics, things to do in college instead of studying, and murder. In fact, the godfather of sabermetrics has read hundreds of books about true crime. "What's fascinating about crime stories," Bill says, "is the process of moving from the known facts to conclusions about the unknown facts. It's like sabermetrics in that you take a set of known facts and try to infer from them what is unknown. It's the same process but a different set of methods."

Some of the best crime stories are those in which no one knows what happened. Likewise, some of the best biography subjects are the ones you can't figure out. In the movie *Chan Is Missing*, a man named Jo searches for his missing business partner, Chan Hung. Everyone he talks to has a different idea of who Chan is. Jo realizes, "The problem with me is that I believe what I see and hear. If I do that with Chan Hung I'll know nothing, because everything is so contradictory."

I felt that way about my search for Bill James. And, as Jo says about a shadowed picture of Chan Hung, I still can't see him. "Another person's view of me is like a mirror," Bill says, "but it's never a true mirror; there's always something out of proportion. Suppose you looked in the mirror and your nose was three times too big, and your left eye was twice the size of your right eye. This is how I feel about other people's views of me."

When writing about Bill's work, it's extremely difficult to keep your beliefs from getting mixed with his. Also, most of his ideas are parts of a larger framework, so abstracting them causes distortion. In that sense, they're like the game itself. "Baseball is an infinite puzzle," Bill says. "You can never really understand why teams win and why they lose. You can understand a little bit more, and a little bit more, but you can never exhaust the subject."

He chronicled his efforts to understand in an essential body of baseball books: twelve editions of the *Baseball Abstract,* the first *Historical Baseball Abstract,* three editions of the *Baseball Book,* three *Player Ratings Books, The Politics of Glory* (republished as *Whatever Happened to the Hall of Fame*), the *Baseball Managers* book, and two editions of the *New Historical Abstract.*

Bill is baseball's pioneering "social scientist" and most influential analytical writer. "I hear from people all the time whose lives were influenced by him," says Rob Neyer, an ESPN.com columnist and one of Bill's former assistants. "College professors, lawyers, scientists . . . Bill didn't just teach people how to think about baseball. He taught people how to think about the world."

When I was fifteen I was playing tennis-ball baseball at a friend's house when he announced he'd found a book by a guy in Kansas who wrote about baseball in a way we wouldn't believe. This was my first encounter with the mind of Bill James, from the 1983 *Baseball Abstract* introduction:

> Hi. My name is Bill James, and I'm an eccentric. . . .
>
> The reason that I am eccentric is that I spend all of my time analyzing baseball games. Well, not *all* of my time—I have a wife to neglect—but most all of my time. I count all kinds of stuff that lots of people are sort of interested in, but nobody in his right mind would actually bother to count. I devise theories to explain how things in baseball are connected to one another. . . .
>
> Like baseball itself, this book is just here for you to enjoy. This is a book for those who abandon themselves to the game, for those to whom the hurried and casual summaries of journalism are a daily affront. It is not for people who already know all about baseball, but for those who want to learn.

I wasn't conscious of it at the time, but that appealed to me as an approach to life as much as a way to look at baseball.

Twenty years later I was working as a copyediting supervisor at a New York book publisher when a Rob Neyer manuscript came in, co-authored with Bill James himself. I had worked with Rob on his *Baseball Lineups* book, and I was jazzed to interact with his former boss—mostly out of admiration, but also out of perverse curiosity.

Back in 1987, at my first publishing job, my boss saw me reading an *Abstract* and informed me that the author was "difficult." My next gig happened to be with the publisher of the *Abstract*s, Ballantine Books. When I suggested to colleagues that they were lucky to work with Bill James, the eye rolls were deafening. Finally, at the Neyer/James publisher, word was that Mr. James accepts no copyediting.

A tangent about tangents: *New Yorker* writer Malcolm Gladwell told Rob Neyer in 2003, "Bill James did something which I've never forgotten and which has influenced my writing ever since. He mastered the tangent. He would go off on some seemingly unrelated topic (usually about Amos Otis), which only much later would turn out to be totally on point. I try to do that as well, only I'm not nearly as good at making it all turn out later to be totally on point."

I know what he means about not making it all turn out, but in the spirit of the Bill James tangent, let me tell you about the tangential philosophical stumper "Who's the bigger jackass?" Around the time I was expecting the Neyer/James manuscript, a friend I'll call Bob was at a crosswalk in Chinatown when a guy on a scooter ran a red light and almost hit him. Bob was standing off the curb, talking on a cell phone, but felt that scooter guy had cut it aggressively close. Bob took off running and caught up at the next light. Scooter guy said, "What are you going to do, hit me?" to which Bob answered, "Yes," and body-punched him. No injuries, no cops. Later, the story drew a split response from friends and family that came down to the question of who the bigger jackass was.

After the Neyer/James copyediting got under way, I queried Bill about whether we should fix "inconsistencies." He didn't care to discuss specifics, but he e-mailed some thoughts on the general topic:

> I have a special problem with copy editors, which is that I am very strongly opposed to consistency in use of the language.

I understand that this is unusual. I understand that I am a minority, and that most people think (actually, most people simply ASSUME, without thinking about it) that consistency in use of the language is preferable to inconsistency. It isn't. Inconsistency is vastly preferable to consistency, for many reasons. This is not a casual observation; it is a strongly held philosophy, central to my career. When confronted with a question of "how should I write this," very often I will resolve the issue by simply doing it the opposite of however I did it last time.

I understand that this is unusual; I understand that copy editors are assigned to search out inconsistency and get rid of it. But you need to understand:

1. I have very good reasons for doing things the way I do them.
2. My name is on the book; the copy editor's name isn't.
3. I know vastly more about the effective use of the English language than the copy editor does.

So . . . I don't want any bleeping policies. OK; you have to have SOME policies. Neyer can have as many policies as he wants on his part of the book; I don't want them. My policy is: I wrote it that way for a reason, leave it alone. And I don't have time to go through the book line by line explaining to some college journalism student why I did everything the way I did it. Leave it alone.

Consistency is boring. Inconsistency is interesting.

Inconsistency challenges the reader.

Inconsistency draws criticism. Criticism is valuable. The more criticism you attract, the more you irritate people, the more you puzzle people, the more successful you will be.

This had me wondering which of us was the bigger jackass. One coworker suggested the Lester Bangs perspective—"part of the whole exhilaration of admiring somebody for their artistic accomplishments is resenting 'em 'cause they never live up to your expectations." True, but I was thinking Bill might be on to something. You remember

Toonces, the driving cat, from *Saturday Night Live*—"Honey, are you sure it's okay to let the cat drive?" Knowing a few things about copy-editing cats, I couldn't blame Bill for wanting to hold the wheel.

Long story short, it struck me that the bigger jackass was me, and I decided to write this book. "I have grave doubts about whether or not I am interesting enough to write about at any length," Bill told me, "but that's not for me to decide. As long as you don't call me on the telephone, we'll get along fine."

A few weeks later I e-mailed to tell him the proposal had sold. No response.

I tried again, nudging. "My publishers are curious how you reacted."

"Tell them I was not visibly upset," he replied.

Puzzled, I forwarded his response to Neyer, who offered, "My guess is, he could handle the notion of a biography before it was going to happen, but now that it *will* happen, he wishes he could disappear into a giant hole."

Sometimes I saw him looking for that hole. He kept telling me, "I don't tell stories," because, he said, "My father was very much a story-teller. Not a good storyteller, unfortunately. He lived in a small town where everyone knew each other and told stories about each other. Once I left home, I didn't know who or what he was talking about. But that never stopped him."

Reluctance aside, Bill was patient and helpful. He never tried to look behind what I was doing. Unfortunately, he can't offer details about the work he does for the Sox. What he can say runs along the lines of "I'm doing a study of college pitchers from the past, trying to figure out what features of their careers predict success as a profes-sional." But before he was an insider obligated to keep secrets, his observations and ideas worked their way into the baseball discussion, changing the way the game is seen and played.

If the hardest part of writing a book is gaining access to stories, the second is guessing what readers know. Bill advised, "I think you're better off to assume an intelligent audience and challenge people to keep up." I've also tried to keep in mind something he wrote about baseball guidebooks from early last century: "In later years the editors of baseball guides would become faceless company men, concerned only with compiling the standard elements of the form and giving no one cause for offense, but at this time guides were still personal, fun, and informative; editors would digress into amusing sidelights or challenge the reader with original ideas, as they saw fit."

Late in the process I worried about not doing justice to his work. "This is an inevitable part of writing a book," he counseled. "When you start you have in your mind this wonderful, radiant book. As you get near the end the real product seems leaden, desultory, flea-bitten, and ragged. It seems not only short of your image of what it should be, but ridiculously, absurdly short. I felt this way about every book I ever wrote. It doesn't mean anything . . . just come to terms with the real book, and carry on."

The Mind of Bill James

1

Who's Bill James?

Like **William Shatner** singing "Rocket Man," bad lineups have a perverse appeal. In 1980 the Chicago White Sox drew just 399 walks and scored the fewest runs in the American League. Manager Tony La Russa rested some of his regulars for an August game in Baltimore, and so . . . Leading off was Bruce Kimm, with an on-base percentage of .290. Batting second was Greg Pryor—lifetime OBP .291. Up next were Jim Morrison and Lamar Johnson, then Kevin Millar's uncle, Wayne Nordhagen. You get the gist.

White Sox starter Steve Trout had taken a 1-0 lead into the sixth, but an error put the leadoff man on, and Baltimore scored two unearned runs. In sum, Trout gave up no earned runs in a six-hit complete game and lost 2-1. It's not unusual for a good pitcher on a bad team to get shafted in the won-lost column, but Trout's season was, as Bill wrote, "ruined by extremely poor offensive and defensive support."

That winter Trout and the Chisox couldn't agree on a contract, so they headed to salary arbitration, with Trout represented by the Hendricks brothers of Houston. Having read the 1979 *Baseball Abstract*, they had hired Bill James as a consultant, a notably progressive decision. Randy Hendricks says, "The White Sox had argued Trout wasn't very good in 1980. In rebuttal I introduced an exhibit of the won-lost records of other starting pitchers in the division, with Bill's method for determining what their records should have been. It had about a 90 percent correlation to actual won-lost records. The method showed that Trout's record wasn't true to the quality of his season. He should have been something like 14-11, not 9-16."

From across the big table in a Chicago hotel conference room, assistant general manager Dave Dombrowski, with wrinkled brow and questioning tone, inquired, "Who is Bill James?" Randy Hendricks explained that Bill James was a sabermetrician who did studies and analysis on the quantitative performance of baseball players.

Bill later wrote, "The White Sox argued that Trout was not in shape and ready to pitch after the strike, but we had an exhibit detailing his first eight appearances in the second half of the season. In those eight games, he walked only eight men in forty-seven innings and had a 3.06 ERA."

Randy says, "Teams despised what they saw as outsiders, troublemakers. It was a real culture battle—tough guys against analytical guys. Career baseball people saw us as unworthy. Like in any society, there was a fear of change, of loss of control."

Bill's basic approach—to isolate a question, then look at what the evidence shows—naturally put him on the arbitrator's wavelength. He may have been the least important guy in the room, the lowest in the pecking order, but when he made a point, no one could say, "You never played baseball, what do you know?"

The Hendricks team won the case, and while many baseball insiders would learn to curse his name, they no longer needed to ask, "Who's Bill James?"

2

Sweet Home Mayetta

On the day I was born," Bill would write, "Tommy Henrich hit one of the most dramatic home runs in baseball history"—a World Series Game One walk-off that gave the Yankees a 1-0 victory over Brooklyn. Born in Holton, Kansas, on October 5, 1949, George William James grew up in Mayetta, a town of about two hundred at the edge of a Potawatomi Indian reservation.

Years later his friend Mike Kopf would rib him about not using his first name, then passing it to his youngest son, who also doesn't use it. Bill says that it's something he and Reuben have in common with the George Kenneth Griffeys. He also notes that Junior is the *second*-best player to hail from tiny Donora, PA, Stan Musial being number one.

Bill was the youngest of six: four sisters and a brother. His parents, George and Mildred, were married about sixteen years before he came along. Bill's mother was sick with cancer throughout his early childhood, and in the winter of 1954, when Bill was five, his mother died. He doesn't speak of it much, saying only, "I have a few scenes with her that I remember." Older sister Carol took on much of the parenting burden until she left for college. She says, "Dad was depressed a lot after our mother died, understandably." Bill's wife, Susan McCarthy, adds, "Bill didn't always get the attention a mother would give. There was a lot of heartache there."

In the early 1950s, George James ran a cream station, an agriculture-based business that linked local farms and butter plants. "I kind of grew up in the cream station," Bill says. "One of my brothers-in-

law, who's dead now—he was twenty years older than I was—said that
the first time he met me, I was five years old, sitting in the cream station playing checkers with an old man.

"I identify with Bob Dole—not politically, I'm not a Republican—
because his dad ran a cream station in Russell [Kansas] when he was a
boy. He was influenced the same way I was, by growing up among
farmers. Dole said that he'd always identified with Eisenhower
because he spent time in a cream station as well. There's something
about that role in life that was an interesting way to meet the world."

In the 1930s, cream stations handled two-thirds of the butterfat
sold from state farms. But by the time Bill was born they were on the
way out. "Unfortunately," Bill says, "my father had no business sense.
He bought the cream station in '48 or '49, after it was apparent that it
was not thriving and would never thrive again."

The spring after his wife died, George was trimming tree branches
with some other men. A branch supporting the branch he was on was
chopped by mistake. He fell, breaking his back. "I missed being an
orphan by an inch," Bill says. His father's health was never the same. "I
was too young to understand what was happening," Bill says, "but it
made my childhood complicated and difficult."

Joyce Cochren was Bill's neighbor and classmate. "We were com-
petitive," Joyce says, "challenging each other with books we could read
and hoped the other couldn't. I tried to get Bill to learn to skip and
ride the old scooter, but he resisted with the same words he used in
high school as a reason for not doing certain homework assign-
ments—'It's stupid!'

"There were always things he chose not to spend time and effort
on. In the second grade he tried to convince the teacher that he was
right about something. When he failed, he told me quietly that she
was stupid. I felt she should be privy to this information, so I raised my
hand, went to the desk, and reported the remark. The teacher asked to
see him in the cloakroom, but he wouldn't tell me what she said."

The James family didn't own a television until Bill was ten. Summers were easy, with swimming lessons, two weeks of Bible school,

but little else organized. Bill says, "We rode bicycles, played sandlot baseball. There was an empty lot a block from the house. I loved to play baseball, but I had no ability."

In *Feeding the Green Monster,* Rob Neyer wrote, "I have a friend, a brilliant man who has written many books about baseball, whose mother died when he was a boy. He's never told me so, but I suspect that he lost himself in the comforting intricacies of baseball." Bill says, "That's probably true. But your mind just latches on to something, and it would whether there were a void there or not. There's a large random component to personality, and I just happened to discover baseball cards at the right time."

In spring 1961 the Post cereal company issued a series of baseball cards printed on the boxes. Bill implored his father to buy cereals the family didn't like, just so he could add to his collection. "I can remember as clearly as anything," he later wrote, "sitting at the table one evening trying to explain that I had decided that the most similar cards belonged to Jim Davenport and Elston Howard. My brother Bob couldn't figure out what the hell the point was and who cared."

Bill wrote that when he was in sixth grade his teacher used to take him aside and try to talk him out of wasting his time. "'William,' he would say, 'you're a bright enough little kid. You've got lots of charm and poise, and you're regarded as a leader around here. You hold your liquor fairly well, and you haven't wet your pants during school hours all week. So what's all this crappola about the baseball statistics?'" Bill would write years later:

> In my childhood I knew a master storyteller who had lived his life as a rodeo cowboy. A professional athlete, a man who did his work in front of the cheering or indifferent crowds, exactly at the same time as did Bob Meusel and Gene Robertson and Alex Ferguson, he retired and did rope tricks at rodeos and retired and delivered milk to us and retired and committed suicide at eighty-two, two years ago, and nobody knows or cares anything about him *because he has no numbers.* When I am dead, Wade will be

forgotten because he has no autobiography in Macmillan, and Alex Ferguson will be remembered as long as there is baseball because he is a part of it.

The variety of stories that can be told is infinite. It is not that the numbers fill out a story which is known from other sources, but that the bits and pieces of knowledge which we have about the ballplayers flesh out the numbers *which are the true story*. There is no other fiction so absorbing and no other poetry so hypnotic.

When he was thirteen Bill began doing roofing work with his dad. "It was a lot of responsibility for someone my age," he says, "but I see now what my father was thinking: A teenage boy needs watching, and the only way I can watch him and make a living is to bring him to work with me." Years of summers spent doing manual labor, yet still being in danger of failing shop class, convinced Bill he needed to find a cerebral career path.

Bill and Joyce attended Mayetta Rural High School. She says he wasn't much for activities that required running or coordination: "He had a slow, deliberate gait that told you he was in no hurry to get where he was going. His area of great activity was his brain. It never stopped. He loved to throw around big words. Sometimes he threw one in that didn't fit, just to make his statement sound impressive." One morning Joyce walked in expressing unhappiness over something someone had said or done. Bill said, "Your propensity for using inter-rogatives to express your disdain for the aforementioned individuals is a pure delight to one who shares that view of those individuals." Like his future readers, some classmates laughed and agreed. Others groaned or looked puzzled. But that was just Bill being Bill.

In high school he went through a phase of talking in accents, especially British. The next step was to invent his own language. "We were studying Spanish," Joyce says, "but that wasn't the language he wanted to use. I had to tell him I didn't understand 'Bill James' and if he wanted an answer he would have to speak a language I understood.

His smile told me he didn't want an answer, he just wanted to enjoy being the mysterious guy no one could quite figure out."

Fred Zweifel, another classmate, says, "Bill tried to play sports but was one of those guys who grows far ahead of their physical maturity. I'm sure he was six-four by the time he was a freshman." There were five boys in the entire class, so Bill played center on the basketball team. "I have memories of him out there with a bunch of guys a foot shorter," Fred says, "Bill grabbing a rebound or taking a pass, with his elbows reaching out at the same level as everyone else's head. He didn't have coordination or speed, but he paid close attention, and often had things to say about what I had or hadn't done. He had this great sense of humor, dry and subtly sarcastic."

Bill was adept at math, of course. He played with numbers, doing fractions and calculations, some by hand and the rest by slide rule, and kept them in spiral notebooks. Joyce says, "Bill loved it when people inquired about his endless pages of digits. Our questions never brought a straight answer from him. Now, of course, we realize he was laying the groundwork for his life's quest."

The first time young Bill realized he had an uncommon analytical ability was one afternoon in the early sixties, when somebody was trying to break the land speed record. Bill says, "The announcer said that in order to do this, the driver would burn up his fuel halfway through the ten-mile stretch he was traveling." Bill's dad didn't understand why that should be, but it was clear to Bill. "If you're burning rocket fuel," he explained, "the thrust it provides is greater than the mechanical capacity of the vehicle to express it. As long as you're burning fuel, you're going to accelerate. As soon as the fuel stops burning, you're going to begin to decelerate. The fastest point in the ten-mile stretch is the point when you're about to burn out your fuel."

3

Jayhawk Bill

B **ill left home** for Kansas University in Lawrence in fall 1967. He says, "I grew enormously during that time, in part because of the classes, but more from the social experience. I lived in Stephenson Hall, a scholarship hall inhabited by fifty-two mostly dorky guys who were pretty good students and came from low-income families."

Bill and friends used to spend hour after hour sitting in chairs in the entry area, a kind of foyer. Bill says, "We played a trivia game called Botticelli . . . I don't know if you know the game . . . you start out:

I have a K.

Is this person real?

Yes.

Is this person living?

Yes.

Is this person male?

Yes.

Mike Krukow?

No.

Is this person famous?

Yes.

Is this person more famous than the governor of Kansas?

Yes.

Is this person a movie star?

No.

Is this person an entertainer?

Define entertainer.

Stage, screen, TV, music.

No.

Is this a sports person?

Yes.

Is this a baseball player?

No.

Football player?

No.

Basketball player?

No.

Hockey?

No.

Is this person an athlete?

No.

Oh, so it's a sports person but not an athlete?

Yes.

Ewing Kauffman?

No.

Is this person a coach?

Yes.

A football coach?

No.

A basketball coach?

Yes.

A college basketball coach?

Yes.

Mike Krzyzewski.

That's it.

"I spent a billion hours doing that. When the Botticelli games broke up we would go play volleyball. Every afternoon when the weather permitted we were out on the concrete playing volleyball from three to suppertime, about six. The volleyball games would break up when somebody would heave water balloons out of the third-floor bathroom window . . . what was it they would yell when they did that? I don't remember. I never threw water balloons, even once; I was always on the receiving end.

"There was a basketball court three blocks away; we'd grab a basketball and go over there three or four times a week. We had endless Risk games. One of my buddies got nicknamed 'Onger,' which was an abbreviation of 'Warm Onger.' To this day his wife still sometimes calls him the Onger. We played bridge and hearts and spades and poker and an infuriating three-person card game called Sergeant Major. Mostly hearts.

"We had an old Ping-Pong table. I played about ten million games of Ping-Pong and can still beat my kids at Ping-Pong. There was an old black-and-white TV—this was before cable, of course, but that was a bigger deal to me than to some of the other guys because I had grown up in a house without television. We used to get pizza and beer and watch the late-night movie and make rude comments. The stations would sign off about one, which was when I started to study.

"I learned an awful lot from those wasted years. Occasionally I studied or went to class, not a hell of a lot of either. And the bull sessions, those midnight-to-three-a.m. discussions which jump effortlessly from Harry Truman to James Bond movies to life in outer space. I sat in on as many of those as anybody. I tell my daughter, who is a college freshman, not to feel guilty about those late-night bull sessions; she may be learning more from them than she is from the classes . . . certainly from sociology. You learn how people think; you take positions and have to defend them, and you learn how you think. I'm a firm believer that many people get more out of going to college than they do out of going to class."

There's a group photo in the 1968 *Jayhawker* yearbook that shows freshman Bill, lanky and young, hair combed, suit-and-tied. He looks like a model student of the 1950s. But the real Bill didn't fit that image. "I was never that good a student," he says. "And baseball was a wedge that began the unraveling of my college career." You can just about trace that unraveling to the day: October 5, 1967.

It was a great year for the Red Sox until the seventh game of the World Series. Carl Yastrzemski won the AL Triple Crown and Jim Lonborg won twenty-two games. In Game Two of the Series, against St. Louis, Lonborg didn't allow a hit until two were out in the eighth. Midway through, Bill had a class to go to, but he decided, *I'm not missing this.* The Sox lost the Series, and Bill ended up on the path of academic non-description. "I do not say this with pride," he says, "but my obsession with baseball—not baseball statistics, but baseball—always took precedence over my education."

BJ and the A's

The summer after Bill's mother died, the Philadelphia A's moved to Kansas City to begin a thirteen-year run of godawful baseball. "That was my childhood," Bill wrote. Not only were the A's "never in any *danger* of having a winning record," they were losers in all but nine of their seventy-eight months in Kansas City. "I was obsessively curious about why the A's couldn't win," Bill says. "Each spring the announcers assured us that this season was going to be better, but it never worked out. I figured it couldn't just be the announcers, because there were different announcers every year."

The announcers weren't the only ones. "The A's changed players every two months," Bill says, "so it was hard to get attached to any particular one." Minnie Minoso was his favorite opposition player, and Ed "The Glider" Charles was his favorite A. The Glider was pushing thirty by the time he made the majors, but was a steady producer to the extent it was possible, considering that the fences were constantly being moved in and out at the behest of owner Charlie O. Finley. "Everything Finley did pissed people off," Bill says. "That was his gift; the man was a pisser."

Arnold Johnson, who owned the A's before Finley took over in '61, was friendly with Yankees co-owner Del Webb. They had an arrangement by which the A's funneled their best players to the

Bronx. Bill wrote, "If you look at the 1958 Kansas City team, you might note that the top three home run and RBI men were Cerv, Maris, and Lopez; the team leader in strikeouts, innings, and several other pitching categories was Ralph Terry. By 1960, all were with the Yankees."

Kansas City had an inferiority complex, and "the pinstripe pipeline rubbed the city at the rawest spot Johnson could have found."

> To a child, none of this quite made sense. . . . Why did so many people hate the Yankees? Why were so many people angry at the owner, when the radio broadcasters (of course) said that he was such a fine man and that what he was doing was in the best interests of Kansas City in the long run? Why did they root for the team if they didn't like them?
>
> The notion of an inferiority complex is difficult for a child to figure out on his own in the best of circumstances. Having never visited either Kansas City or New York, I could have had no sense of the difference between one city and another. The history of the Yankees' overlording of baseball meant nothing to me. A child has no way of understanding history because his concept of time is too limited; he can't imagine what is meant by a period of years. I could gather from it only that our team did not win very often, and that some people felt we were being taken advantage of. I rejected the idea that we were being taken advantage of because it seemed to me to be related in some way to self-pity.

Johnson died in 1960, and Charles Oscar Finley bought the A's. Bill described this period as the era of false promise, when the A's looked committed to youth. He wrote, "I was a full-fledged fanatic by now, rarely missing a game, often pacing a harrowed pattern around the front room as the A's wrestled to preserve their victories, more often sitting doggedly through the last out of a depressing rout." Each season began with the same promises made by new announcers. Each summer Bill felt that "at any moment the breaks would change, the momentum would switch, and the river would begin to flow uphill."

He says, "I don't know why it mattered to me if the A's lost 103 games or 104, but at the time it did." By year's end, the focus always went to small individual goals. "The A's had a lot of people who hit .301," he wrote. "The announcers had nothing else to talk about, so they'd start finding out what the players' goals were about the All-Star break, and the rest of the year was consumed in watching them try to reach these. They usually had an exciting battle for the team leadership in wins . . . plus once in a while somebody was trying to stay among the league leaders in doubles."

Bill noted that two recurring motifs in the *Abstract*s were that poorly run organizations leave promising young players on the bench in favor of established mediocrities and "tend to project their weaknesses onto their best players, and ultimately will dwell not on what the player can do, but on what he *can't*." The A's embodied those errors in their dealings with Manny Jimenez, Jose Tartabull, and others. Bill has surmised that this made a deep impression on A's players who later became managers, such as Dick Williams, Dick Howser, and Whitey Herzog.

Finley fixed on the idea that the A's could win by following his theories about what made the Yankees winners. He traded several of Kansas City's best players for a couple of power hitters, then ordered that the A's home park be reworked to the dimensions of Yankee Stadium. This was both physically impossible and against the rules of baseball. "And third," Bill wrote, "the whole idea was nuts." Thwarted by league officials, Finley had a line painted on the outfield and ordered the public-address announcer to say, "That ball would have been a home run in Yankee Stadium," whenever a fly ball was hit beyond it.

"In addition to being ugly and smelling bad," Bill wrote, "the Kansas City A's had a bad personality. Charles O. Finley considered himself to be a master showman, and the team fairly swarmed in cutesy promotions and special events. . . . Sheep grazed in the grass beyond the outfield; they were joined later by a mule. One year a cellar-bray-tion (a mule brays, get it?) was planned for the day that the A's got out of last place, but they never did. A mechanical rabbit popped out of the ground to deliver clean baseballs to the umpire." Finley feuded with everyone, from the press to the players to the league to the city, and spent virtually his entire time in Kansas City threatening to move.

In 1969 the expansion Royals set up in Kansas City and won sixty-nine games, a respectable number for a new team. The Royals got Lou Piniella from the expansion Seattle Pilots. He won Rookie of the Year. In one of the most lopsided trades ever, they delivered Joe Foy to the Mets for Bob Johnson and Amos Otis. Johnson proved to be one of the best rookie pitchers in the league, and the next year he was part of a deal that brought Freddie Patek. A.O. became Bill's favorite player.

In their first years of existence, the Royals were able to get Piniella, Otis, Patek, Cookie Rojas, John Mayberry, and Hal McRae for next to nothing. Bill wrote that when the team did make a bad deal—Piniella to the Yankees for Lindy McDaniel—"they paid that one back with interest in 1976 by suckering the Brewers out of Darrell Porter and Jim Colborn for three guys who were about even to Jim Colborn."

What the Royals management accomplished can be compared to what Red Sox management did in 2003 when they brought in David Ortiz, Bill Mueller, and Mike Timlin as free agents. Mark Bellhorn came in a trade with the Rockies, Kevin Millar came at the start of spring training for cash from the Marlins, and pitcher Bronson Arroyo was claimed off waivers.

Bill wrote that the Royals were "extremely fortunate" in that era; "nobody is *that* smart." The same could be said of the Red Sox, who put Manny Ramirez on waivers and tried to trade him to Texas.

They were lucky to fail, so he could go on to become their World Series MVP. As astute as Red Sox management has been, you can't ignore the factors they had nothing to do with, such as the Varitek-and-Lowe heist, the signing of Pedro, and the development of Nomar.

The Royals of the 1970s also hit upon the best kind of good luck an organization can have, in George Brett. "No matter how smart you are, no matter how good your system is, when you find a George Brett you're lucky," Bill wrote.

Whatever the mix of luck and brains, the Royals front office was able to give the people of Kansas City a team to rally around. Bill wrote, "Whereas the A's organization was rather a grimy, dirty machine, grotesquely inefficient and with a personality nobody liked, the Royals tended to the other extreme; they seemed antiseptic, colorless, mechanically efficient, and with not much personality to like or dislike. This was a very welcome change. We had moved from the slums to the suburbs." Still, the team seemed to him to be a product created for public consumption, and only years later did he regain "the creative innocence required to abandon my emotions to the flight of the team."

Bill's first days at KU coincided with the A's last in Kansas City. Detached from baseball on an emotional level, he was sharpening his analytical skills. "I transferred my interest in baseball from a team to the game itself," he says, "and more or less misused my education to learn to analyze baseball."

His passion for the sport was reconstituted. "The period of my psychic separation from the emotional level of the sport corresponded to the period of my education, and so it happened that I began to borrow ways of looking at the game not from sportswriters, announcers, and other fans, but from the academic disciplines of history and the social sciences."

He opted for a dual major of English and economics. "I started taking what they taught me in economics class and applying it to baseball," he says. "That's more or less how I became what I became." He noted that the marriage of baseball analysis and economics didn't work perfectly. "Still," he says, "this doesn't stop me from doing the best I can." Economists use mathematical modeling techniques to figure out whether the things they posit are true. Bill didn't invent mathematical modeling, obviously, but he did dream up his own applications. "I learned that economists used mathematical models, and it then occurred to me that a simulation game was a mathematical model of baseball, and could thus be used to study real and significant issues about the game."

The Other Major

Bill's love of literature certainly comes out in his baseball writing. In the '84 *Abstract*, under the heading "If There Were No Professional Baseball, What Would This Manager Probably Be Doing?" he joked about A's manager Steve Boros: "Assistant professor of English literature, University of Michigan; a campus legend, author of three unpublished novels and the short story 'Time Was When a Rose Was a Rose Was a Rose,' which was collected along with works by Saul Bellow, Eudora Welty, David Niven, and Reverend Leroy in the *New Zealand Anthology of Good Stories by People Who Drive on the Wrong Side of the Road*."

Bill says, "I love Philip Roth, but, interestingly enough, struggle through *The Great American Novel* with no real interest. I also loved Bernard Malamud—but not *The Natural*. I am certain this reflects some unattractive territorial protectiveness on my part, or, worse yet, projections of insecurity. If truly talented writers start writing about baseball, where will I be?"

He once wrote of manager Dick Williams, "Sometimes in literature a hero forms a sort of bond, good or malignant, voluntary or involuntary, with some object or image (automobiles, freight trains, playing cards, locked doors) that are part of everyone's life but which seem to haunt him and protrude inescapably into his fate. So it is with Dick Williams and second basemen." (Williams had a proclivity for "weird comings and goings" with second basemen. Bill wrote that some of these, "such as the 1984 decisions to release Juan Bonilla and shift Alan Wiggins in from left field, have been courageous and brilliant. Some, such as the time he tried rotating four men at the position and pinch hitting for them whenever they were do at the plate, have been funny. Some, such as the 1973 decision to resign as manager of the A's over the shabby treatment of Mike Andrews, have been courageous and sad. Some, such as the dogged determination to play Rodney Scott in Montreal *and* San Diego, carried to the extent of claiming that Rodney was the best player on his Montreal team and pouting publicly when he couldn't have him for the Padres, have been courageous and stupid.")

This *Abstract* literary reference comes from the '82 entry on Mookie Wilson:

> Talk about your eerie coincidences. His real name is William Wilson, but they can't call him that, for obvious reasons. There is another major league player who does and doesn't do exactly the same things that this guy does, and who is the same age and color, and that man's name is Willie Wilson. To use the same name would invite unnecessary and unattractive comparisons. Edgar Allan Poe wrote a story about a man who was haunted by another man of the same name, same build and talents and face. The idea was that you were supposed to catch on that his personality had split, and he was merely projecting himself into another character of the same description. The two men's names? William Wilson. Swear to God.

And this one touches on a recurring theme of the *Abstract*s, that every baseball season will show you something you haven't seen before.

Do you remember the story of the Devil and Daniel Webster? It's a story about a man who sells his soul to the devil for earthly success, but when the time comes to face up to his responsibilities, pack a trunkful of Coppertone and prepare for a long, dry summer, instead of just saying "Well, OK, you're the Devil and a deal is a deal," he says "Nuts to you, I'm not going," and he calls in Daniel Webster to argue for him.

Well, the Phillies remind me of that story. The Phillies began to evolve into an old ballclub four or five years ago, and a lot of people (including yours truly) have been waiting for them to collapse ever since. What you're supposed to do when you begin to accumulate thirty-five-year-olds on your roster is start to look to the future, begin breaking in some young talent, so as to cushion the decline phase—like the Dodgers have done.

What the Phillies did instead was to start bringing in more old ballplayers, beginning with Pete Rose in 1979. Ahah, we all said: you'll pay for this. Trying to stretch out your good times by a couple of years, when you could be going to church on Sunday and bringing along some younger talent; you'll burn in the second division for this, Philadelphia.

But when the moment of their reckoning arrived, and the aging of the talent became critical, the Phillies made a unique response: They sent for Joe Morgan. Instead of saying, "OK, you're right; we've got to start paying for this now," they brought in even more, even older ballplayers to prop up the team until the next generation of talent was assembled. They challenged their liability head-on.

4

Drafted Last

America was deep into Vietnam when Bill got to KU. "I participated in some protests in '67 and '68," he says, "but gave it up after I realized that the protests were being manipulated by the leaders for their own agendas."

In December 1969 there was a draft lottery for men born from 1944 through 1950. Numbers ranged into the hundreds. The higher the number, the better. Bill's came up 24. If the draft continued past his senior year, he would likely be called into service.

U.S. troop involvement was winding down by 1971, but the draft stayed in effect. With graduation fast approaching, Bill could have tried the ROTC, joined the National Guard, or gone "doctor shopping" to come up with a medical excuse. Instead, he sat tight and waited to be drafted.

He went into the army at the start of December 1971. "I believe I was the last person drafted from the state of Kansas," he says. "They had us raise our hands and swore us in. Then the officer in charge informed us that, because enlistments were ahead of schedule, they had temporarily stopped the draft, right after my group. But they never did have to resume, and then the draft was ended."

Bill had a harder time than most getting through basic training. "You have to understand," he says, "as a soldier, I failed every test you can fail. I simply had no ability to do any of the things the army wants you to do. I couldn't do push-ups. I couldn't shoot a rifle worth a crap. I couldn't march fast or climb obstacle courses, I couldn't assemble and reassemble a rifle quickly, I couldn't keep my shoes shined or my shirttail tucked in. I was constantly singled out, in training, as the guy who didn't get it. I very seriously did not think that, if I wound up in Vietnam, I was coming back."

Bill doesn't tell stories, but he has one he likes to tell about being shipped out. He says, "When I was completing the final stage of draftee training, they marched us to a center to pick up our unit assignment. The address on my assignment was an overseas shipping center in San Francisco, which meant Vietnam. Then—I swear this is true—we marched back to the training company and, for the first time in weeks, were allowed to turn on the television. Richard Nixon was on, and he was announcing new policies aimed at ending the war protests. One of the new policies was that draftees would no longer be sent to Vietnam. But, Nixon specified, draftees who already had their orders for Vietnam would have to go, but no new draftees would be sent there.

"I couldn't believe it! They got me *again*. I already had my orders—had had them for ten or fifteen minutes before the policy was announced. At this point I was absolutely convinced that I was going to be the last soldier killed in Vietnam. I was going to take a bullet, and just as I went down Henry Kissinger was going to come running up waving his arms, saying, 'It's over, it's over. Stop shooting.' But fortunately the army was too disorganized at that time to keep track of who had received their orders when, so when I got to San Francisco they weren't sending any draftees to Vietnam. They changed my orders to send me to Korea."

Bill got to Korea in September 1972. He'd been trained as a military police sentry dog handler, but the first of his first sergeants said, "If there's anything I don't need, it's a college-educated dog handler. Can you type?" Bill says, "They spent eight months training me to be a dog handler, but the day I got there I became company clerk."

Bill says the main thing he took from his time in the army was the opportunity to work with a first sergeant named Clarence Bray. "He was a fine man, a Kentuckian with a high school education. He knew how to organize and get things done. This probably sounds stupid, because, as anybody knows, I am not at all organized, but you should have seen me *before* I worked with Sergeant Bray. I'm ten times better organized now than I was before. I learned at least as much from him as I did from any professor."

Army Analogies

The army gave Bill fertile fields for future *Abstract* analogies, like this one about Red Sox second baseman Marty Barrett:

In the military, drill sergeants and other power mongers will set up little tests for you, make you do some stupid, irrational, and painful thing just to find out how you react to it. If you pass their little test, then they'll always think you're OK, regardless of whether you're worth a hoot or not, because they have reached a prior conclusion that this is the moment at which they're going to find out about you.

I was at a game in KC last May in which Barrett had a couple of hits early, just took pitches on the outside corner and guided them softly over the first baseman's head, the two hits being identical. When he came up the third time I was saying to myself that now they'll make him hit the inside pitch, and they did. The pitcher threw him two pitches on the inside corner, and he turned on the second one and hit the thing a mile (well, maybe 430 feet) for his first major league homer. I was really impressed by that, although logically I knew that it didn't mean any more than anybody else's first home run, because in my mind I had made a prior decision that this was Barrett's test as a major league hitter.

Bill did his basic training at Ft. Leonard Wood, Missouri, and advanced training at Ft. Gordon, Georgia, then went to Lackland Air Force Base in San Antonio. As you'd expect, the army didn't make much use of Bill's talents, and he would later liken it to the Seattle Mariners' front office. In the '88 *Abstract* he wrote, "The Seattle Mariners treat talent as if it were a free resource." He explained that the Seattle farm system was as good as any, but their best ex-prospects were having big years for other teams:

About 5:00 one winter morn some sixteen years ago I rolled out of bed with 130 equally disaffected strangers. We gathered in front of the barracks, made a formation, and marched over a mile. Spreading out, we meandered down a half-mile grass strip between the two lanes of a highway, "policing the area," which is military talk for picking up all the little bits of paper and trash. This took maybe twenty minutes, but with the formation and the march back it took well over an hour, every day. I estimated that the Army was spending about $1,800 a week ($7,800 a month) to keep the paper picked up on this little stretch of grass between the two lanes of a highway.

The problem was that the generals were in the habit of thinking of manpower as a free resource. Economists used to refer to things like air and water, which could be used by anyone without charge, as free resources. They were assumed to be available in unlimited supply. At one time grazing lands were a free resource. Probably at some point in the early history of man, the land was a free resource. Now it is realized that even air and water are limited, and I don't think economists even use the term anymore.

Military officers didn't use the term, either, but when I entered the army I was paid something like $70 a month. If one man got killed or served his time or ran away, they just drafted another one; they didn't worry about what it cost. My monthly salary rose rapidly, however, not because I was a good soldier but because Congress was regularly raising the salaries of lower-ranked enlisted men. This was toward the end of the Vietnam era, and it no longer seemed viable to draft men and pay them nothing. The society would no longer accept it. With the draft discontinued, soldiers were being paid substantial sums of money to reenlist—and the generals, once those men had reenlisted, were ordering these expensive soldiers to march in circles about eighty hours a month, at a cost of billions of dollars.

Being treated for two years as if I were essentially worthless impressed a lesson upon me: the more talent available to you, the less respect you have for it.

"The practice of 'policing' a highway was common," Bill says, "and I did that at all stops, but the place where I did the most of it was Ft. Gordon."

In the '84 *Abstract* Bill wrote, "Military jargon exists to disguise the fact that they don't have the foggiest notion of what the hell they're trying to do. The army is run by people whose vision extends as far as the due date on their next report; the officers are largely intelligent men, locked into a command structure that so totally isolates the commanders from the commandees that they have no real concept of how it is that their decisions will impact on other people's lives. An insane fascination with rotating people in and out so as to emphasize that no one is irreplaceable makes it impossible to develop long-term goals or undertake long-term projects; no one will start anything that's going to take three years because no one expects to be where they are three years from today. Better to show progress on paper today than show it in the field in five months. . . . So what happens in the army? A lack of vision leads to a compulsive need for change, change for the sake of change. All decisions are made according to what things look like on paper. People lose a sense of where they are going and what they are doing, and eventually lose the sense of their own worth."

At one point Bill was with a company when a new first sergeant came in, and still there a year later when the next one arrived. He wrote in the *Managers* book that both first sergeants, on their respective arrivals, wanted to show their intent to make things better for the men. The first tried to do so by taking down some old curtains hanging in the NCO club. Later, when the second came in, he put the same curtains back up to make the same point. The process was duplicated with the mess hall seating arrangement and the timing of the daily exercise routine. And each time it worked.

In the *Guide to Managers* Bill asserted that baseball managers tend to lose their effectiveness the longer they stay with one team. There are exceptions, of course, but almost all managers who spur a leap forward will suffer a step back. Bill put a great deal of thought into the question of why this should be, finding that there are many reasons interacting "in ways that makes them impossible to classify." But, he noted, if a manager is successful, the success changes the needs of the organization, making that manager obsolete in the process. A new manager can make changes that pull his team out of a rut, but it's almost impossible for him to avoid getting in a rut himself down the road. The rare manager who can keep winning with one team over a period of years is the one who doesn't get stuck on one side of the axis between, say, a style that's high or low pressure. Most teams swing between extremes. Bill cites the Yankees' success in the years when low-pressure Bob Lemon and high-pressure Billy Martin were exchanged for each other.

"I believe, rightly or wrongly," he wrote, "that low pressure is better than high pressure, young is better than old, and using the bench is better than not using the bench." (Sounds like Terry Francona.) He believes there are long-term advantages to stability, but that few managers are able to do the job well enough over the long haul for organizations to benefit from the advantages. "It's a universal curse," he wrote, "from which only great managers are exempt."

5

The Wizard of Sabermetrics

Bill got out of the service in fall 1973 and made his way back to Lawrence. He dreamed about the army for years after. "They weren't pleasant dreams," he says, "and I don't miss them." He rented the first apartment he saw. His plan was to sleep and watch television to decompress. Carol says, "The apartment was awful, and I wondered why he lived in it. He told me years later that he felt he was barely sane when he got out of the army, and woke up after several months, thinking, What am I doing in this awful place?"

He enrolled back at KU in January 1974, in the education school, and took small jobs, including one with Pinkerton Security as a guard at different places, one being the Stokely–Van Camp pork-'n'-beans plant. He had put on weight, but he swapped a food addiction for a walking addiction and managed to trim down. Good thing, since he was about to meet the love of his life.

Susan McCarthy, a radiant philosophy major, worked two summers at Stokely's. She came on in the early evening and went home before sunrise. She worked at the end of the packing line, where the rail cars were loaded. "Not many people came past my area," she says. But there was a tall, bearded young security guard who passed her station each night and sometimes would stop to talk. Susie says, "We'd talk about books and classes; and once I mentioned I was going to a Royals game with my family. He didn't reveal his baseball passion to me at that moment, but he gave me a quizzical look like, 'Could she be a baseball fan?' But he didn't ask, and I didn't volunteer that I didn't like baseball."

Susie usually took a food break around 10 P.M. One evening, August 1, 1975, Bill came over to where she was sitting outside eating cantaloupe. She offered him some, but he said he was watching his weight. *That's stupid*, Susie thought. When he asked her out, she said yes, which made it quite a day for Bill, as he also delivered to *Baseball Digest* what became his first national article.

"Winning Margins: A New Way to Rate Baseball Excellence" came out in the November 1975 *Baseball Digest*. It explained that major league statistics levels change so much from decade to decade, you can't tell the great from the not-so-great without adjustments. In 1930, for example, Ray Kremer of Pittsburgh logged an ERA over 5.00 while striking out just fifty-eight batters, yet he led the National League with twenty wins. Meanwhile, the team's first baseman, Gus Suhr, drove in 107 runs—a total that would have topped the league in, say, 1968—yet he finished 84 RBIs off 1930's league pace.

To compare players from different eras, Bill suggested looking at the margin of difference between a league leader and the number two man. Dazzy Vance in 1924 struck out 262 batters. That would have put him third in the NL in 2004. But the second-best total in '24 was barely half of Vance's. In other words, the raw number says pretty good, but the winning margin says absolutely dominant. It's not a perfect method, but it shows the type of thinking Bill was doing at twenty-five.

Psychology

Bill considered going to graduate school to study psychology, which is surprising considering some of the things he's written on the subject. For example, the Houston Astros had a very strong home-field advantage in 1979 and '80, and some said it came from the Astrodome psyching out opponents. Bill wrote:

> Twentieth-century man uses psychology exactly like his ancestors used witchcraft; anything you don't understand, it's psy-

chology. If we can't deal effectively with criminal behavior, we throw it off on the psychologists. If we don't know what a disease is, it's psychosomatic. If we don't know why one team has a large home-field edge, large numbers of people are sure to assume it's psychological.

He points out, "There is a parallel between baseball and psychology, in that I'm not a fan of traditional wisdom in either. When people discover a little of the pattern by which things are put together, they tend to overreact, to overstate the value of the knowledge. This is true in psychology. The human mind is so complicated, it would be high praise to say our understanding of it is fragmentary. Psychology is certainly an interesting subject, but I have limited confidence that professional psychologists know what they're talking about."

Does that mean they shouldn't be mucking around in there at all?

"No, I wouldn't say that," Bill says, "but I do think practicing psychologists have done as much harm as good. On the other hand, what is scorned as 'pop psychology' has done a lot of good. There's a line in one of Saul Bellow's books that we have a name for everything except what we really think and feel. What some demean as psychobabble has made a tremendous contribution to the culture in creating a vocabulary to let us talk about what we think and feel. It's still far from where we ought to be, but way ahead of where we were when I was a child."

I hate to say it, but baseball isn't kind to people with emotional problems. People often imagine that playing baseball for a living must be an easy job, but it isn't. The pressure is incredible, the working conditions often difficult. Talented players with emotional problems rarely come around in that environment.

It's probably off the subject, but did you ever think about this: that psychology is the great failure of the twentieth century. Psychology, it seems to me, has made us all grand promises, which it has been manifestly unable to fulfill. We have placed in psychology the faith that our fathers placed in God, in country, in *doing what was right*. Psychology has largely supplanted the concepts of manhood and honor and eaten into literature and manners, but what has it done for us? We were all supposed to gain insight into ourselves, to understand why we are who we are and what we can do about it. We're more confused about who we are than we've ever been.

"Criminal" psychology—remember that idea? It was going to teach us how to deal with criminals. Forty years later criminals are taking over the world, and we don't have any idea how to deal with them. Nobody can get through college without a class in developmental psychology—but tell me the truth: are we doing a great job with our children? If educational psychology is such a wonderful thing, how come our educational system is such a mess? We confess to psychologists what we used to confess to priests, but is their absolution worth any more?

I'm not suggesting that we should get rid of psychology, only that maybe we should begin to ask it to pay the rent. Anyway, back to baseball . . . when a young player exhibits the signs of emotional instability, don't bet on a handy psychologist to pull him out of it. It's probably a good idea just to stay away from him.

That was written fifteen years ago, and Bill now says, "I wouldn't take my own fulminations on the subject too seriously. As much as anything, I was being a devil's advocate, and I suppose that the complaint I had about psychology could as well be lodged against sabermetrics."

Still, he says, "In the late 1970s I edited a little sabermetric research journal called the *Baseball Analyst*. There was a lot of speculation about why so many home runs were hit in Atlanta, which was called 'The Launching Pad' although the dimensions there were just the same as they were in, for example, Busch Stadium or Royals Stadium, which were poor home run parks.

"We had a guy who wrote articles for us, Robert Kingsley. He was a retired engineer. (At that time the entire community of sabermetric researchers was like six guys.) Kingsley studied all of the possible reasons why more home runs were hit in Atlanta rather than St. Louis or Pittsburgh or other parks, and concluded that none of them were sufficient. Therefore, he concluded, it was psychology. The hitters went in *expecting* to hit home runs, they took home run swings, and the result was home runs. In St. Louis the pitchers would go in there expecting to get ground balls, and the result was ground balls.

"He looked at the effects of the altitude, but he thought they were negligible. This was about 1977. At that time nobody understood the impact of altitude on the way the ball travels. We didn't really understand that until about 1980, when another of the early researchers, Dick O'Brien, did a clever study that showed that the difference was in fact explained by the altitude.

"That experience, in a way, crystallized my feelings about psychology. In our society, we use 'psychology' as an explanation for anything we don't understand. Robert Kingsley couldn't find any rational explanation for the difference, so he concluded it was psychology. This is precisely the way people identified witchcraft for hundreds of years. The widow Mueller walked by about 3:00 as I was milking my cow, the milk turned out to be sour, there's no reason why that milk would be sour . . . it must be witchcraft.

"My point was, in order to show that something is a psychological effect, you need to show that it *is* a psychological effect—not merely that it isn't something else. Which people still don't get. They look at things as logically as they can, and, not seeing any other difference between A and B conclude that the difference between them is psychology.

"We don't understand why the Red Sox played better without Nomar than with him, so we credit it to clubhouse psychology. We don't understand why Joe Torre is successful, so we claim that he is a master psychologist. This is illogical, and it isn't really any different than attributing it to witchcraft. People used 'witchcraft' to explain why babies died in their cribs and why cats act weird. Using 'psychology' in the same way isn't any better, and it isn't a service to *real* psychology. It is actually *defending* real psychology to resist the bastardization of the term."

In 1971 a Lawrence resident opened a theme restaurant-bar based on a baseball-simulation game called Ball Park. "Some people lived out there," Bill says. "I didn't have the money to do that, but it helped me to see how interested people were in this stuff." During this period he was obsessed with figuring out how an offense works or doesn't work, how to better evaluate a trade, and so on. "I had thought about these things," he later wrote, "but to win that damn little league I had to know."

An important figure in Bill's table-gaming days was Dallas Adams. "He was the first person I corresponded with who genuinely shared my interest," Bill says, "and the two of us spent a thousand pages or more batting back and forth the ideas that would eventually form the basis of my career."

KU professor Jim Carothers still plays in a Ball Park league. He remembers the first time he met Bill. "At the time, he was in a league in which the loser of the ongoing season would be able to draft Ted Williams as a rookie the next season. He was put off by the idea of his competitors losing on purpose. I could see he was a young man who had a strong sense of ethics."

Around this time his sense of ethics first bumped up against the Elias Bureau, which compiled and processed statistics for the National League. "There was a research project I wanted to do that required accounts of games," Bill says. "I contacted the teams, who sent me to the league, who sent me to Elias. At first I couldn't get an answer from them, and when I did, it was along the lines of 'We don't deal with people like you.'"

Bill found that the writing life wasn't going fast enough and began working on what he called The Secret Project. He doesn't like to talk about things before he does them. "If you talk about something and it doesn't work out, you look foolish," he says.

"When we were first getting to know each other," Susie says, "he wasn't too open about wanting to write. Since most writers end up failing, he hesitated to call himself one. He had a file box, and in it he was putting the things he wanted to do. After I'd known him awhile he finally showed me some of it. What he wanted to impress upon me, I think, was that he had some ambition and wasn't going to end up as a security guard."

Susie offered to show samples of Bill's writing to her father, a college English professor. She says Bill bristled at the idea, although he understood she was trying to help. He didn't want to be seen as a struggling writer, and he didn't want to be in the position of asking for permission to be a writer.

Since he didn't start writing it until January, Bill's *1977 Baseball Abstract: Featuring 18 Categories of Statistical Information That You Just Can't Find Anywhere Else* wasn't ready for sale until the season was a month old. "He showed it to me," Susie says, "and I was impressed in a way, but I didn't know quite what to make of it." A small ad in the back of *The Sporting News* netted a few sales at $3.50 apiece.

Bill opened with monthly batting records for players and teams. "The records of rookies are particularly interesting," he wrote. "You can 'see' Hector Cruz learning to hit major league pitching, watch the league catch up with Jason Thompson." Bill was seeing patterns and stories in the data—even if they weren't there. He says, "I once thought that players had predictable patterns within seasons, but now I think much of it is random. I still believe that *teams* have predictable patterns."

The image of Bill working on his secret project at night in the bean factory might evoke William Faulkner writing *As I Lay Dying* on the night shift in a power plant. His employer, however, didn't see it that way. Bill says, "Pinkerton's decided to get serious and banned me from doing my research while on the clock, at which point I quit that job and went to work for Stokely's itself."

From about January 1977 through May 1978 he worked three jobs, not including *Abstract* author: Bucky's hamburger joint, Stokely's, and 7-Eleven. He didn't always have a car running, so he walked from one job to the other during a brutal winter. He eventually shifted to the loading dock at Stokely's, later tapping the experience for an *Abstract* allegory comparing the problem-solving methods of a co-worker, "Vito Kowalski," with the California Angels' use of free agency:

> Vito believed that one should never use an ounce of intelligence so long as one had the option of using a pound of force. We'd have to unload a railroad car, and since rail doors don't work very well, usually about a third of the job is getting the thing open. They can stick, jam, or lodge in about thirty places, but if you step back and look at them a second you can ordinarily figure out where the problem is and apply a crowbar to it. Vito would have none of that. His method was to grab hold of the handle and pull like hell, and if that doesn't work you pound on the handle with the crowbar, and then you hook up the handle to a forklift, a chain hoist . . . on up to, presumably, a stick of dynamite. He would rush at breakneck speed from one of those remedies to the next, and nowhere along the line would he ever give a millisecond pause to stop and consider what the problem was.
>
> It's not that Vito was dumb. He wasn't dumb. He was bright. And, from the habit of using his muscles, strong as a rhinoceros. But the very idea of considering how to approach a problem, whether a rail door, an awkward traffic pattern, or a problem with a supervisor, seemed to profoundly embarrass him. It was unmanly or something.
>
> Vito eventually wound up in the state pen, charged with rape, which I kind of hate to bring up, because it ruins the atmosphere and all, and besides that it strains the analogy to the breaking

point. But up to that point the California Angels were, it seems to me, a perfect baseball counterpart to Vito Kowalski. What so many baseball fans find unacceptable about free agency is that it simplifies the formula for building a winner; instead of spending x amount of dollars here to acquire a pool of potential talent and doing this and that and the other to bring the talent around so as to win maybe five years later, you simply pay the money and get the player. . . .

But it is so graceless, so inefficient, so brutal. It's not that the Angels' methods cannot eventually work; Vito would eventually get the door open, at some cost to the equipment. The Angels believe in taking direct, forceful action to deal with the problem at hand, at whatever cost. Vito would unhesitantly use a forklift to get the door open; the Angels will unhesitantly trade ten years of shortstop play for two months of relief help if what they need at the moment is a reliever. Any advantage to be gained by reflection, patience, or acumen is regarded as practically dishonest.

I wondered if Bill ever had trouble working with the equipment. He said, "When you drive a forklift, you drive it backward a lot, and occasionally you run into a pallet of food products. You try to avoid this, but it's not a big deal. The worst that happens is you dent a few cans of beans. But one time I was leaving the plant at about one in the morning, and I backed into someone's car, because I was still in that frame of mind."

The second edition of the *Abstract* was almost double the size of the first. "I did the second one because I didn't do a good job on the first. I knew if I started earlier and worked harder, I could do more things." He did a detailed capsule of every team—not the type found in the typical annual. If you didn't know that Rod Carew was the AL batting champion, this wasn't the book for you.

Highlights from the '78 *Abstract* included:

- ◆ The assertion that Roger Maris's record was breakable, based on the idea that if George Foster were playing in a "normal" home park, he'd have hit sixty-five.
- ◆ The suggestion that teams were prone to overusing their knuckleballers. "Look up Wilbur Wood. He pitched a lot, and effectively, but I think it wore him down."
- ◆ In 1977 fewer errors were made against good teams than bad—not what you'd expect. Bill speculated that this was caused by teams playing their best lineups against good teams. Thus they made fewer errors but were still more likely to lose.
- ◆ The vaunted Orioles defense and pitching looked a lot less impressive outside of their home park. And, in what he called "the most shocking contention in this book," Bill wrote that due to the offense-inflating effects of Fenway Park, the supposed big-hitting Red Sox were, in fact, a team with outstanding pitching and a mediocre offense.

Susie finished school and moved away for the summer of 1977. Bill wrote her just about every day and went to see her several times. She moved back to Lawrence in the fall, after they decided to get married. "Neither of us wanted anything big or formal," she says. "Or traditional, for that matter. We sat in Bucky's and, eating a soft-serve ice cream cone, talked about how we could have a wedding without inviting our extended families. Our solution was to invite parents to the ceremony and have a reception for siblings later.

"There is a tiny little community ten miles from Lawrence called Stull that had a lovely old Methodist church and not much else. We had the ceremony there on a Friday afternoon. My mother made my floor-length green dress. Bill wore a tux he'd had made in Korea. He insists he offered to buy me a bouquet, which he says I turned down. I don't remember that part. For the wedding, though, I felt like I needed to be holding something, so that morning we rushed around to nurseries and found a small green plant which filled in for the traditional bouquet. (Kind of strange, I know.)

"Bill recited a passage from the Bible, and I chose a poem by Rilke. We did have a wedding cake later, but no one had even thought to plan a meal or anything, which seems strange to me now. Bill and I left that evening for a week-long driving trip to the Ozarks, and on our return, my mom hosted a gathering of our combined siblings."

When they got back from their honeymoon in November 1978, there was a letter from Dan Okrent, a writer/editor who was working on a masterpiece called *The Ultimate Baseball Book*. He'd read an *Abstract* and had written to express interest in writing an article about Bill. "I was ready to say I just can't do this again," Bill says. "That's when Dan's letter arrived."

Dan helped Bill score the plum assignment of writing *Esquire's* 1979 baseball preview, with four pages of team capsules that were pure early James. He wrote that the Twins were hurt by their owner's "penury, tactlessness, and racism." He sniped that "Dan Ford is arguably a hitter, but he plays outfield like a blind man staying overnight in a friend's apartment." The quip that Rick Cerone was to catching more or less what the late Thurman Munson had been to aviation was deleted for "taste."

Esquire ran a half-page profile of the "twenty-nine-year-old fanatic who, did he not really exist, could have been invented by Robert Coover." (Not the last time Bill would be associated with Coover's *The Universal Baseball Association, Inc., J. Henry Waugh, Prop.*) There was a photo of Bill wearing a Royals helmet, cocking a rolled-up *Abstract*. With wacky grin, shaggy beard, and goggle-size glasses, he looked like a half-in-the-bag coal miner, which he obviously wasn't, or the world's biggest baseball nut, which he arguably was.

The 1979 *Abstract* was skinnier than the 1978 edition, having print on both sides of the pages. "We were making progress," Bill quips. It introduced the account-form box score, a redesign of the standard box score that takes less space and has more information. Bill knew there was little chance of it catching on, and it didn't. He reintroduced it in 1983, writing, "I can build a better box score, and I have. I can't force anybody to use it."

As in previous editions, fielding was a significant focus: "The largest differences between fielders today are not in their various abilities to handle a baseball which is hit toward them, but in the speed, reaction time, and positioning skill which they employ to get to where the play is, and thus to have a chance on the ball."

In the 1978 book he had introduced a way to calculate the percentage of balls in play that a team's fielders turn into outs—the Defensive Efficiency Record (DER). In the '79 edition he confirmed that DER correlated with run prevention and winning percentage. The formula was complex, however. "A lot of people still use DER," he says. "It's common, and I use it for one thing or another every day. But the simplified versions of it that other people have advanced are better than the complicated form that I used in the seventies."

He wrote that there comes a point in the technical analysis of baseball records at which confidence in it begins to flag. "So why do I do it?" he asked, then answered:

> People who say they don't trust the records or that they are suspicious of statistical analysis are simply not thinking about what they are saying. Are people suspicious of the statistics which say that Lou Brock is a great base stealer, or of those that say he doesn't hit as well as he used to? The difference between a .275 hitter and a .300 hitter, even once a ballplayer is well established, is simply not visible. It is a difference which can be seen in the record books—an extra hit every two weeks—and nowhere else. The difference between a batting champion at .330 and a runner-up at .325 is nothing.
>
> And because of that, people who don't study the records become the prisoners of them. What is Hack Wilson doing in the

Hall of Fame? He has no more business there than the Pope has at Caesars Palace. He was put there because people read the raw numbers—190 RBIs, 56 HR—without understanding them, without making any attempt to put them back into the context from which they came, without considering the impact in the games in which they were compiled.

Without any exception, anyone who tells you that statistics lie is going to turn around in the next sentence and quote you a half-dozen of them. To understand baseball without reference to its statistics is an absurdity, like understanding American politics without reference to elections. The only choices are—use the statistics carefully, or use them loosely.

Dan Okrent was working on the article about Bill for *Sports Illustrated*. He and Bill went to a Royals-Twins game in Kansas City on September 11, 1979, and Dan spent a few days in Lawrence.

"The first version of the article was ready by early 1980," Bill says. "This began a bizarre series of scheduling and canceling of publication. *Sports Illustrated* had a fact-checking arrangement with the Elias Bureau, and there was tension between me and Elias."

The piece was picked over by a fact-checker who succeeded, for the time being, in squelching publication. One sticking point was that some of Bill's numbers were off by a hit or two. Elias wouldn't provide Bill with official statistics, so he was getting them from teams or from his own counts based on unofficial box scores. In one instance he had written that a Reds player hit .350 against lefties, which turned out to be off a few points. "It was irritating as hell to me," Bill says, "because Elias wouldn't give me the official stats."

Another bone of contention: the trading record of the Cubs. In the 1978 *Baseball Research Journal*, Bill had described his method for "scoring" trades. He evaluated each player's seasons and reduced "the contributions of all the players exchanged to a single ratio." With this method it was clear that despite their reputation as rotten traders, the Cubs hadn't traded poorly—Lou Brock notwithstanding.

"My understanding was that people at *SI* were choosing up sides," Bill says. "But I had no control over it. 'It's going to run,' they'd say. 'No, it's not.' 'Yes, it is.' It wasn't fun for me. I was working in a factory."

Susie says, "I look at some people as they're starting out—the husband's going to do this and the wife's going to do this and they're going to live here and have two kids. It all looks so orderly. We didn't do anything like that. We had no idea what Bill was going to do or what I was going to do or where we would live. We planned nothing. So we tried not to put too much weight on the article, because it could have turned out to be nothing."

6

Monkey Wrench

Before 1980 there wasn't a proper name for Bill's work, so he came up with *sabermetrics*, in honor of the Society for American Baseball Research. Founded in 1971, SABR fosters baseball research and discussion. Bill has said, "I would never have invented that word if I had realized how successful I was going to be. I never intended to help characterize SABR as a bunch of numbers freaks."

Bill tried to make it clear that numbers weren't the subject of the discussion. "The subject is baseball," he wrote. "The numbers bear a relationship to that subject and to us which is much like the relationship of tools to a machine and to the mechanic who uses them. The mechanic does not begin with a monkey wrench; basically, he is not even *interested* in the damn monkey wrench. All that he wants from the monkey wrench is that it do its job and not give him any trouble."

But the craftsman can't be faulted for finding magic in his tools. "When the numbers melt into the language," Bill wrote, "they acquire the power to do all of the things which language can do, to become fiction and drama and poetry."

Am I imagining things?

Do not the numbers of Ted Williams detail a story of fierce talent and, by the char of their ugly gaps, the ravages of exquisite frustration that ever accompany imperfect times? Do not the numbers of Roberto Clemente spell out a novella of irritable determination straining toward higher and higher peaks until

snapped suddenly by an arbitrary, but now inevitable, *machina*?
Do not the stressed and unstressed syllables of Willie Davis'
prime suggest an iambic indifference? Is there not a cavalcata in
Pete Rose's charge? Is there no union of thrill and agony in Roger
Maris' numbers? How else can one explain the phenomenon of
baseball cards, which is that a chart of numbers that would put
an actuary to sleep can be made to dance if you put it on one
side of a card and Bombo Rivera's picture on the other.

Before the *Abstract*, baseball fans understood a fixed set of statistical verities. A few metrics told us all we thought we needed to
know. Sportswriters and broadcasters transmitted the wisdom *and*
misperceptions baseball professionals disseminated—the game's "Kil-
imanjaro of repeated legend and legerdemain," Bill called it. Baseball
fans grasped the basic syntax of the box score, but the building blocks
of a more descriptive language existed, below the surface, in the
records.

The data needed to test much of baseball's traditional knowledge
always existed, but opinion and lore lorded it over research. It's so
much easier to form an opinion than to study a question, like the difference between making babies and raising children. "Perhaps the
central tenet of my career," he says, "is that hard information is much
more powerful than soft information. Whenever you add hard, solid
facts to a discussion, it changes that discussion in far-reaching ways,
and sometimes in unfortunate ways." Rather than start with an opinion and build a case, Bill began with the question and searched for
evidence to help answer it.

For example, the object of a baseball offense is to create runs. "A
hitter should be evaluated by his success at that which he is trying to
do," Bill wrote, "and that which he is trying to do is create runs." As
simple as that sounds, it's easy to overlook, because there are statistics
that can be seen as ends in themselves. Batting average is the classic
example. Bill lamented that end-of-season statistical summaries listed

teams in order of batting average. "It should be obvious that the purpose of an offense is not to compile a high team batting average," he wrote.

How, then, to measure run creation? The ideal would be a formula by which the elements of a player's batting record could be expressed as runs. But why not simply look at runs scored and runs batted in? Because individual counts of runs scored and batted in are distorted by context; for example, a player who comes to bat behind teammates who are on base a lot will drive in more runs than a player batting behind teammates who aren't. The RBI statistic tells you something about the hitter, but not purely.

Looking for a formula to express a stable relationship between the number of runs a team or player scores and a combination of his statistics, Bill tinkered until he came up with *runs created*, which in its basic form is:

$$\text{(Hits + Walks) (Total Bases) / (At-Bats + Walks) = Runs Created}$$
Or, the slightly more advanced:
$$\text{(H + W – Caught Stealing) (TB + .7 Steals) / (AB + W – CS) = RC}$$

Think of a player's (or a team's) offensive value as if it were a rectangle, with the ability to reach base (as on-base percentage) being one dimension and ability to advance runners (as total bases) being the other. Batting average makes up a big portion of both, so it gives an immediate sense of the size of the player's rectangle. But you have to adjust for walks on the OBP side and extra bases on the TB side. Otherwise, you'll overrate the players with high batting averages but little power and few walks, and underrate players who have low batting averages but walk a lot and/or have power.

> Don't argue with me—just look at the facts. In 1984 Greg Brock hit .225, yet he scored 33 runs and drove in 34 while making just 219 outs. Per 27 outs, that's over eight runs scored or driven in. Enos Cabell hit .310, yet he scored only 52 runs and drove in

only 44 while making 330 outs. Per 27 outs, that's less than eight runs scored or driven in. If the runs created formula is wrong, and if Brock in fact is not a more productive offensive player despite an average 85 points lower, then why does that happen? I know that the Dodger brass thinks that Brock has been a washout and the Houston brass thinks that Cabell has been a big hit, but they're human beings just like you and me, and they're wrong in this case.

In 1963 and '64 the Boston Red Sox were managed by Johnny Pesky, and Dick Stuart was at first base. In the '82 *Abstract*, Bill took up the question: Is a .260 hitter with 35 home runs as valuable to his team as a .320 hitter without? Bill called it Pesky/Stuart, because they were known to discuss the issue "at great length and full volume" on the team bus.

The question of who's more productive between the Cabell and Brock extremes is separate from the Pesky/Stuart question. Pesky had a high on-base factor, Stuart a high advancement factor. "Ah, yes. Pesky/Stuart," Bill wrote. "They were arguing about nothing." In their respective three best years, Pesky created 299 runs while using 1,257 outs. Stuart created 300 while using 1,259. Pesky may have been the better overall player. "But," Bill wrote, "that isn't what the argument was about. As hitters, the only thing to choose between is the needs of the team. If you were leaving people on base, you'd need Stuart; if you were having trouble getting on base, you'd need Pesky."

Two caveats about baseball statistics:

First, they're contextual, or, as Bill put it, "not pure accomplishments of men against other men," but "accomplishments of men in combination with their circumstances." For example, ballpark architecture is a monumental factor in the formation of statistics. While this fact was known and understood to varying degrees for decades, Bill played a sizable role in quantifying park effects and publicizing their importance. He wrote:

On a personal level, no one has been more affected by this than Jose Cruz, the great outfielder of the Houston Astros. When I say that this man is a great hitter, I mean that he is a great hitter—as good as, maybe better than, hitters like George Brett, Dale Murphy, Jim Rice, and Bill Madlock. If you look at their stats in road games over the years 1981–84, it is obvious that, as long as all players were in neutral parks, Cruz was the best hitter among that group; he outhit Rice, Murphy, and Brett during that period by more than thirty points (in road games) and also had a higher slugging percentage than any of them.

But when the players went home, Dale Murphy went home to Atlanta, Jim Rice went home to Fenway Park, and George Brett went home to Royals Stadium—and all three of them magically became much better hitters. Jose Cruz went home to the Astrodome, the worst hitter's park in baseball, and magically lost thirty points off his batting average and 80 percent of his home run power.

And because that happened, the public at large never realized that Cruz was the great hitter that he was. Cruz's statistics have defrauded him. They have not told his story true and fair, but through an unfriendly interpreter known as the Dome. Cruz's stats, if interpreted by the network of standards which are used to transmogrify baseball statistics into language, and thus make them meaningful to the public, simply fail to reveal the true quality of the man's bat.

The second is that when the public's faith in a set of metrics solidifies, it's tough to break. "Given an option, all men prefer to reject information," Bill wrote. "We start out life bombarded by a confusing, unfathomable deluge of signals, and we continue until our deaths to huddle under that deluge, never learning to make sense of more than a tiny fraction of it." Misguided faith leads to stubborn repetition of foolish decisions.

Will someone please explain this to me? In 1981 the Oakland A's stole ninety-eight bases, fourth highest total in the American

League, but hit a league-leading 104 home runs and posted the best won-lost record in the league. In 1982 they soared to a major league leading total of 232 stolen bases, but dropped to sixth in the league in home runs and fell off to a dismal 68–94 record.

After the season, team prez Roy Eisenhardt announced that the A's were going to rebuild their team concentrating on, in the order he said them, speed, pitching, and defense.

Basic runs created isn't the absolutely most accurate conceivable metric,* but it's a better distillation of run production than the fashionable on-base plus slugging. "OPS amounts to taking the elements of run creation and putting them together wrong," Bill says. "They shouldn't be *added* together, they should be *multiplied*. A team with a .400 on-base percentage and a .400 slugging percentage would score more runs than a team with .350 and .450, although both add up to an .800 OPS. I don't see that it's easier to figure than runs created, and it's certainly less accurate. It has become standard information. I think it's doing that to make me feel old."

Of course the components of OPS are meaningful. Bill explained, "There are two statistics, which, by themselves and without the aid of any considerations about base stealing, clutch hitting, or gravity waves, will predict the number of runs scored by a team. Those two statistics are on-base percentage and slugging percentage. A team which does well in those two areas will always do well in runs scored, no matter what else they don't do. They can be slow as the devil, they can be terrible bunters, bad clutch hitters, stupid base runners, and completely inept at hitting behind the runner. They will still score runs. A team which does poorly in those two areas will always do poorly in runs scored, no matter how well they do anything else."

The importance of on-base percentage is now clear to most, even to those who downplay it. Bill notes that the central insight of the on-base discussion is that the hitter, more than the pitcher, determines when a walk occurs.

*There's a thorough explanation of this in Bill's 2002 book *Win Shares*.

The Real World Is Complicated

Bill wrote in 2005:

First, it is always better to use a broad base of information than a narrow base of information. The habit of sorting statistics into "meaningful" statistics and "meaningless" statistics is an unfortunate and destructive way of evaluating the statistical universe, first because it causes us to discard information that we could use, and second because it causes us to turn a blind eye to the biases and distortions of those statistics that we have labeled "reliable."

Labeling certain statistics "reliable" and others "unreliable" simply does not describe the real universe, in which

a. All statistics contain biases, many of them unknown, unmeasured, and impossible to remove by statistical adjustments, and

b. Virtually all statistics are meaningful at a certain level.

The "Runs Allowed" statistic (for pitchers) contains many, many potential biases which we are helpless to remove. Suppose that we have two teammates, pitching 160 innings each because of injuries. One pitcher is injured in April and May, and thus pitches 75 percent of his innings in hot weather; the other pitcher is injured in July and August, and thus pitches 75 percent of his innings in cold weather. Since the weather dramatically affects the run scoring level, the actual run context of the two pitchers is very different—but we are powerless to adjust for this.

Suppose that one pitcher, by the luck of the draw, happens to pitch twice in Colorado, not at all in San Francisco, while the teammate happens to pitch three times in San Francisco, not at all in Colorado. Such things happen all the time. This biases the runs allowed context at a very significant level, but we have no ability to adjust for this or remove the bias.

Suppose that one pitcher happens to pitch three times against the Yankees, not at all against the Royals, while the other pitcher pitches 37 innings against the Royals, 6 against the Yankees. This biases the run context in a way that we are powerless to adjust for.

Suppose that one pitcher, because his manager believes him to be well suited to his home park, pitches 110 innings at home, 50 on the road, while the other splits his innings the other way.

Thus, to rely too heavily on the runs allowed rate is dangerous, since the runs allowed rate can be—and sometimes is—strongly influenced by unseen contextual factors. The runs allowed rate simply cannot be treated as a pure and reliable measure of a pitcher's contribution.

Suppose, on the other hand, that we ask the question "Is the winning percentage meaningful?"

Well, if you have two teammates, one of whom is 15-11, the other of whom is 8-15, is it likely that 15-11 pitcher is actually a better pitcher?

Yes, of course it is likely. It is probably . . . what, an 85, 90 percent shot, given no other information?

Thus, the won-lost record of the pitcher certainly **is** meaningful at a certain level. It may well be that the runs allowed rate is **more** reliable and more meaningful than the won-lost record, but it is certainly **not** true that the one bit of information is 100% reliable, nor that the other is zero percent reliable.

The harder and more confusing question is whether the won-lost record is meaningful *independent of the runs allowed,* or whether the "meaning" of the won-lost record is entirely subsumed by the runs allowed rate.

The argument against won-lost records, I think, is that *won-lost records have no predictive significance independent of the runs allowed rate.* In other words, if you take two teammates with the same innings pitched and the same ERA, but one of whom finished 15-11 while the other finishes 8-15, there is no evidence that the pitcher with the better won-lost record will perform any better in the following season. The 8-15 pitcher is just as likely to win 20 games in the next season as the 15-11 pitcher.

I understand this argument, I think, because I invented this argument. I was, for several years, so far as I know the only person on the planet who believed in this argument. The extent to which won-lost records are predictive of future won-lost records *independent of runs allowed* is zero percent—therefore, the won-lost record is not independently meaningful.

This is a common type of argument in sabermetrics. Various forms of this argument are used to demonstrate that clutch hitting does not exist (because measures of clutch performance independent of actual batting skill have zero reliability from season to season), that catchers have little impact on run prevention (because catcher's ERAs do not deviate reliably from team ERAs), that hits allowed by pitchers are not meaningful (because hits allowed, independent of other factors, are unstable from season to season), that deviations from expected wins and losses by teams are not meaningful (because the Pythagorean expectation for wins and losses predicts next-season success better than the actual won-lost record does), and for many other purposes.

But this argument, in some of these cases, is much, much less convincing than I once believed it to be. I have come to understand, by modeling the problem in various ways, that it is much, much, much more difficult than I realized to determine by this method whether or not a skill factor does exist. Suppose that there were a catcher who saved his team 2/10ths of a run per nine innings—30-plus runs a year, a very large factor in the evaluation of that player's contribution to his team—and suppose that you had several years worth of catcher's ERAs and pitcher/catcher combination ERAs to study to determine this. Could you identify that catcher's defensive contribution, in the data?

The correct answer is "absolutely, positively not." You absolutely could not identify that good defensive catcher, with even 55 percent reliability, or anything approaching 55 percent reliability, even given several years' worth of data to work with. It *seems* like one should be able to do this, but it is actually impossible, even given near-ideal conditions to work with (good and bad defensive catchers splitting time evenly, etc.).

It is a problem of shifting plates—trying to make a stable measurement against a rapidly shifting base. It is much, much harder than it seems—hundreds of times harder. Therefore, all of the conclusions which rely on this "departure from shifting plates" type of analysis are suspect.

Baseball people traditionally *believe* that there is an "ability to win" in some pitchers—that some pitchers can win games 8-6 and 1-0, while other pitchers can lose the same games 10-8 and 2-1. While I am skeptical of this argument, the proof that it is untrue is vastly less convincing than I once believed it to be. The argument to dismiss the won-lost record is unconvincing—therefore, at least from my standpoint, the won-lost record is back in the game.

To depart for a moment into a philosophical blind alley . . . simplifying the universe is a necessary but dangerous habit of thought. It is necessary to simplify the universe, because the external universe is vastly more complicated than any image of it that we are capable of holding in our minds—therefore, it is necessary to reduce and eliminate the complications of the real world in order to form any understanding of it.

But simplifying the universe is also dangerous, because some of what is left out of our image is nonetheless real and significant. This is the essential problem of political parties: that both parties, both "bents" of political philosophy, simplify the universe in order to make sense of it. Republicans believe that we must all be responsible for ourselves and those near to us; Democrats believe that we must all help to take care of one another. Both principles are absolutely true, but both are simplifications of a more complicated universe. One is no more true and no more useful than the other. Democrats defend their simplification by labeling individual responsibility as selfishness; Republicans defend their simplification by labeling sharing as irresponsibility. Both parties thus trundle happily along with political philosophies that manifestly fail to explain the real world.

When I was a young writer, I simplified the baseball universe by declaring the runs allowed to be meaningful, and the won-lost record to be meaningless. A great many people have now bought into this simplification.

But as a more mature writer, I have come to understand that the real world is more complicated than that. The question is not which statistic is "reliable" and which is "unreliable," but rather, what degree of trust we choose to put in each one. Certainly the degree of trust that I place in runs allowed rates is much higher than the degree of trust that I place in won-lost records—but not by a margin of 100 to 0. In the last book I used 85 to 15, and I am more likely to go to 80-20 than I am to go to 90-10. It is a complicated world. A statistical system which understands this is better than a system which denies it.

A delusive idea regularly proffered about Bill is that he advocates "baseball by numbers," whatever that means. But most statistical analysts will tell you that numbers don't tell the whole story. W. Edwards Deming famously said, "In God we trust; all others bring data." But he also said, "Data will provide you with about 3 percent of what you really need to know." Bill says, "Statistical images simplify the real world. This clarifies the picture, which is useful, but the problems come when people insist that the real world is as simple as the statistical picture.

There's an argument that sabermetricians make the world too complicated, but that's not necessarily true. They may actually be doing the opposite: oversimplifying the complex."

That said, statistics are an essential part of understanding a complex game. Bill wrote in an early *Abstract*:

> Consider a single moment in a pennant race, a July moment in a minor game against a meaningless team, but a moment in which a ball is hit very hard but caught by an outfielder who is standing in the right place, but before it is caught it must be hit, and before it is hit it must be thrown, and before it is thrown this pitch must be selected, and this pitcher must be selected, and this batter must be selected, and there are reasons why he was selected to throw and why he was selected to hit, and there are reasons why this pitch was selected and why it was thrown this way and why it was swung at and why it was hit and why, finally, the outfielder chanced to be in the right place, so that in the single moment of a pennant race, there is a complexity that surpasses any understanding.
>
> A game consists of dozens of batters and hundreds of pitches, and a season for one team consists of hundreds of games, and the league consists of a dozen or more teams. And how many details can you think about, to add up to a pennant race in your mind?
>
> Is it not obvious, then, that it is only in stepping *away* from the pennant race that we can develop a vision of it? No one could remember at any one time a significant portion of the at-bats that Mike Fischlin has in a season—even Mike Fischlin's wife. How then, remember the season?
>
> That is why statistics have such a place in baseball. Statistics look at games by the hundreds, and without the details. And that is why everyone who is a baseball fan—everyone, everyone, *everyone*—reads the statistics, studies the statistics, and believes what he sees in the statistics. Without them, it is impossible to have any concept of the game, save for meaningless details floating in space.

7

National *Abstract*

For the cover of the 1980 *Abstract*, Susie drew an ape contemplating a baseball, *Thinker* style. Bill introduced *sabermetrics* as a term and asserted that the most important addition to the *Abstract* was platoon statistics—batting records versus left- and right-handed pitchers.

In the '81 edition—the last self-published *Abstract*—Bill theorized that big, thick sluggers—the Greg Luzinski body type—tend to wear out quickly, having shorter careers than you otherwise might expect. "I think it should be kept in mind when evaluating the career expectation of, say, Bob Horner," he presciently wrote.

On underachieving Cleveland outfielder Rick Manning: "Patience with a young player, yes, but not this much patience. There is a place for *im*patience in the building of a baseball team, too. All of us, baseball players included, have a tendency to coast for as long as we can, and never to find out what we can do until we have a time of crisis. If I was running the Indians, I'd create a crisis for Rick Manning in a hell of a hurry. If he finds himself, great; if he doesn't, we've got a baseball team to run."

On then-commissioner Bowie Kuhn: "My perception of Bowie Kuhn is much like Gore Vidal's perception of George Washington—an incompetent commander with an uncanny knack not only for surviving his own fiascos, but for rising through them, a man stolid and dull and gray all over, but with a 'serpentine cunning' (Vidal) that makes him an incomparable politician."

Of the "sabermetric-type material" Thomas Boswell was doing for *Inside Sports* (e.g., the Big Bang Theory and Total Average), Bill wrote that the important "truth" of the Big Bang Theory, that the winning team will score more runs in an inning than the loser will in all nine, was not true at all. Bill felt that the idea had merit, nonetheless, in World Series play.

He wrote that the problem with TA was that if you figured *team* Total Averages, the teams came out "all mixed up": Teams that actually scored 600 runs ranked ahead of teams that had scored 700. "The world needs another offensive rating system like Custer needed more Indians (or, for that matter, like the Indians needed another Custer)," Bill wrote. "What we really need, as I wrote three years ago, is for the amateurs to clear the floor."

> I don't mean to sound harsh or negative about the work that Boswell has done. He is a first-rate writer, and I would happily say that he was a first-rate sabermetrician if I thought that any of you would believe it. If, like most of the nation's sportswriters, he had never developed a single idea about how baseball games were won, if he had never done a half-hour's research to check his idea, then I would not be criticizing him. It would hardly seem wise or fair to single him out for criticism because he did have a single idea, and he did do a half-hour's research, give or take ten minutes. The best ideas are those which have one saying, "Well, I wonder why nobody else ever thought of that?" Boswell has yet to come up with such an idea. But I would give a week's pay to have Boswell working for a K.C. newspaper, where I could read his stuff regularly. He's good.

Inside Sports **ran** an article in May 1981 titled "Baseball Nuts," about five people who "care more deeply than most" about baseball. One of the five was a tall, bearded fellow in Kansas who self-published an atypical baseball annual and played Ball Park, the baseball table game. The reporter, visiting Bill in Lawrence, sat in to watch a Ball Park game.

Bill remembers, "On my team were Joe Gordon, Spud Chandler, Harlond Clift, Dixie Walker . . . some of the all-time greats. I asked him how many of the two teams' players he'd heard of, and he said Lou Gehrig, who was on the other guy's team. He was the only one. The irony was that the reporter had a BBWAA card and could vote in Hall of Fame elections."

Dan Okrent's profile of Bill in the May 31, 1981, *Sports Illustrated* perfectly balanced the statistics factor with an appreciation of Bill's "almost poetic" writing and quirky charm. Okrent wrote, "Driving home one night with a friend from a Royals game in Kansas City, James stopped for a lonesome red light while delivering a brilliant soliloquy on the statistical evidence of shortstop Freddie Patek's decay as an effective player. The traffic light changed to green and then it changed back to red. It changed to green again, back to red and back to green again before James' disquisition ran its course and he returned to earth. 'Oh, the light's changed,' he said, and proceeded calmly down the road."

Susie says, "We've always been very grateful to Dan for seeing the merit in Bill's work and the *Abstract.*" Okrent's push to bring Bill to a larger audience didn't stop there. He connected Bill with an agent and prompted the publisher at Ballantine Books to bid for the right to take the *Abstract* national. Bill says Ballantine paid him $10,000 for the first national *Abstract.* When it did well he got a contract for four years "for a reasonable amount of money." With the advance as a down payment, he and Susie were able to buy an old house in Winchester, Kansas.

"You'd think I would have been completely focused on what was happening in my career at that time," he says, "but I wasn't." His dad had been diagnosed with cancer. His brother, Bob, a truck driver, had been found dead in the cab of his rig a few months earlier, cause of death unknown. Bill says, "We should have asked for an autopsy, but we didn't, and one was never done." Then a close friend of Bill's was killed when a tornado hit south Lawrence. Bill says, "He was riding his bike when he realized the tornado was coming. He rushed inside a building at the last minute. Apparently there was a reinforced part and a nonreinforced part. He was in the wrong part."

Even in the best of times, the yearly book crunch—between the baseball season's end and the manuscript due date—was like a "psychological trauma" for Bill, Susie says. The time and brainpower that went into the *Abstract* were extreme, and the schedule was brutal. As pressure mounted, Bill would pretend it wasn't happening. He started reading books unrelated to baseball, eating too many Pringles, and drinking too much Diet Pepsi. But once he got on track he was unstoppable—working fifteen hours at a stretch, sleeping four.

The book crunch was a winter phenomenon, and winter in Kansas can be as cold as Neptune's moon. Bill wore zip-up coveralls over his pajamas, and an electric blanket over that. Susie played a vital part in making sure her husband didn't go completely cuckoo. Bill wrote, "I love my work at two o'clock in the afternoon, but it does wear a bit at four o' clock in the morning after morning, and I've no idea how anyone else can endure it. But Susan McCarthy does and at the heaviest moments finds new burdens to pick up, which gets the work done."

The first national *Abstract* manuscript was written longhand by Bill. Susie typed it on an electric typewriter she kept at home for typing bills for the local law firm where she worked. The manuscript was edited first by Dan, then by Peter Gethers—editor for the entire run of *Abstract*s and *Baseball Books*. Pete says that Ballantine was "sort of a failed company" at the time, but the *Abstract* revived it. The first edition was a success, but it tested the production staff. "It was a nightmare for everyone," Gethers says. "I've never worked with another author like Bill. He has random quirks that he defends with a rigid system of justifications. If he spelled a player's name one way on one page and differently on another, he wanted it left the way he'd done it. If we tried to fix it, he'd go ballistic. If we made a suggestion he didn't like, he'd write an e-mail that said, 'Whoever wants it this way is a moron.'"

Susie says, "Publishing the books at home he could print what he wrote, just as he wrote it. To have someone he didn't know come in and start giving advice was difficult for him. He knows what he wants to do, and if there's any suggestion to the contrary, he tends to take offense. Since I used to read everything and did a lot of his typing, I learned early on that it was a risky business to point out even spelling errors. I just corrected them and went on. If I thought a sentence was poorly worded or needed punctuation, I learned to keep my opinion to myself." Once, one of her professors called to say he enjoyed the book but couldn't resist passing along one thing he wished were different. "He thought it was a little lazy to use cuss words," Susie says. "I told Bill about his advice, but of course it didn't do a damn bit of good."

Reactions to Bill and the *Abstract* pointed to the gap between intellectualism and jockism, and, to an extent, to a generational split. Maybe such generalizations aren't worth making, but the bottom line is that this stuff wasn't for everyone. You can see where Bill was coming from in his first choice of an assistant. Jim Baker, a New Jersey native in his early twenties, had devoured the first national *Abstract*. He answered an ad in the SABR newsletter and took a written test.

Jim was working as a swingman in a mental facility in Piscataway, alternating day and night shifts with days off in between. Bill flew him out to Lawrence, and Jim remembers thinking, "Wow, a liberal arts major being flown to an interview." Among the questions, Bill asked Jim if he played chess. "Life's too short for chess," Jim replied. Jim flew back to Jersey, loaded up his 1965 Wildcat convertible, *Das Boot*, and drove to Kansas to begin his new job.

Bill had an office on Kentucky Street in half the first floor. The other half housed a Gestalt therapy practice. The bathroom was in that part of the building, and Jim heard strange things during those trips. The office was listed in the phone book as *Baseball Abstract*. One evening a drunken Rotisserie player called. "Is this the man?" the caller wanted to know. "Is this Bill James, the man himself? My team's got all these macho guys, Latin guys. What should I do?" Jim was lonely, so he talked to the guy. "We did get some strange calls," Bill says, "but Jim took a lot more of them than I did."

Bill and Jim shared a passion for baseball, junk food, and humor. Bill remembers Jim reworking a *Family Circus* strip in which the grandmother had cleared off the lower shelves of her tchotchke collection to keep little hands from touching. One kid was crying and the other was pointing to the empty shelves. Jim rewrote the caption to read, "Aww, Grandma sold all her figurines to buy crack."

Jim did some great writing in the '84 *Abstract* and the first *Historical Abstract*, then moved to New York hoping to write for *Saturday Night Live*. He ended up writing a novel about a mailman who steals mail. Later he moved back to Kansas to work for the Major Indoor Soccer League. Now he has a column at BaseballProspectus.com. Among his many moments of comedic brilliance there, he coined the term *invisimé* for the things you leave off your résumé, in partial tribute to Wally Backman.

Irascible Bill

In the national *Abstract* days, certain players and types were regular targets of Bill's ire:

Doug Flynn's reputation as a fielder preceded him, but his bat was a no-show. In the '84 *Abstract*, Bill wrote, "Doug Flynn does just as much to destroy the Montreal offense as Tim Raines can do to build it."

Abstract readers counted on Bill to shoot straight, and he was hardest on players whose only claim to a roster spot was that they'd hung around long enough to be called veterans. Owning up to the "worst prediction of the '82 season"—naming Jack Perconte as a potential Rookie of the Year—Bill wrote, "Who looks worse, me or [manager] Dave Garcia?" Perconte had started well, gone into a small slump, and promptly lost his job. "Sat on the bench for whom?" Bill wrote. "For a couple of past-thirty journeymen utility players, players who have established beyond the furthest remove of doubt that they are *not* championship quality ballplayers. What is the point? How can anyone be that blind?"

Of second baseman Duane Kuiper, who rarely got on base (and when he did was the worst base stealer in the league), Bill wrote, "It's absolutely incredible that a player this bad could be given 3,000 at-bats in the major leagues." Of third baseman Ken Reitz, who was "slower than a lot of dead guys," Bill wrote, "He's something: career run totals are 5, 40, 48, 43, 58, 41, 42, 39, and 10. You see those and you'd never believe he was a regular."

Bill had no patience for the Omar Moreno type—speedy, but with a low OBP and no power. He tagged Moreno as "the worst lead-off man in baseball" in the '83 *Abstract*. In the '84: "Ecch. Unless Buddy Biancalana happens to make the Royals, Omar Moreno is the worst player in the major leagues. There can be absolutely no excuse for writing his name on a lineup card."

Bill did much to discredit the use of low-OBP players as leadoff men, but you still see this type at or near the tops of lineups. He railed against using "bat control" types in the two-hole, and noted the tendency of managers to put a second baseman in the second spot in the batting order. Let's leave this player generic:

> A classic "bat control" second hitter. He hit only .257, and his batting average represented 73 percent of his offensive value, as his peripheral stats were awful (included two stolen bases and eight caught stealing). So why would anyone say "bat control" as if these words were a magic wand, and jam an unproductive player right in the middle of your offense?

In the *Abstract* era, no type was less loved than Alfredo Griffin's: "He stops every ball that comes his way, and every rally, too." The traditional reasoning is that it doesn't matter that he doesn't hit if he makes up for it in the field:

> I can't stand it when people say that if he does the job with the glove it doesn't matter what he hits. *Of course* it matters what he hits. . . . Whenever you hear that when you have one thing, this doesn't matter or that doesn't matter, and you'll hear it fifty times this year, you're listening to baseball games go flying out the window.

Rodney Scott was a second baseman in Montreal. When the Expos fired manager Dick Williams in mid-1981, Williams went to San Diego. Bill was one of Dick's biggest fans, but not when it came to Rodney Scott.

> Williams was fired in Montreal because he became locked in a struggle with his players and his front office that came about in large part because of his irrational insistence that a .210 hitter with no power who is none too swift on the double play and who frankly did not belong on a major league roster was, believe it or not, the best player on the team.
>
> Yet having been finally released from this struggle, having been eventually and deservedly fired because of it, and having directly and deservedly rehired by another team because when not dealing with Rodney Scott he is a wonderful manager, what does he do? He attempts—no, he *demands*, insists, sits in his office and throws a temper tantrum when his attempt is thwarted—to take this problem to San Diego with him.
>
> I find it a wonderful instruction on the usefulness of emotional attachments in decision making that this man who is ordinarily as canny a judge of talent as there is could form a blind spot so large that it would hide from him such monstrous ineptitude.

No player took more hits than Enos Cabell. Bill and Enos had mutual friends, and one fall Bill visited them just days after Enos had. Bill reported that Enos left him an "unfriendly but good-natured" gesture, through an intermediary. Bill wrote, "Everybody tells me that Enos is a hell of a good guy, and you know, you can tell he is. His abilities being what they are, would he be in the major leagues if he wasn't?"

Of course, Sparky Anderson also got Bill's ire up, and when Cabell became one of Sparky's Tigers, Bill let fly with both barrels:

> When Enos Cabell was hot early in the year, you'd ask Sparky Anderson about him and Sparky would say "Enos Cabell is a *we* ballplayer. You don't hear Enos Cabell saying 'I did this' and 'I did that.'" I think that's what drives me nuts about Sparky Anderson, that he's so full of brown stuff that it just doesn't seem like he has any words left over for a basic, fundamental understanding of the game. I want to look at a player on the basis of what, specifically, he can and cannot do to help you win a baseball game, but Sparky's so full of "winners" and "discipline" and "we ballplayers" and self-consciously asinine theories about baseball that he seems to have no concept of how it is, mechanically, that baseball games are won and lost.*
> I mean, I would never say that it was not important to have a team with a good attitude, but Christ, Sparky, there are millions of people in this country who have good attitudes, but there are only about 200 who can play a major league brand of baseball, so which are you going to take? Sparky is so focused on all that attitude stuff that he looks at an Enos Cabell and he doesn't even see that *the man can't play baseball.* This we ballplayer, Sparky, can't play first, can't play third, can't hit, can't run, and can't throw. So who cares what his attitude is?

*Believe it or not, Bill had written in 1979 that Sparky was "obviously" a good manager.

Bill felt that to an intelligent reader, it would be clear that his intent was not to hammer on Enos Cabell, but to make the point that ball games are won and lost on the field of play. Attitude, leadership, talent, desire, and experience are valuable *if you turn them into results on the field*. Bill wrote, "If you don't turn them into results, and Enos was not at the time, they're meaningless words. . . . If you lose a ballgame on the field you cannot win it back in the clubhouse, and anybody who thinks you can is a loser."

Once, one of the agents Bill worked for, Tom Reich, threw a party Bill attended, and Enos was there. Bill says, "I was introduced to him and there was no look of recognition in his eyes and I thought, 'Thank God.' But I was talking to him later and he made a joke about something I'd written. He knew exactly who I was. He was just classy in handling it."

When the '83 *Abstract* hit the paperback bestseller list, Susie remembers, "Bill and I were in the backyard of our Winchester home playing with our two collies, when a beat-up old pickup drove up and parked. A man got out and came up to our chain-link fence and said, 'Is this where'—he looked at his notes—'a Bill James lives?' We didn't try to run and hide. He told us he had a delivery from his liquor store in the nearby town of Oskaloosa. We were puzzled, the man seemed puzzled, but we told him we hadn't ordered anything. 'Someone from New York called and ordered this for Bill James. I was supposed to deliver it, too.' The man went back to his truck and brought back a case of whiskey. We asked if there was a note and he said no. Neither Bill nor I care for whiskey, but under the circumstances it seemed best to accept it and ask questions later. Turns out Random House wanted to acknowledge Bill's first book on the bestseller list and help us with our celebration. They had wanted to send champagne, but the small rural liquor store didn't have twelve bottles. Plenty of whiskey in stock, though. Living in isolation as we did, we hadn't even thought of having a party, but at least the liquor store owner graciously allowed us to exchange the whiskey for some wine."

By the mid-eighties, the *Abstract* and its author had become a cultural marker. *Newsweek* once called the *Janus Report* "the sexual equivalent of the *Bill James Baseball Abstract*." There were references to "the Bill James of education policy," of suicide, of movies, elections, comedy, weather. . . . A book review in the *Chicago Tribune* praised an author for being to politics what Bill James is to baseball: "a mix of historian, social observer, and numbers cruncher who illuminates his subject with perspective and a touch of irreverence."

The salient references were to what Bill calls a willingness to take small questions people care about, but that no one takes very seriously, and take them seriously. The stereotypical references were to the "guru of statistics" image, which Bill never liked, as he made clear in the introduction of the first *Historical Baseball Abstract:*

> I write an annual book about baseball called *The Baseball Abstract*. It's kind of a technical book, at times, and there are a couple of essays in it every year that are not real easy to understand; it's sort of like *Street & Smith's Baseball Annual,* only it's for adults. I invent all manner of different ways of measuring things, estimating things, describing relationships within the game, and I use these to analyze almost any question about baseball that comes up. Some people like it, some people don't. I was once described by a now defunct publication as "the guru of baseball statistics," and by Sparky Anderson as "a little fat guy with a beard . . . who knows nothing about nothing."* Actually, I'm seven inches taller than Sparky is, but what the heck; three out of four ain't bad, and it sure beats being described as the guru of baseball statistics.

To see Bill James' contribution to baseball writing as being mostly about statistics is like seeing Babe Ruth's contribution to baseball

*Sparky says, "Bill does a great job at what he does. Everybody gets mad once in their lifetime."

playing as being primarily about home runs. The "Sultan of Swat" was an on-base leader ten times, an ace pitcher for five seasons, etc. The "Sultan of Stats" wrote passage after passage that shows baseball as life in microcosm.

The Cleveland Metaphor

Sports metaphors tend to be cheesy, but Bill pulled it off by sending up the idea in his exposition on the tragicomedy of the mid-eighties Cleveland Indians, whom he suggested be renamed the Cleveland Blahs. From the '86 *Abstract*:

> The Cleveland Indians remind you of one of those movies that is supposed to be a metaphor for Life, and the only thing you can think of while watching it is that if this is life I'm sure glad it isn't mine. In Life, as in the Indians, we seem to waste so much of our talent, we seem to spend so much of our time bashing ourselves against entrenched and immovable forces. We make blind decisions about our lives and look back on them in awe of our own stupidity. They should call themselves the Cleveland Metaphor, or simply the Cleveland Life. I spent many years rooting for a terrible team, and I watch this team with a certain sympathy. But I'm sure glad it isn't mine.

Weather . . . or Not

We've all known someone so focused on the problems of a thing, she completely forgets the good stuff. Back when the San Francisco Giants played in Candlestick Park, there was a movement to build a domed stadium. Bill wrote in the '84 *Abstract*:

> What is it, exactly, that attracts people so to the idea of putting a roof over a park? I know people who have lived in Minneapolis and gone to a good many baseball games there, and what they remember most is the weather, the wonderful warm evenings,

sitting there at maybe seventy-five, eighty degrees on a June evening, feeling in your face the same wind that carries the ball in from the track.

And yet, incongruously, it was the weather that they wanted to keep out. Sometimes people become so problem-oriented, so focused on the worst part of a thing, that they fail even to see that in shutting out the bad weather, they are also shutting out the good weather, and that there is at least as much good weather as bad. An odd psychological mechanism at work here, the perception of weather as inherently negative, something to be avoided.

The Saddest Thing

Before he loved the Red Sox, the Royals had Bill's devotion. This paragraph from the '92 *Baseball Book* speaks to the broken hearted:

> The Royals now must face the fact that after four years of rebuilding they have nothing going for them; they are at the *beginning* of a rebuilding cycle, not the middle or the end. And that is what will be hard for them and their fans—to accept that what is gone, is gone. It looked good, but it didn't work, and nothing now can be saved from it. While anyone may be a year away from a miracle, they must face the fact that they are not a year away from having a good team, but three years. They need to face the fact that *they need to start over.*

Losing a Step

Sometimes when we're getting old, we cling to a self-image that isn't hitched to reality. Bill wrote about that in an '87 *Abstract* essay, "The Fastest Player in Baseball," which is what Willie Wilson was . . . eight or nine years earlier.

> It being observed last summer that Willie Wilson didn't seem to run quite as well as he used to, Wilson replied that yes, he did

think he had lost a stride but that he didn't think anyone except him could tell the difference. First of all, this isn't true (anyone can see the difference), but this comment struck me because the evidence of Wilson's loss of speed is all over the statistics. Wilson, who used to steal eighty bases a year, now steals thirty or forty. Whereas he once stole successfully in almost 90 percent of his attempts, now he's in the range of 80 percent. Whereas he once went to the plate over seven hundred times and grounded into only one double play, he now grounds into one a month or so. Whereas he used to hit several inside-the-park home runs homers a year, he hit none in 1986. Whereas he once scored 133 runs in a season, he scored only 77 in 1986. Whereas he once made 3.4 plays a game in the outfield, last year he made 2.66. Whereas he used to hit twelve triples a year, he hit only seven in 1986. How could anyone not "see" that he had lost a step?

Bill's books are full of passages that intermix the art of writing and the science of sabermetrics. Yet he's a hundred times more likely to be tagged as "stat guru" than "writer." George Plimpton wrote that Christy Mathewson once said, "A pitcher is not a ballplayer," and "what he meant was that a pitcher is a specialist, an artist, with all the accompanying need of consolation and encouragement." Bill hasn't suffered from *zero* encouragement, but he isn't in the writers' wing of the Hall of Fame, and you won't find him in collections of the best sportswriting. That's in part because he's seen primarily as "the ultimate stat freak"—the baseball equal of seeing Jonas Salk as the ultimate test tube freak.

Bill's influence among readers of baseball books can be compared to, say, Lou Reed's in popular music. Not every new act from the last thirty years owes a debt to Lou's first band, but just about every good act does. Brian Eno had a classic line about that band: "Only five thousand people ever bought a Velvet Underground album, but every single one of them started a band." Those who immersed themselves in the *Baseball Abstract* grew up to spread Bill's influence in every arena that involves thinking or writing.

The depressing gaggle of televised baseball's so-called analysts inflicted on us by FOX, ESPN, and the lot appear to have read and understood about as much Bill James as the typical *American Idol* winner has listened to and absorbed Lou Reed. The clichés and recycled non-insights issue forth in a water-torture drip drip drip from the mouths of "those druids," as Bill has referred to them. If you're familiar with *The Matrix*, it's possible to interpret the Agents as infectious, replicating clichés. At one point Morpheus tells Neo that the Agents are guarding all the doors and holding all the keys. Bill wrote, "Clichés are the soldiers of ignorance, and an army of sentries encircles the game, guarding every situation from which a glimmer of fresh truth might be allowed to escape." Bill James was the closest thing to Neo that the baseball matrix has seen.

Tim O'Reilly, founder of the country's largest independent publisher of computer books, notes that the *Abstract*s had the freshness and personality people like to claim for blogging. For example, this bit on Greg Luzinski:

> So what do they call him? The Bull. How is it possible for such an original form to become recognized by such a worn moniker? The bovine image is an acceptable starting point, although over the years he has become less bovine and more porcine. But how about Beef or Slaughterhouse or something? That works, doesn't it—Slaughterhouse Luzinski? The problem with The Bull is that it sounds like it was decided upon by a 7 to 4 vote in the Phillies' front office, which, come to think of it, it probably was.

Bill's love of politics came into play when he wrote about the fact that the Angels kept changing double-play mates in the early eighties:

> Rarely this side of Jimmy Carter does one see such a classic illustration of how it is that a series of perfectly rational short-term decisions can mount up to an irrational pattern. It's not that the Angels look ahead at the eighties and say, "Well, what we want to do with our double-play combination in this decade is to change

it every year. We find that our players play more exciting defense if they are totally unfamiliar with one another." It is simply that the Angels don't have the attention span required to set up a plan of action in 1982 and act on it in 1983. They never look ahead at all. . . . And thus the future is, and will always be, a continual surprise to them.

His gift for pinpointing the key question at the heart of a debate and animating tenets of economics and statistics—or, in this case, logic—comes out in the Robin Yount commentary of the '83 *Abstract*:

I am reliably assured that Robin Yount is not, in addition to his other virtues, a brilliant man, but he made the one most perceptive comment that I heard on television in the summer of 1982. When asked who he thought should vote for the All-Star game, the players or the fans, he said, "I can't really answer that question because I don't know who the game is supposed to be for. I don't know if the game is supposed to be for the fans or if it is supposed to be for the players." You see the point? You know those people who run around saying that the players should elect the All-Star teams because look at this vote and look at that one and there are all kinds of people who don't deserve the honor who wind up in the starting lineup? Those people are making an assumption, without even realizing that they are, that the purpose of the All-Star game is to honor the players, and therefore that the desire to honor the right people takes precedence over the desire to put in front of the fans the people the fans want to see. Is the game basically an honor for the players, or is it basically an entertainment for the fans? The answer you select to that question will tell you who ought to elect the teams. People simply leap over that question and construct their reasoning from beyond it; Yount sliced up the argument with a deftness that William Buckley should envy.

That passage holds a clue to how Bill organizes his thoughts. Bill's friend at the *Kansas City Star*, Joe Posnanski, says, "I think this is a big part of his genius. He doesn't skip steps." His logic may not always be flawless, his conclusions not always airtight. But in general he makes a concerted effort not to skip over evidence in a rush toward summation.

Bill interwove psychology, social science, and history in commenting on the baseball gambling scandals of 1918–20, of which he wrote, "What is rarely mentioned about the Black Sox scandal is that it was merely a part of its time, a time in which corruption was gaining rapidly in American society."

> In society at large we use sports to express and defend our values, as well as to teach them. Strange as it seems, the reaction of the public in the period after the War to End All Wars was, in essence, that it was one thing when the police were corrupt, that it was one thing when juries were bribed and judges kept on retainer, that it was one thing when elections were rigged and politicians let contracts go to the highest briber, but when *baseball players* started fixing games, well that was just too much; something had to be done about it. And it was; the expulsion of the crooked players was a symbolic purging and cleansing of society which set the stage for the many other purgings and cleansings which are remembered now as the Teapot Dome scandal. It is so odd that this is remembered now not as the period when governors took bribes to free criminals, but as a time when a few baseball players threw the big game.

If there had been a movie theater in Mayetta when he was young, Bill might have become a film critic. The *Abstracts* contain scattered movie references, including this lesson for man-a-gers in this 1983 comment on Ted Simmons:

> One of the many wonderful moments in the movie *Ragtime* occurs just after the terrorist group has seized the library, and Jimmy Cagney, the police chief, has arrived on the scene. A stranger breaks through the crowd and informs Cagney with

great urgency that he is curator of the library, and that it is a priceless collection that must be handled with the utmost care. Well, says Cagney, why don't you go tell those fellows that? To which the poor man replies, are you trying to be funny? And Cagney replies, my good man, so long as those guys are in there, you are not the cur-a-tor of anything.

I was just amazed last summer by the intensity of the anti-Herzog, pro-Simmons sentiment in St. Louis. The Cardinals had the best record in the division in '81 and were in contention all the way last year, but every time they lost two games in a row all the Simba-ites would come out of the woodwork.

But look at the situation as it must have looked to Herzog. You've got a highly talented team that isn't winning. The team doesn't hustle; it doesn't execute fundamentals; it doesn't play very good defense. You've got a player who is universally recognized as the leader of that team. He is a public idol. He is on the board of directors of the art museum. He is, reportedly, good buddies with the owner. He is a .300 hitter with power. But, unfortunately, he is a catcher, and he is not a good one. So you sign another catcher, and you tell him that, for the good of the team, he is going to have to move. And he says, "No, I won't do it. The hell with what's good for the team." What are you going to do?

I don't know what you'd do, but I know what I would do. If I had to trade that man for five cents on the dollar, I'd trade him. You don't have to be in baseball to relate to that circumstance. Suppose that you are the new manager of an office, or a loading dock, or the new plant manager in a factory, and things aren't running worth a hoot, and people are bitching and moaning a lot instead of working together, and you approach your highest-paid employee, who is also the most popular, visible man in the organization, and who is also a friend of your boss, and you tell him that you are going to assign him some different duties. And he tells you to stick it. What are you going to do?

De facto authority, that is the message. You either get rid of that son of a bitch, or you accept the fact that he is running the show and you are not. If Whitey Herzog didn't have the guts to run Ted Simmons out of St. Louis, he might as well have quit on the spot. Because if he didn't, from that moment on he was not the man-a-ger of anything.

Hemingway said the most essential gift for a good writer is a built-in, shockproof shit detector. Bill has the gift, and it's woven into his style. He wrote about Aurelio Lopez:

> This guy must have one of the greatest arms that God ever made. He's thirty-five, threw about nine million pitches in the Mexican League before he came to Los Estados Unidos, where he has been working sixty games a year since 1979, and he trains on beans and beer with three side orders of meat, and he can still blow his fastball by good major league hitters.

The *Abstracts* were dotted with wordplay and commentary on language, like this classic from the '83 comment on Royal Frank White:

> Did you ever notice that players named "White" are almost always black, and players named "Black" are usually white? Why is that? The last White major leaguer who was actually white was Mike White, who played for Houston in the early sixties. Since then we've had Bill White, Roy White, Frank White, and Jerry White, all of whom were black; Mike White probably would have been black except that his father played in the majors in the thirties and they didn't allow you to be black then. The Royals also had a Black on their roster, Bud, who of course is white; in fact, the Royals had to set some sort of record by having four colored people on their team, White, Black, Blue, and Brown. Scott Brown is not any browner than anybody else, Vida is definitely not blue, nor for that matter is Darryl Motley. I suppose that it is the nature of names, as with Peacekeeping Missiles and Security Police, to disguise the truth more often than they reveal it.

Horace Speed stole only four bases in his career. Vic Power was a singles hitter, Bill Goodenough was not good enough, and Joe Blong did not belong for long.

Bill was making good money for the first time, but the period of the 1984 and '85 *Abstracts* were "surely the most unhappy years" of his adult life. He fell short of his own expectations, and he didn't know how to handle the expectations that came with new fame.

Criticism, too, was hard to handle. Bill was one voice (albeit with an amplifier—the *Abstract*), but the carping that came back at him was multitudinous. Pete Gethers says, "Bill has all the things you want in a great writer: funny, insightful, poetic, and mean as hell when he wants to be. He's a nasty critic, brilliant and harsh, but he's very sensitive to criticism."

By 1985 he'd begun to pull out of his depression. That year Villard published the first *Historical Baseball Abstract*. "This was his magnum opus," Gethers says. "He was obsessed."

Bill explained that at some point in the research he started to believe that baseball history was as much about small, colorful characters and moments as it was the story of big stars and great events. The first part was broken into decades and scattered with little-known facts and stories. A sample from the 1800s:

- In 1883 a Philadelphia zookeeper started using homing pigeons to deliver scores by the half-inning around the city.
- Play in the 1890s was not merely dirty but violent, with umpires in need of police escort.
- Contributing essays on player dress from the different eras, Susie reported that women who played baseball in the 1890s were called "fair base ballists."

The second part—player comments and ratings—divided players into peak and career values. Bill made the point that in evaluating greatness, it makes sense to decide whether you mean greatness in the peak years or over the full career. For example, Bill rated Roy Campanella as the greatest catcher in peak value, with Yogi Berra fourth. In career value Berra was first, Campanella seventh.

In center field, he had peak: Mantle, Cobb, Mays; and career: Cobb, DiMaggio, Mays. Mays' rating was controversial, but Bill noted, for example, that Willie played in four World Series, winning once and posting a .282 slugging percentage, while Mickey won eight of twelve and slugged .535. That's just one point in the discussion, however, not the center. Ten years later in the *New Historical Abstract*, based on Win Shares and not separated by peak and career, Bill would rate Mays first, Cobb second, Mantle third.

The first *Historical Abstract* stands as one of the essentials of any baseball-book collection. The *New Historical* in some ways beats it, but many who read the first before the *New* maintain it's the best baseball book ever written. When the printed book hit Pete Gethers' desk, he put a copy in the mail with a note to Bill: "Call me as soon as you get this." Two weeks went by without a response. "I was a wreck," Pete says, "thinking he hated it." Pete finally got his author on the phone and inquired. Bill hadn't even looked at it. The package was sitting unopened on his desk. Bill gave it a flip-through and said, "It looks fine."

The '84 *Abstract* heralded the launch of Project Scoresheet, a nonprofit venture to make score sheets of every major league game available to the public. Bill was bugged that the official scoresheets of major league games were "jealously guarded possessions of the bureaus which compile the official statistics."

An analyst, a historian, a biographer, or Bill James couldn't, for example, find out how many inherited runners had scored on a reliever; how well a player hit when leading off an inning; or whether Eddie Murray tended to "let down" in blowouts. What was the difference in a player's batting average with a fast runner on first? How much better did a hitter do against a pitcher the second, third, or fourth time through the order?

There were endless questions, and the data existed to answer them, but it was held as proprietary by the bureaus. Bill saw this as both a restraint of free trade ("I would sell for about $12 the same information that the Elias Bureau sells for thousands of dollars," he wrote) and an unfair labor practice, in that ownership wanted to have better access to information for use during salary negotiations. Bill wrote that he had considered a legal challenge, "but one of my goals in life is to die without ever being involved in a lawsuit, and anyway lawsuits are expensive even when they are successful and expensive as hell when they are not successful, so the questions about the legality of the National League's position are not really germane."

> What is germane is that it is wrong. The entire basis of professional sports is the public's interest in what is going on. To deny the public access to information that it cares about is the logical equivalent of locking the stadiums and playing the games in private so that no one will find out what is happening. It is stupid and counterproductive. But baseball has been doing this for fifty years and they're not about to stop unless someone stops them.

His plan wasn't to bring together volunteers to compile scoresheets that were *as good* as the official ones. He wanted to create a *better* system. "Want to know how many pitches are called strikes against the home team and how many against the road team? We'll find out," he wrote. "Wondering what the connection is between the number of pitches thrown to a leadoff man and the number of runs scored in an inning? We can get it if we want to." Beyond his own desire for the information, why would he bother? As he saw it, the fans were baseball's rightful owners. He wrote, "It is a small way of asserting that we're not waiting for them to do whatever they see fit."

Kenneth Miller was the first project director of Project Scoresheet. He handed it off to John Dewan, who, with his wife, Sue, built the network. Soon they were embroiled in controversy. In 1985 a company called STATS Inc., which supplied computerized stat services to a handful of teams, was about to go out of business. Pioneering saber-metrician Dick Cramer took it over and, needing investors, contacted Bill, who took a small stake. Bill recommended John Dewan as a potential partner.

John and Sue bought in and started getting STATS into business shape, but John kept running Project Scoresheet. A volunteer network of scorers, headed by a new partner in a for-profit business based on the collection of game data . . . it was asking for trouble. "Project Scoresheet had a board of directors," Bill says, "and John didn't agree with them about what direction to go. There was a huge tug-of-war, in which I was the rope."

In the '88 *Abstract* Bill called it "stupid squabbling over absolutely nothing." But in March he found himself acting as mediator for a hearing to resolve the issues. He ruled that the data belonged to both sides, and Dewan should cut ties with Project Scoresheet. STATS, under Dewan, sold out to News Corp. at the top of the stock market bubble in the late nineties.

Dewan later started Baseball Info Solutions, current publisher of the *Bill James Handbook* statistics annual. Because so many people think of Bill as Mr. Stats to begin with, and the *Handbook* is cited in newspaper columns as "the latest Bill James book," the idea that Bill James equals statistics is as strong as it's ever been. Bill says, "I wrote a proposal for that book about 1988 or 1989, based on my perception of the need for such a book—an accurate perception, I believe. I proposed the book to John Dewan and Don Zminda at STATS, and they said, 'Okay, can we put your name on it?' And we did. Yes, it does perpetuate the idea of Bill James as a statistician, and yes, this annoys me, but . . . it's there. It's not a marketing thing, in a sense, because I did create and design the book, but it is in a sense. I didn't sell my name to them; I sold the idea and my name went with it."

Tensions between Bill and the Elias Bureau were wound tighter than an aged base stealer's hamstrings in the middle *Abstract* years. In the '84 book he introduced a method for rating relief aces and dismissed the system that the Elias Bureau "foisted off on *Sports Illustrated*" in their season-opening issue in 1982. "When the only way that you know of to evaluate players is by average rank," he wrote, "and you're too lazy even to weight the categories being averaged so as to allow the most important information to have a proportionate impact on the rankings, it's a good sign that you're probably in the wrong line of work."

But being in the wrong line of work never stopped anyone from jumping someone else's train. In spring 1985 there appeared the *Abstract*-ish *Elias Baseball Analyst*. Its main purposes, Bill wrote, were "to make money, steals my ideas, and make as many disparaging comments as possible about me." The *Analyst* took potshots at the *Abstract*, referring to "arcane formulas with strange-sounding acronymic names," while claiming to serve as "the state of the art for a variety of imitators."

What it served to do was to let loose a torrent of numbers with the significance of a watermelon. Bill says, "Statistics derived from twenty or thirty trials don't really mean much, and there are few situations in which I would make a decision based on them." On the other hand, there's no magic sample size to go by. It's a matter of weighing all the factors and making decisions on the body of information. But in general if a weak hitter is 6-for-17 against a pitcher, and a strong hitter is 1-for-17, the information can be less a help than a harm if a manager bases his lineup selection on it.

Bill wrote in the late eighties, "*The Elias Analyst* has ripped off my methods and my research so closely that many passages fall just short of plagiarism. They use methods that are nearly identical to my methods, repeat research that is virtually identical to my research, and sometimes write it up in phrases that vary only slightly from my phrases—without giving me any credit."

In the 1987 essay "Wake-Up Call," he reported that Elias was going to take over compiling the American League stats and issuing the official "red book." Bill called the league office to ask whether this meant that information would be disappearing from the book. They assured him Elias had promised none would. Bill wrote, "I knew that was bull-shit, and sure enough it was." He found that "thousands of pieces of information had been eliminated," and the book came out a month later than it had before.

> Hey! American League, wake up. If you don't watch the product that's being put out with your name on it, I will guarantee you that product is going to deteriorate. In five years, you'll look at the booklet one day and say, "Hey, whatever happened to that record of the Grand Slam Home Runs that we used to have in our stat summary, or that Club Pinch Hitting chart, or that chart of Average Game Times?" And you'll call the stat bureau, and they will tell you that it wasn't specified in the contract. That is not a generous woman that you are in bed with, Dr. Brown. Keep an eye on your pockets.

Rancorous though it looks, Bill says, "It wasn't personally directed at Elias, but at the idea of making the game accounts private property. I did my best to open things to the public. I wasn't entirely successful. There are still things that are hard to get. On the other hand, we haven't been entirely a failure."

Susie was about four months pregnant when the Royals won the World Series in October 1985. In March she threw out the "first ball," as it were—a baby girl named Rachel. Two weeks later Bill had to leave for a twelve-city book tour. "It didn't seem right to be away from home," he says. He was growing more detached from the *Abstract*: "Some of the fizz had gone out of my writing." With a baby in the house, he had less time to sit and think about baseball. Yet he was pushing to produce more material on tighter deadlines, thanks to competition from books geared toward Rotisserie leagues. The first national *Abstract* had been at the publisher in mid-December. It was in stores the first week of April 1982. By 1985, they wanted the manuscript to be in by mid-Novem-ber—just three weeks after the World Series. Bill says that if he could do it over, he would tell the publisher, "You do what you want, but I'm not sending the book until January 15th."

Excerpt from the '86 *Abstract*:
Phil Niekro

In the edited passage below, Bill illustrated how *old* forty-seven-year-old Phil Niekro was in 1986. "When I came up with the idea," he says, "I knew it would work in print, and I was so proud of it that I told two or three people what I was going to do, which is very unusual for me; I never tell people what I am writing or going to write. But they didn't get it, at all, when I explained it to them; they just looked at me blankly like, 'Why would you do that?'"

We can do this by teams . . . let's do the Cardinals. You probably know all the current Cardinals; Steve Braun is the oldest of them. Mike Torrez, who started with the Cardinals and then pitched for everybody else before dropping out of the game, was older than Steve Braun. Rick Wise, another peripatetic pitcher of similar talent, was older and earlier than Torrez. Steve Carlton is older than Wise, for whom he was once traded. Jose Cardenal, who patrolled the Cardinal outfield behind Carlton, was older than Steve. Tim McCarver, who caught for that team, is older than Jose Cardenal. Ray Sadecki, a teammate of McCarver's in his early days, a twenty-game winner on the 1964 Worlds Champions, was older than McCarver. You may remember Dick Nen, who hit the gigantic home run which buried the Cardinals the year before that, 1963. Nen was older than Sadecki. If you think hard enough, you may remember Julio Gotay, the Cardinals' shortstop before they traded for Dick Groat. Gotay, who was most famous as the man who dropped his mail in a green-painted trash bin for several weeks before Curt Flood discovered it, was older than Dick Nen. Von McDaniel, the Cardinals' pitching sensation of 1957, was older than Julio Gotay. But Phil Niekro is older than Von McDaniel.

Phil Niekro is older than Tommie Aaron, except that Aaron is dead and you can't get any older than dead. I remember a few years ago at spring training, when Tommie was a coach with the Braves, he was hitting fungoes one day, his claim to alphabetical supremacy stretched across his back. Susie and I were sitting and watching him. A little woman about fifty yelled out from behind us, sounding for all the world like a character in the background of an old movie, "Haank. Oh, Haannk." She had a camera. At length, Tommie turned around, and gave a dutiful, patient half-smile. She took a picture and yelled, "Oh, thank you, Hank." Then he died, a year or so later.

Phil Niekro is older than Martin Luther King or either of the Kennedys were at the time of their assassinations. Phil Niekro is older than Boog Powell. Phil Niekro is more than ten years older than I am.

Funny thing, though. He doesn't look a day over sixty.

The ***Boston Globe's*** Bob Ryan posited in 1984 that Bill could be as important to baseball as Alexander Cartwright, "who codified the game," and Babe Ruth. It's been much noted that Bill James didn't invent statistical analysis in baseball. That's true, of course, just as it's true that baseball existed before Cartwright codified it and that Ruth wasn't the first player to hit the longball chicks dig.

But all three epitomize what Japanese artisan Kaneshige Michiaki meant when he said, "Tradition is always changing. Tradition consists of creating something new with what one has inherited." Michiaki explained that people sometimes confuse *tradition* with *transmission*. Copying what came before is transmission. Producing something new while incorporating what came before—*that's* tradition.

Bill is baseball's Thomas Paine, who pointed out the internal contradictions and misconceptions of Christianity when the idea of examining the Bible as an objective text, let alone looking at it critically, was heresy; or its Martin Luther, nailing his rail against corruption, the 95 Theses, on the door of the church at Wittenburg. In other words, his place in baseball tradition is as a questioner of the status quo. There's no better example than his '88 *Abstract* essay "Revolution."

As you're probably aware, Major League Baseball enjoys a government benefit other U.S. businesses don't: exemption from antitrust laws. In "Revolution" Bill called for an end to the exemption. There's no substitute for the full essay, but you can get a sense of where he was coming from.

> The minor league system as it exists today is an abomination in the sight of the Lord. Players are assigned to the minor league team at the last minute without the team having any say in who wears their uniform, players spend two weeks at a city and then are moved around like checkers, anonymous young men playing to develop skills rather than playing to win, teams in great cities drawing a couple of hundred fans a game, pennant races with no meaning, no connection between city and player, player and fan, fan and city. They have really, truly reached the point at which they don't care about winning.
>
> If you're selling a sport and the players don't care about winning, that's not a sport. That's a fraud. Minor league baseball today is exactly what the 1919 World Series was: a charade, a rip-off, an exhibition masquerading as a contest. In one of his books Earl Weaver tells about one time when he was managing in the minor leagues he had a sluggish first baseman that the major league team was trying to make into a third baseman. The guy couldn't play third base, and Weaver knew if he put him there he would cost him the pennant race. Earl wanted to WIN. In desperation, he finally started sending the major league team phony box scores, showing the guy playing third base when he was

actually playing first, living in terror that a scout would catch him and he would get fired—for trying to win.

That's a disgraceful situation. Baseball, for most of the cities in the nation, has been reduced to the level of professional wrestling. By this horrible system, then, most of the nation is deprived of having real baseball. . . . The Memphis team works for my team, the Kansas City Royals—but why should Memphis have nothing so that Kansas City can have everything? Why should Memphis not be allowed to keep a good ballplayer, so that Kansas City can have them all? It's not right. It's unethical, it's immoral, it is corrupt. We have no right, as Kansas City fans, to use Omaha, Memphis, and Fort Myers as our servants. Every city, whether a great city or a small city, should have its own proud team, the best team that it can support. There should be leagues, and there should be pennant races, and there should be civic pride invested in them. And they should serve no master except the urgency of competition.

In fall 1987 the NFL players were on strike. The owners used substitute players. Bill noted that there isn't a wide divide between an NFL player and those who are almost good enough but have to work regular jobs. But in baseball there is a huge gap between the major league players and those who are in the regular workforce. Filling that gap are the minor leagues.

Minor leaguers good enough to compete with major leaguers see themselves as standing in line. "So the second-level baseball players are not going to cross the picket lines, nor the third-level players either," Bill wrote. "That means that in order to play replacement games, you would have to dip way, way down into the talent pool."

Also, "THE EXISTENCE OF THE MINOR LEAGUES forces the owners to deal with the players on generous terms, and forces them to pass on to the players a great deal of the income that in football the owners are able to keep for themselves."

The major leagues did not create the minors. The National League established itself in the major cities, and the other leagues were left, in general, to the smaller cities. Bill wrote:

> At first there was no reserve clause. This was a sort of primordial soup for baseball, an original chaos in which the land itself was liquid, and the players would just drift from team to team as suited themselves. So the owners said "We've got to get organized here. We can have competition between different leagues, yes, but we can't let these players move around from team to team just however they want. Let's construct a reserve arrangement." Organized baseball began, then, in an attempt to deprive the players of negotiating power.

By the early twenties every minor league team was *required* to sell its players to the majors. In return, the majors agreed not to draft players right from high school. Soon the majors forgot their end of the deal, and as the gap between majors and minors widened, minor league owners agreed to become farms for growing future major leaguers.

At first the big league teams tried not to exploit their power flagrantly. "In about ten years," Bill wrote, "that, too, went by the boards, and if a player was hitting .385 at AAA ball and the minor league team was a half game ahead with two weeks to play and the major league team needed him to pinch-run once a week, they'd just take him away."

> Historian Dee Brown has written that probably at no point in our history did white Americans intend to do to American Indians what they actually did. It was a process, extending over a couple of centuries: One generation would make treaties, and the next generation would amend them, cut them back a little bit, claim a little more land, and the generation after that would forget about the treaties altogether, so that, looking at the entire pattern over a period of generations, one would swear that there was a conscious decision to drive the American Indian into the ground.
>
> The history of the relationship between the minors and the majors is very similar: One generation would make agreements,

and the next generation would amend those agreements, and the third generation would renege on them entirely or forget that they had ever been made. The minor leagues, originally independent competitors of the major leagues, were by tiny degrees and yearly increments reduced into mere servants, living on crumbs, sustained by the major leagues for their own uses like a farmer keeps chickens, just for the eggs.

An irony of the system is that the system—established and maintained to suit the greed of the owners—traps them into paying higher salaries because the talent supply is restricted. "Like a tyrant suffocated in bed by his own hired thugs, major league baseball has choked nearly to death all of the other leagues, and now finds itself kneeling before its own hired help," Bill wrote.

And of course the system lets owners manipulate municipalities. "It's an appalling situation, the most blatant abuse of monopolistic power," Bill wrote. Were leagues able to compete, cities wouldn't be at the mercy of the owners.

Bill argued that free competition would increase total attendance of pro baseball games by tens of millions, maybe hundreds of millions. While more people could make a living through baseball, the days of multimillion-dollar salaries might end.

What would happen to the quality of play? Isn't talent stretched thin already? Bill wrote, "Now there is a truly preposterous argument. This nation could support, without any detectable loss of player quality, at a very, very minimum, two hundred major league teams."

Think about it. If we had 240 major league teams, each team would represent about a million people. Do you have any idea how many people a million people are? Start counting people that you meet on the street sometime. If you live in New York and ride the subway, start counting the people on the subway. It will take you years and years of counting people that you meet on the street and in the subway to reach a million. You trying to tell me that's not enough people to pick twenty-five ballplayers out of?

The best players would naturally gravitate to the biggest cities and best leagues, and that's fine. "The small teams should be able to sell the rights to players while they are under contract, and the contracts should run out at regular intervals because men are not chattel to be moved around without their consent. It's one thing if it happens naturally, and quite another if it happens by force—the difference between rape and chemistry," Bill wrote.

He contended that if Congress were to force Major League Baseball to stop acting as a monopoly, the current structure would break apart. Two ways it could be done: (1) Order the existing major leagues to break into four competing leagues, instructing them not to coordinate their activities in any way except to organize a "national championship." No negotiating TV contracts together, no reserve clauses to inhibit player movement, and no collectively deciding which cities get teams. (2) Order the majors to divest themselves of the minors, "and prohibit them from continuing to engage in predatory and monopolistic practices with regard to teams in other leagues—as they have done for a hundred years." In time, the competing leagues and teams would act in their own selfish interests, as they should.

Bill wrote, "If the first approach was selected, the major leagues should also be required to divest themselves of their minor league affiliates, or at least most of them. If the second approach was selected, the regulation should prohibit the existing majors from expanding for a period of fifteen to twenty years," Bill explained. Some minor league owners would complain that they were being cut off from their main source of support, which was their major league "partner"; that would be true, in the short run. "It would snip the lifeline, and force the team to scramble for survival on its own, by doing novel things like promoting, putting together a good ball team, getting into a pennant race, and trying to win."

Well, I hope I've made you think, anyway. I hope I have made you realize that the world in which we live is not the only possible world, nor even the best of all possible worlds. I am not arguing for these changes because I want to be provocative; I am arguing for these changes because I believe they would make baseball healthier, more exciting, and more fun.

Competition isn't always pretty. Teams would fold, go bankrupt sometimes, use nearly naked usherettes in a cheap attempt to boost attendance, pull out in the middle of the night without paying their debts—all of the things that businesses do. Baseball would be less stable. It would change more rapidly than it ever has, in part because each league would be learning from the experience of the other leagues. But it would be changing because it would be growing, and it would be growing toward a baseball world which is larger, stronger, smarter, richer, more diverse, and more fair to fans. It can happen.

Hey, buddy, I love tradition, too.

How could Bill claim to love tradition while agitating for such radical change? The answer is in the distinction between the sport and the monopoly. The *sport*, he argued, would be growing "larger, stronger, smarter, richer, more diverse, and more fair to the fans" if set free. This isn't to depict him as crusading for the dismantling of the current structure, but to illustrate the extent to which his perspective on the game was, truly, revolutionary.*

Bill still says yes to the question of whether antitrust exemption should go the way of the brontosaur. "I was once on a panel with an antitrust lawyer and an economist," he says, "and that question was asked to us, to me first. I said it wouldn't make any difference. The economist jumped in and said it would force sweeping changes in the game, and he outlined what those would be for several minutes. Then the lawyer jumped up and said that we were both wrong, that it would cause far-reaching changes in the game, but they would be almost exactly the opposite of the ones outlined by the economist. The truth is, nobody

---

*In the '80 *Abstract* he quoted Thomas Carlyle from *The French Revolution*: "Meanwhile it is singular how long the rotten will hold together, provided you do not handle it roughly. For whole generations it continues standing, 'with a ghastly affectation of life,' after all life and truth has fled out of it: so loth are men to quit the old ways, and, conquering indolence and inertia, venture on new."

knows what difference it would make, and nobody *can* know, because that would be determined by the interaction of this event—removing the exemption—with other events. Nobody knows what those other events would be, so nobody has any idea what the effects would be."

Cutting back on his baseball writing, Bill was fulfilling a promise he'd made to Susie to spend more time with the kids and give his wife time for her own work. With a third child in the bullpen, the Project Scoresheet/STATS conflict, and annoyance with the side effects of his creation, he decided to "break the wand"—to make the 1988 book the last. Pete Gethers remembers, "It broke my little heart when he quit, although by that time it was almost a relief. I say it with total affection. I think he's a genius. But it's hard to work with an author who's not having fun. I think in some ways he liked it more when only a couple thousand people were reading his books. He didn't want to be the 'guru of statistics.' But people are dumb and they latch on to labels."

Bill later elucidated another reason for quitting the *Abstract*, in "Notes upon Watching a Small Boy with a Music Box."

> My little boy has just turned two, and he is trying to figure out a music box. It is a baseball music box, on which a small figure pivots with a tiny bat, swinging at a white cloth marble while the tinny sounds of "Take Me Out to the Ball Game" leak from below.
>
> The music box has two operating mechanisms, an on/off switch which one pushes and pulls, but also a handle which must be wound to provide power. This is too much for a two-year-old boy to deal with at first. He pulls the switch and the music starts; he pushes it and the music stops—but then, when the tension winds down, he pulls the switch and nothing happens. Isaac is frustrated. "Broke," he says, handing me the worthless machine. "Ball payer broke."
>
> He will, of course, soon figure out the concept of two switches. But I am struck by this: that ideas are harder than machines, and many people will never master the two-switch concept as it applies

to a logical inference. I find this to be an undeniable lesson of sports talk shows. A caller argues that a baseball manager makes no difference. Look at Whitey Herzog, he says; he was supposed to be such a genius a few years ago, but why can't he win now? The caller has not mastered the two-switch concept; the on/off switch must be turned on, but the energy must *also* be there.

If Ralph Kiner is in the Hall of Fame, demands a voter, shouldn't Roger Maris be in there, too? The argument is perfectly satisfactory to him; one switch operates all machines. Indeed, the entire intellectual life of many sportswriters is a search for master switches. Baseball is 90 percent pitching, sportswriters argue, not because this makes any sense or because there is any evidence to support it, but because it reduces the terrifying complexity of the sport to a single switch. To win a pennant anymore you have to have a strong bullpen—never mind that a dozen teams have won titles in the last ten years with conspicuously weak bullpens. The key to winning on artificial turf is speed.

If only one could hold an idea in one's hand and play with the switches, I think, how quickly the arguments would advance. In the real world, arguments go around and around, advancing almost imperceptibly from generation to generation, and this is another way of explaining why I stopped writing the *Baseball Abstract*. After ten years, I realized the impossibility of advancing complex ideas in a world that only wanted to know where the switch was.

8

The Exploding Sabermetric
Inevitable

From 1977 through 1981 the self-published *Baseball Abstracts* reached a cadre of cutting-edge fans and agents. With help from Dan Okrent, Bill signed with a New York publisher for the 1982 edition. Until he broke the wand in 1988, the *Abstract* was, in the words of George Will, "the most important scientific treatise since Newton's *Principia.*"

Bill's efforts to bring more objective analysis into baseball were as well taken by insiders as Galileo's theories about the solar system were by the Holy Church. But the big bang set off by Bill and a handful of fellow sabermetric pioneers would inevitably change baseball, as he predicted it would.

In 1984 he put together a study of power pitchers and night games, sorting all current American League pitchers into "cells" according to strikeouts and walks per nine innings. He found that pitching under the lights helped control-type pitchers to some degree, but helped power pitchers to the statistical extent of "a whale among minnows." Were major league managers using power pitchers at night to their advantage? Looking at usage patterns, Bill found the answer was "Not to any significant degree."

And that is the potential value of sabermetrics to a major league team. Every major league manager has probably heard the thought expressed that power pitchers are most effective when the lighting is least effective; we've known that since Vander

Meer. But without studying the issue from the outside, without stepping back and measuring it, how could he ever know how to evaluate the theory, how much weight to put on it? We can't know that, and so he can't use the knowledge. And I'll tell you for sure, Don Zimmer ain't going to take the time to look up no pitchers in cell C3 and figure out what happens to them. But other things being equal, a manager who has respect for knowledge is going to beat the crap out of a manager who doesn't. And that's why sabermetrics is an inevitable part of baseball's future.

In time the ideas started to gain support among a few insiders. Bobby Valentine, young for a manager at thirty-five, was a self-described James disciple. He worked with Craig Wright, a sabermetrician and friend of Bill's, while managing the Texas Rangers. Valentine says, "Bill's influence has been profound."

Bill wrote in 1978 that "dramatic successes in baseball are imitated and come to shape the way the game is played in future generations." That was in reference to Rod Carew's batting stance, but twenty-five years later, in the blockbuster book *Moneyball*, writer Michael Lewis chronicled how baseball's new wave of quantitative analysis took shape in Oakland, depicting the *Baseball Abstract* as the storm that started it.

Sandy Alderson, hired to be the A's general manager in 1981, was an ex-Marine and Harvard Law graduate—in that sense nothing like Bill James. But he was also in his mid-thirties, not a baseball lifer, and something of an iconoclast. On the lookout for a "theory of baseball" that would give him an edge, he found it in the *Baseball Abstract*. Alderson later told writer Michael McCambridge that he didn't tout Bill and his "theory," because "I subscribed to it so strongly that I didn't want anyone else to think about it."

Current A's general manager Billy Beane considers Alderson his mentor. Michael Lewis reported that in 1995 Alderson introduced Beane to the *Baseball Abstract*. "That was the big moment," Beane said, "when I figured out that all the stuff Sandy was talking about was just derivative of Bill James."

Billionaire commodities trader John Henry led a buyout of the Red Sox in 2002. Rob Meyer had read that John Henry had an interest in sabermetrics. Rob contacted him and discovered that Henry had been a fan of Bill James since the *Abstract* days. Rob e-mailed Bill to let him know that he had given his phone number to Henry, and said sorry if Bill would rather he hadn't. Bill replied, "Any time a billionaire asks you for my phone number, go ahead and give it to him."

In late 2002 the Red Sox brought Bill on as a senior consultant, before hiring Theo Epstein as general manager. Bill describes his job as, in effect, what he has always done: to look at problems from a distance and try to see the size and proportion of each element. When the Sox hired Bill, Henry expressed disbelief that it had taken so long for a team to make that move.

He later told Rob Neyer, "People in both baseball and the financial markets operate with beliefs and biases. To the extent you can eliminate both and replace them with data, you gain a clear advantage. Many people think they are smarter than others in the stock market, and that the market itself has no intrinsic intelligence—as if it's inert. Similarly, many people think they are smarter than others in baseball, and that the game on the field is simply what they think it is, filtered through their set of images and beliefs. But actual data from the market means more than individual perception/belief. And the same is true in baseball."

Since the publication of *Moneyball*, volumes have been written about conflicts between traditional scouting and the "Bill James crowd." But Bill points out, "There are always an array of options available to the team, and what Theo does, I think, is survey the whole array of options, rule out those that the scouts don't like, rule out those that we don't like, and see what's left. Let's say that you need a first baseman, and there are twelve marginal first basemen that the team could go after. There might be six that the scouts like and six that the stat analysts like, but they won't be either/or; by the law of averages there should be three options that both sides like, and, in my experience, there almost always will be."

Sometimes it's hard to figure out what Bill *really* thinks. Even the most pro-James people don't get him right all the time. What, for example, is the Bill James "theory of baseball"? Bill wrote in the 1986 *Abstract*:

> My basic theory of baseball is that *any* theory of baseball will work if the talent is good enough. A "theory" or a clear idea of how you're going to win is extremely useful to a baseball team, because it organizes the work, clarifies the needs and goals of the team; it provides focus and direction among a dizzying array of options and alternatives. If you're trying to win a pennant it helps to know whether you're trying to win it by pitching or power in exactly the same way that, if you're trying to make a million dollars, it helps to have a clear idea whether you're trying to make the money in real estate or prostitution. Almost every successful organization displays some such presentiment—but it isn't the theory that wins. It's the players.

Michael Lewis points out that one of the insights at the heart of the Oakland A's system is that there are players whose value isn't on the surface. It's a recurring theme in Bill's books, and it's one of his ideas that some people find exquisite, some can accept only in theory, and many refuse to really consider.

Take a Red Sox–related example from the *New Historical Abstract*: Jim Rice and Roy White. By conventional statistical measures Rice was clearly the better player, yet Bill rated White the twenty-fifth best left fielder ever, Rice twenty-seventh. Bill doesn't talk about the rating now that he works for the team that Rice played for, but the fact that White was a Yankee dampens the notion that there's bias at work.*

What makes Bill's thinking so difficult to distill is that he is both scientist/analyst *and* artist/entertainer. Norman Mailer (who, inciden-

---

*Then again, Bill went out of his way in the book to make the point that Rice was seen as an arrogant jerk in his playing days, so who knows?

tally, was one of the early buyers of a self-published *Abstract*—he was looking into biorhythms) points out that both the scientist and the artist are engaged in an effort to "penetrate into the nature of things." But they're also opposed; the scientist is trying to "destroy the fundament of magic," while the artist is trying to "undermine the base of technology." Bill the artist and Bill the scientist were pulling and pushing in the same and opposite directions.

Stepping back further—but still working on White/Rice—the media and the masses focus almost entirely on the scientist aspect of Bill. And society's anti-science impulses are mirrored in insider-baseball culture. Soon after Bill was hired, *Boston Globe* writer Dan Shaughnessy was on a Boston TV show with Rob Neyer. "It's a little troubling to me," he said. "This guy's brilliant, a great baseball writer, has reinvented what people can do with this kind of thing . . . I just don't like statistical-oriented analysis. I think it's overdone. You know what you see. You know players, you don't know players, you should stick with that."

James Thurber once wrote that he had discovered one fact in his lifetime, that "most people want to believe rather than to know, to take for granted rather than to find out." That hits on the essential difference between the Bill James approach and Shaughnessy's. "The point at which I departed from traditional sportswriting was in trying to apply the standard of clear and convincing evidence to baseball questions," Bill says. "What I have always thought about most was the question of 'How do you find better evidence about the issue?'

"I thus tended to make general, expert-oriented questions into narrow, specific questions that had actual answers. I was trying *not* to be an expert. I was trying to say things that were objectively true, regardless of who was saying them, because I wasn't an expert and I didn't want to pose as one. The 'community of experts' resented this, because it implicitly undermined their authority. But from my standpoint, I was never arguing with experts; I was just trying to present evidence.

"In the sciences—which, in all candor, I know very little about, not being a real scientist or a trained scientist—but, nevertheless, in the sciences it is understood that opinions have little or no value. It is widely understood, by scientists, that where there is no clear and convincing evidence, the opinion of the most learned expert is not significantly more reliable than the opinion of a layman. The standard of what we believe is not 'trust' or 'faith' that experts are correct; it is clear and convincing evidence. If an undergraduate with a C average can show by clear and convincing evidence that leading scientists are wrong about something, the scientists will not say, or should not say, 'Who are you to argue with Jonas Salk?' What counts is evidence, not the authority of the person making the claim."

Of course, trying to present evidence embroiled Bill in arguments, and in the process of arguing he often expressed opinions. But, as he points out, there may be a bright line between evidence and opinion—sometimes there is and sometimes there isn't—but there is never a bright line between scientists and experts. "In a sense," Bill says, "the baseball world doesn't really get what I was doing any more now than it did twenty-five years ago. The way they have dealt with this is to accept me as an 'expert'—a different kind of expert. The principle of trusting evidence rather than experts is only marginally more accepted in baseball now than it was then."

These ideas also come into play in areas of greater seriousness than baseball. For example, Bill believes that almost all of the "applied psychology" in the criminal justice system failed to fulfill its promises over the course of the twentieth century, and much of it failed at immense cost to society. He explains, "The psychologists who testify at trial are mostly just high-paid whores giving arbitrary testimony about which there is no professional consensus—and really, everybody knows this. Many studies show, and most lawyers acknowledge, that juries pay minimal attention to the professional testifiers.

"Prison psychologists can no more 'fix' a criminal than they can paint smiley faces on the moon. 'Counseling' a criminal to avoid criminal behavior is precisely as effective as preaching to him. If the criminal chooses to reform, he can reform, but it's hard work. If the criminal doesn't make a decision to reform, you can counsel him until your toes turn green, and it's not going to make a damn bit of difference. Any psychologist will admit, I think, that there is no treatment for a criminal which makes him a non-criminal.

"It is my honest opinion that the judicial system would be better off if they would just get rid of all of this stuff, but it is nearly impossible to do. Who's going to show up at the state legislature ten or fifteen years running to advocate the position that hiring psychologists to evaluate accused criminals at the time of their arrest is a waste of money? Who is going to fund the studies to prove that it's a waste of time and money? Nobody. It's in the system; it's going to stay there.

"The *real* cost of this, though, was in the parole system. Psychologists were, at one time, convinced that they could *tell* how dangerous a prisoner was; they could psychologically evaluate him, and determine whether he was ready to be released into society. It was this belief in the 'filtering' capacity of modern science that caused society to move to a system of parole.

"But it just didn't work. It didn't work, because the most highly trained psychologist in the world has no more ability than you or I to interview a criminal and determine whether he will commit future crimes. There simply isn't any such body of knowledge.

"My favorite illustration of this is the case of Edmund Kemper, a California serial murderer of the early 1970s. Kemper murdered his grandmother and grandfather at about age fifteen, spent a couple of years in a juvenile facility, and was released into society when he became an adult. He had to make periodic appearances in front of his parole review committee, and, after one of these, the psychologist on the committee wrote a glowing report about how well Kemper had adjusted to society and moved on from his juvenile mistakes. At the time of the interview, it was later learned, Kemper had the severed heads of two coeds in the trunk of his car. He thought that added to the thrill of conning the parole board.

"Of course that's a gruesomely extreme example, but the fundamental problem was commonplace. Psychologists simply had no ability whatsoever to fulfill the promise they had made to society, which was to sort through the criminals and figure out which of them were still dangerous. The consequence of this was that prison became a revolving door for prisoners; commit a crime, go to jail, make parole, commit 200 or 300 more crimes before you're caught again."

Bill cautions, "Much of this analysis is dated. Parole has been eliminated at the federal level, and curtailed or eliminated in most states. People no longer believe in the parole system, and no longer trust the judgment of psychologists in relation to it. But a similar series of events has been enacted in our other institutions. In education, for example . . . the educational system is now filthy with psychologists . . . psychologists as counselors, psychologists as testers, psychologists as consultants and designers. It is not easy to see that this is making the educational system a lot better, although maybe I am missing something. Maybe it *will*, in two or three generations, but maybe it won't."

Baseball fans are offered an endless parade of experts—mostly ex-players and managers—but experts and expertise don't necessarily come as a package. In the '81 *Abstract*, Bill wrote:

My strongest impression from the World Series last year was that I had never before appreciated how little the network announcers actually know about the teams they are describing. . . .

So I decided to try the radio, meaning Sparky Anderson. Sparky is full of information; he never lets up, cramming the space between pitches full of inside dope about what each batter does well and how often, how you pitch to and defense each one, that sort of thing. And if there is anyone in the Western Hemisphere who knows less about the Kansas City Royals than Sparky Anderson does, I don't know who it would be—Karen Ann Quinlan, perhaps. Where does he come up with all this stuff? Amos Otis is a dead pull hitter—a 99-percent pull hitter, he said—leaving some question as to why 13 of his 18 home runs went to right field. In the World Series Otis flied out to the outfield four times, once to center and three times to right.

Winding back to White and Rice . . . In criminal cases where a defendant has given what turns out to be a false confession, conviction rates are the same as in cases where the confession was true. Eyewitness testimony is also given far more weight by jurors than is warranted by its reliability, which some studies peg at a scary 50 percent. Just as jurors tend to overweight eyewitnesses and confessions, baseball fans tend to overweight standard statistics and conventional wisdom.

But baseball has a rare capacity for objective analysis, thanks to the depth of its statistical record. Bill wrote, "There may well be no other facet of American life, the activities of lab rats excepted, that is so extensively categorized, counted, and recorded." Yet if not taken with *all* of the evidence, *in context*, standard statistics can be a kind of false confession, backed with eyewitness and expert testimony.

Bill laid out the evidence and concluded that there wasn't an ocean between Rice and White but a stream. If they'd played in the same park in the same years, White might well have come out the better. He played in a pitcher's park in a pitcher's league and was compared unfairly to past Yankees greats. His abilities were subtle but no less valuable. Is it an insult to Jim Rice to say that he was a fine player whose context gave him every edge, and that Roy White was an equally great player whose context hid the truth about him? No. Is it an artful stretch to rank him ahead of Rice? Perhaps.

Here's another Moneyball/A's/Bill James–related insight. In the *Abstract* years, Kansas State University had a basketball coach named Jack Hartman. Bill referenced him on the subject of what *talent* means. "Hartman had a player in the late seventies named Ed Nealy, who was 6-9, very strong, soft hands, but slow and couldn't win a jumping contest against a sack of flour," Bill says. "Hartman loved him, because he was always where he was supposed to be. I remember his quote about him: 'Well, what is talent? Talent is just being where you are supposed to be and doing what you are supposed to do.'

Which is a very different idea of talent than most people have, but it worked for old Ed Nealy."

In this sense, *Moneyball* illuminated A's first baseman Scott Hatteberg as an "Ed Nealy." Of course a team of Ed Nealys probably won't beat a team of Michael Jordans. But, unless your resources are unlimited, you have to compromise and look for hidden value. Baseball, being orders of magnitude more complex than basketball, has more places for value to hide.

Bill says, "Economic questions are essentially about *value*. My work is essentially about value. Economists deal with the problem of finding the right value—the value of a stoplight relative to a speed bump, the value of a house relative to the value of transportation, or the value of an endangered species relative to 10,000 jobs, or the value of a lost suitcase with uncertain contents. I worry about the value of a walk relative to a run, the value of a run relative to a win, the value of a twenty-four-year-old player relative to a twenty-eight-year-old player, the value of a fielder relative to a hitter, the value of a minor league prospect vs. a marginal major league pitcher.

"Value is determined in different cases by different things. Value is related to scarcity, to utility, to potential, to costs, to sales, to productivity . . . all of these things have corollaries in baseball. It's not that I used any economic method as much as the habits of thought—looking at the supply chain, looking at scarcity, finding ways to define productivity. A key concept in economics is that 'somewhere is a consequence.' If you can identify the consequence, you can work your way back toward the value."

By the way, you probably wouldn't think of Barry Bonds as part of any "hidden value" rubric, but when a front office zeroes in on the wrong metrics, even the future best hitter of his era can be underappreciated. In the 1990 *Baseball Book*, Bill wrote of Bonds:

> I'm sure you have heard the rumors that the Pirates are trying to trade him, and I'm sure that, like me, you wonder what the hell they are thinking of. There is always the possibility that the

Pirates, despite their two-year string of bad decisions, know something that we don't—that Bonds has a lifestyle problem of some kind which is inhibiting his development. What is more likely than that is that they are focusing on his batting average (.248), and losing track of all the positives—19 homers, 93 walks, 32 stolen bases, 34 doubles, excellent defense in left field. I don't know that Bonds is ever going to have an MVP season, but I'll say this. If you want to trade him, I'll take him.

The Sox don't operate under the payroll constraints of, say, the A's, but look at some of Boston's lineup next to that of their 2004 World Series opponent. Bill Mueller versus Scott Rolen. Kevin Millar against Albert Pujols. As great as Johnny Damon is, most pundits wouldn't have preferred him over Jim Edmonds. No wonder the consensus prediction had the Cardinals winning in five or six games.

But a basic James principle is that "balanced strength is always preferable to unbalanced strength." The 2004 Red Sox, often labeled a "fantasy league team" by the media, were in fact far from it. Fantasy leagues value steals the same as home runs. Fantasy teams value the saves statistic at a premium. If you were putting together a fantasy team, the Yankees and Cardinals would have been better choices.

Of course, the "fantasy team" barb was supposed to reference Boston's lack of defense, too, but it reveals both the media's fixation on errors as the sole measure of fielding and a failure to realize that the old Fenway Park infield (and Boston weather) created a huge park effect with respect to increased errors.

Heart was the other thing the "fantasy" Red Sox were supposed to lack—especially in contrast to the Yankees, who "play the right way every day," as the New York–area hype machine spun it.

After the postseason, Bill made comments along the lines of, "There is no way in hell we would have come back from a 3–0 deficit to the Yankees without exceptional veteran leadership," in answer to the question of what accounted for the comeback. Some wondered if "Mr. Stats" could be serious, but, in fact, it wasn't at all out of character. Bill once wrote, for example, "To bring together a core of people who want to win and who are willing to pay the price for that; that, I continue to believe, is terrifically important, the heart of a team."

Bill says that there is an arbitrary element to the question of why the Sox won. He explains, "Let's say one team wins a hundred games, the other team wins ninety-nine, and, at the end of the pennant race, the reporter asks, 'What do you think was really the key victory of the season?' Well . . . pick one. They're all critical. And the same here. There are a lot of answers to the question, one no more true than the other. There are a hundred reasons the Red Sox won the World Series, one no more true than the other."

The Sox did have something Bill wrote about in the early *Abstracts* as having a disproportionate effect on the outcomes of postseason series (especially World Series): power. Bill doesn't claim to have a formula for winning in the playoffs, but there is the historical record, and there is logic. Both point to the fact that October games are overwhelmingly pitched by frontline pitchers, and frontline pitchers give up a larger percentage of their runs as home runs than second-tier pitchers do.

The reason: A sequence of events that ends in runs being scored off a home run is shorter than a sequence that puts runs across in other ways. For example, two scenarios: (1) Single, followed by a home run: that's two runs on two hits. (2) Single, steal, single (run scores), double (run scores): that's two runs on three hits and a stolen base, twice as many elements. The second sequence can work, but against a great pitcher it's harder to pull off than the first.

In the 2003 American League Championship Series, five outs from going to the World Series before falling to the Yankees. As even your nephew's hamster knows, a year later the Sox became the first team to climb out of an 0–3 hole to win a postseason series when they stuck it to the pinstripers in the 2004 ALCS. Next they beat St. Louis to bring the World Championship to Fenway for the first time since Babe Ruth was the franchise's ace pitcher.

There's an old carnival scam: "Two pennies more, and up goes the donkey." The way it works is, the barker promises that as soon as two more pennies are added to the pot, his donkey will climb up a ladder. Of course it always takes two more, and the donkey never goes up. Red Sox fans had reason to feel like they were stuck in a perpetual up-goes-the-donkey con, so seeing that ass get off the ground was sweet . . . and all the more so for how the season seemed to be souring two-thirds of the way through.

Trailing the Yankees by eight games in the division, the Sox traded star shortstop Nomar Garciaparra, who wasn't happy or healthy. They slotted in Orlando Cabrera, who was both, but the move was widely criticized. "What about No-mah?" I asked Bill. "A lot of people thought you screwed up."

"I thought a lot of people had an unrealistic view," he said. "The reality is that we didn't own Nomar's future. Nomar owned Nomar's future. Some people wrote about it as if we'd traded six years of Nomar Garciaparra. We didn't own that, nor did we have any great chance of obtaining it."

What about for the rest of the season?

"We'd lost confidence that he was going to help us win. His effort was fantastic. Sometimes he tries *too* hard. But it wasn't working. We had lost confidence that it was going to work."

Was it a panic move?

"Well, if you're trying to start a fire, and you have a box of matches, and you start striking matches and throwing them in there, and the fire's not lighting, you start to feel kind of desperate. We weren't desperate, but we were getting down to our last match. We felt that the team should ignite, but it hadn't. Fortunately, finally it did."

AL Division Series 2004
Sox 3, Angels 0

The Sox blazed through August and September to win the wild card, then swept the division series against the Angels. David Ortiz won the final game in extra innings with a walk-off homer. Bill and Susie were watching the game at home. Bill says that what he'll always remember is the move manager Terry Francona *didn't* make. In the ninth inning, score tied, Ortiz drew a walk. Bill says, "Tim McCarver and Joe Buck, broadcasting the game, felt certain that Terry should pinch-run for Ortiz, try to move the runner into scoring position, and play for one run. Susie was screaming at the television, 'No! No! Don't pinch-run for him! We need his bat!' And Terry, thank God, saw it the way Susie did. The gain in the *chance* of scoring that run wasn't worth taking David's bat out of the lineup." In the eleventh inning Ortiz stepped up and blasted the Sox into the ALCS.

AL Championship Series 2004
Sox 4, Yankees 3

As a lifelong Kansas City fan, Bill came to the Sox with a pre-forged dislike of all things pinstripe. He points out, "The Yankees beat the Royals in heartbreaking fashion in '76, '77, and '78, just as they did the Red Sox. The Yankees used Kansas City as a farm team in the fifties and sixties, just as they did the Red Sox from 1919 to 1930. They took Babe Ruth from the Red Sox, but they got Roger Maris from Kansas City. They got Red Ruffing from the Red Sox, but they took Ralph Terry from Kansas City. They got Joe Dugan from the Red Sox, but they took Clete Boyer from Kansas City."

Rachel McCarthy James, Bill and Susie's college-age daughter, says, "Dad hates the Yankees, and taught us kids to do the same, reading us *The Year the Yankees Lost the Pennant*, et cetera. When I was nine or ten, we were in a toy store and I found a Barbie in a Yankees outfit. I took it up to him, and said, 'We should burn this, Dad!'"

A doll burning may have been in order after Game Three of the '04 ALCS, a 19-8 shellacking. Game Four was close, but Yankees relief ace Mariano Rivera came on to try to save a one-run lead in the ninth. Two batters later, with a pinch-run steal in between, the game was tied 4-4.

Popular history will hail the Dave Roberts steal as the key to the game-tying sequence, but Kevin Millar's leadoff walk was at least as crucial. (Getting the leadoff man on base is the factor most linked to scoring in a given inning.) Rivera had one immediate goal: keep Millar off base. But, respecting Millar's power, Rivera had to pitch carefully, and Millar was unwilling to swing at a pitch off the plate.

Bill says, "All I remember about the steal is that, at the time, I thought he was out. He wasn't, obviously, but from my vantage point in the seats behind home plate, I thought he was out. It was a great play, and it deserves a place on the roster of famous plays from that postseason, of which there are so many."

Bill Mueller's single sent the game into extra innings, where Ortiz ended it with a home run.

Two more wins and it was Game Seven, first inning. Boston took a 2-0 lead on Ortiz's short-porch homer. In the second inning, with the bases loaded, Johnny Damon jacked Javier Vazquez's first-pitch meatball into the upper deck, effectively putting the Sox in the World Series. Susie says, "Bill rarely mistimes a trip to the bathroom, but Johnny was at the plate when Bill left with the score 2-0. I knew it would kill him that he missed the grand slam, but it gave me a chance to try and fool him. Our TV is in the basement, and access is from a staircase walled off from the rest of the room. As he came down, he asked what happened to Damon. I tried to keep the excitement out of my voice and said, 'He hit into a double play.' By this time, Bill was at the base of the stairs, and rather than react to me, his eyes went straight to the score in the upper corner of the screen. He's hard to fool, and yes, he'll check the evidence before he believes his wife."

Grady's Mistake

Near the end of the seventh inning, with Boston in control, my mind drifted back to the eighth inning of Game Seven the year before. Pedro Martinez was 115 pitches into the red, jammed up after back-to-back hits to Derek Jeter and Bernie Williams. The Sox had relief help available, but manager Grady Little left Pedro on the hill.

Scary movies are psychological metaphors. *Halloween*, for example, is about the fact that some problems will keep coming at you until you face them head-on. *The Sixth Sense* is about being trapped between worlds and needing help to resolve the problem. *The Ring* combines those two ideas, and so did this ballgame. As the nightmare unfolded, I wanted to scream, "Look out behind you!" to Pedro and "Help him!" to Grady.

Godzilla Matsui ground-rule doubled and Jorge Posada followed with a game-tying bloop. From there, Aaron Boone's walk-off homer in the eleventh almost felt like an afterthought. A week later I heard a story that said it all.

A devout Red Sox fan got stuck in London on business at the time Game Seven was to be played. He went from pub to pub, looking for one that had the necessary satellite equipment and was going to be open all night. He didn't find any that were good on both counts, but he found one with a satellite and an owner who agreed to stay open for a price. The fan settled in to watch the game.

It was near daybreak in London as Pedro gave up hit after hit and the lead slipped away, the Sox fan raging and writhing in agony while a half-dozen Brits drank away the night. Finally one of the inebriated Londoners looked over at him in concern, looked back at the television, and asked, "Excuse me, sir, but would the rules permit those fellows to employ a substitute for the bowler? He seems to be laboring a bit."

The brutal truth: Grady Little had failed to comprehend what was apparent to a drunk, half-asleep Englishman who had never seen a baseball game before. Pedro was toast.

The media coverage of Grady and Pedro's horror show was misleading in regard to Bill's ideas about pitch counts. He talks a lot about them, but not how you might imagine. "In the 1970s," he says, "when I started writing the *Abstract*, pitchers, a lot of them, would pitch three hundred innings a year. There were pitchers who would pitch twenty or twenty-five complete games a year. Throwing 180 pitches used to be commonplace. Now if a pitcher throws 120 pitches it's a news story. The reason is that people are less averse to losing than they are to being humiliated. Managers are so averse to criticism over a real threat of injury, it's become almost a competition to see who can back off furthest. There's been a paradigm shift in what is perceived to be the dominant virtue. The dominant virtue was toughness and faith in your pitcher. Now the dominant virtue is the manager being careful not to hurt his pitcher. It's not driven by logic or data as much as by accordance with the dominant virtue."

Bill has written that if you're too careful with pitchers, you can *only* be careful with them, and says that pitch limits have been pulled in so far from the practical risk zones that there's no significance to them. Ironically, it was Bill who, in the *Abstract*, wrote that one of his managerial heroes, Billy Martin, used his pitchers the way people used to test for witches. (If she floats, she's a witch. If she drowns, she's not.) The analogy filtered into baseball's collective unconscious, making Bill in part responsible for the obsession with pitch counts he now pooh-poohs.

To the mainstream media, the fact that "100 pitches" is a statistic made it a Bill James concern. *Daily News*ie Bill Madden imagined, "All the way from Bill James' stats silo in Lawrence, Kan., you could hear the wails of outrage." For a healthy pitcher, however, the issue isn't pitch count, it's whether the pitcher is tired. Bill wrote in 1986:

> My theory about motions is that most managers don't have a very good sense of when a pitcher is tired, and that this is probably the one thing in baseball that a fan at home watching the game on TV can see *better*, if he pays attention, than the manager can. The fact that managers don't, in general, have any idea when their pitchers are tired is supported, I feel, by the things they say about it—for example, that the pitcher's readings on the radar gun have not dropped, or that what they look for when a pitcher is tired is when he starts dropping down, not coming over the top. . . .

Most importantly, *the movement of the trailing leg is often the first indicator of when a pitcher is tired.* When a pitcher gets tired, he'll start to conserve energy by diminishing the force with which he propels himself forward; the end result of this will be a dramatic reduction in the movement of the trailing leg. *Many managers pay no attention to this, and will allow a pitcher to stay in the game, even with men on base and the game on the line, when it is very obvious, from the movement of the trailing leg, that the pitcher is tired.*

Bill says, "I still think that managers are not well positioned, in the dugout, to see the 'tells' of pitcher fatigue, but that situation is different than it was twenty years ago in this way: Starting pitchers now are pulled out of the game much earlier relative to their fatigue. Twenty years ago, managers would leave a tiring pitcher in the game; now they come out as soon as the manager suspects that they might possibly be getting tired. So it's not really a question of the managers seeing things or not seeing them; these things just don't happen anymore, the way that they did twenty years ago."

We Have Arrived at the Blunder

As a Sox fan, I searched for understanding in a baseball universe that seemed bent on thwarting me. In the wake of Pedro's meltdown, I turned to my baseball bibles—my old *Abstracts*. There was something familiar about Grady's blunder. I found it in Bill's account of the 1985 Cardinals-Royals World Series, with Charlie Leibrandt as Pedro and Dick Howser as Grady Little.

Leibrandt took a 2-0 lead into the ninth inning of Game Two. After a leadoff double, he got two outs before allowing an RBI single: 2-1 Royals. He was dominant until he got tired, at which point it didn't matter what he'd done—he wasn't the same pitcher. Sound familiar?

A bloop double put the tying and winning runs in position for the Cardinals. Bill would write:

Then came the decision that I really, sincerely, seriously, can't understand. By this time, we in the right field bleachers were tearing our teeth out, wondering why Quisenberry was not in the game, wondering why, if Howser had lost faith in Quisenberry, Joe Beckwith was not in the game, or if not Beckwith then Gubicza, or if not Gubicza then almost anybody would do.

After an intentional walk, Terry Pendleton lofted a pitch into the left-center gap, and that was the ballgame. Bill wrote, "What Howser said was that they had made a decision before the inning that Charlie still had his good stuff—his readings on the radar gun were good— and that it was his game to win or lose. To me, it sounds like saying that you let the house burn down because you'd made a prior decision to ignore the smoke alarm."

What is a managerial blunder, to begin with? Is it a decision about the odds in the game that is wrong on the percentages? No, it can't be, because *none of us knows exactly what the true odds are* in any given game situation. None of us knows, and none of us ever will know, not a hundred years from now when they have computers that will fit on your fingernail and spit out the history of the universe at a billion words a second, none of us will know for sure what the odds are because each unique situation contains a thousand variables, at least a hundred of which will not have had enough trials to be evaluated. In short, no one can ever know how this pitcher will pitch this batter under these exact lighting conditions when this pitcher is tired. We will know much more about it later than we know now, but we will never KNOW.

But we do know what the book says. What we know is how an ordinary manager would handle this situation in an ordinary case, and we know WHY he would do it that way. These are three elements of managerial blunder:

It is a move which goes against the conventional practice,
It occurs at a key moment of the game, and
It doesn't work.

World Series 2004
Sox 4, Redbirds 0

Game Four, ninth inning, two down: Boston closer Keith Foulke glove-stopped Edgar Renteria's comebacker and underhanded to first, spawning celebration hangovers across Red Sox Nation. "Our seats were on the third tier," Susie says, "between third base and home plate. There were some Boston front office people sitting in another area of the same section. Bill and I were sitting on the back row of our section.

"With the final out there was chaos, hugs and kisses, congratulations all around. We talked with the people around us for a bit and then headed downstairs to get a better view of the on-field celebration. I must say the Cardinal fans showed a lot of class. I know I have never hugged so many strangers in one night. We stood in the back of the main level and watched the various presentations. I suggested to Bill that he join the Red Sox celebrants on the field. He hesitated but said he didn't think he should. I'm not a very forward person either, but I was thinking about the historic nature of the night. He was part of it. I kept edging him downward to get a better view of things.

"We tried calling the kids but had a hard time getting a signal. Rachel finally got through to us. I described the scene and she said, 'Tell Dad he's got to go on the field. He should be there too.' I told her I had tried to convince him; but with both of us working on him, he relented. We were standing five or six rows behind the Red Sox dugout when Lucinda Treat, the Red Sox' house counsel, spotted Bill. She asked the security guard to let him through. However, Bill had left his press credentials back at the hotel and the guard refused to let us through without proof he was bona fide. Lucinda didn't give up, though, and brought over a big Red Sox security guy who pointed at Bill and authoritatively said, 'Let him through!' The gates opened and we were on the field.

"Out of the crush of people, Theo Epstein emerged. He gave us a big bear hug. He was totally soaked with champagne and beer. My stellar memory from the World Series came moments later. I hadn't met John Henry before. Bill introduced us after they had exchanged congratulations. John poked his index finger repeatedly into Bill's chest and said, 'You're a World Champion.'

"John was pulled away, and Bill and I walked around the field, meeting and talking with people. At one point, Curt Schilling and Pedro came dashing across the field, trophy in Pedro's hand. My favorite player, David Ortiz, was being interviewed feet away from us. Bill and I noticed people scooping up some of the dirt from the base paths, so we followed suit, stuffing a few handfuls into my jacket pocket.

"It was such a beautiful, magical night, we didn't leave the field till about midnight. We walked to the hotel where many of the players were staying. The place was mobbed by Boston fans. We each had a glass of wine and talked with a guy who had made the trip from Boston but hadn't gotten into the game. The streets were mostly deserted as we walked back to the car. At 2 a.m., we looked for an all-nighter to get something to eat. Steak 'N Shake had to do for Bill's first meal as a World Champion."

Bill and I are talking over eggs and coffee on the eve of the first 2004 presidential debate.

How do you feel about roller coasters?

"I remember when our son Isaac was seven," Bill says. "We went to the Six Flags near St. Louis, where there's this Batman ride. I'm like, 'I'm not getting on that.' And seven-year-old Isaac is standing there explaining to me, 'Dad, have you read anything in the newspaper about people being killed on this ride? All of these people are riding it, and none of them are getting killed.'"

There's a real conflict there between the evidence and the gut. What about flying?

"I'm okay with it, but I was on a plane to Boston the other day, and a woman next to me said, 'I'm not good with planes, but I get through it with a Darvon and a couple of Bloody Marys.'"

I wonder if she was picking up a car at the other end. You worked on some kind of lawsuit involving Thurman Munson's plane crash?

"I did quite a bit of work on it. The case involved his widow and the people who had taught him to fly, or failed to do so."

You were on the widow's side?

"No, the opposite. The issues in the case as I remember it can be summarized this way: Thurman, in the last few moments of his aviation career, made so many mistakes that, his widow claimed, he couldn't possibly have been properly trained; and the people at the flight school said he'd made so many mistakes, you couldn't possibly blame it on them. I don't remember exactly, but from the time he took off until the crash, he made a dozen major mistakes, or about that. I was going to testify about where Thurman's career was going, if he hadn't died. I would have argued what I think is self-evidently true, that his best years were behind him. But the case settled before it reached that point."

You've had some bad experiences with lawyers?

"Well, I'm not complaining. Some of my best friends are lawyers. Susie threw a surprise party after the Red Sox hired me. I got home from a KU basketball game and there were about fifty people in the house. At one point a small group got into some legal discussion, and it kept drawing in more and more lawyers. Eventually there were about twenty of them standing there."

How about the presidential debates? After four years, shouldn't people know what they think?

"It's kind of like judging a veteran by spring training."

What do you think about NAFTA?

"Free trade has both benefits and costs. Different people have different opinions about the trade-offs. There's no sure way to know except to let it happen and find out. But I'll tell you what I think. I think the benefits are overstated. There's been a consensus between Republicans and Democrats that the benefits outweigh the costs. My instinct is that this has become an article of faith, so people have stopped thinking about it."

I'd like to understand how a complex issue so quickly goes from open question to article of faith. Is it that people need to get as many things into the answered column as possible?

"That's it. Nature abhors a vacuum. People have to have an explanation, and if the only one available is a bad one . . . 'Well, it's the best we got.' The same thing happens in baseball. Somebody says something that makes intuitive sense. If there's no clear, quick refutation to it, it becomes accepted truth."

Bill says that after NAFTA was passed with broad bipartisan support, he heard a political analyst say that in American politics we have a stupid party and a greedy party, and when they get together they do something stupid and greedy. It reminds me of the *Simpsons* episode where Dole and Clinton are revealed to be slathering space aliens masquerading in human suits. The crowd is agitated, but one of the aliens reminds them, "You have to vote for one of us; it's a two-party system." That settles them right down.

We've created a process by which no one in his right mind would want the job. Should we be trying to get the best person, not feeding the egos of career politicians?

"Like Cincinnatus," Bill offers. "You know that story? Cincinnatus was a Roman general who'd retired to his farm. Rome was going to be attacked, but the Senate couldn't decide who should be in charge, so they said, 'Let's just sit down and figure out who has the best credentials.' Cincinnatus was out plowing his field when a messenger rode up to tell him he'd been named dictator."

How'd it work out?

"As far as I know, it worked out fine. He still has towns named after him, so he must've done okay. I used to think Colin Powell was that guy, someone right for the job but who didn't seem to want it. But then he got involved. . . ."

What about Mario Cuomo?

"Cuomo's a very bright guy, and he played baseball in the minor leagues—certainly a point in his favor."

How about Bob Dole? He's smart, but with a mean streak.

"Dole's a natural comedian. He would've been an effective president. He isn't that conservative; politically the difference between Dole and Bill Clinton is about two degrees. Dole has a mean streak, but is a mean streak a bad thing in a president? I don't know that it is. I have a mean streak, too. I go back and read things that I wrote years ago, and I'm astonished at how vicious I was. So I relate to Bob Dole in that sense."

Is that because writing is solitary—it lets you detach from the subject as a person?

"That's it. It's an unfortunate thing, and I fault myself for it. I wrote something about Doug Flynn that was so nasty, he not only was angry at me, he stopped speaking to the media in general."

You sure it wasn't Duane Kuiper—"a pathetically inept offensive ballplayer"?

"I'm fairly sure it was Doug Flynn. He's reportedly a very nice man. I should've thought about the fact that I was criticizing a real person. There were times I forgot that."

I remember you writing, "Kansas City designated hitters don't get on base very much and don't hit for power, but they're nice people." A writer can't worry too much about offending people, right?

"I still feel bad about it, but maybe that's my perspective now that I'm famous and people take shots at me. I took my shots, so I guess they're entitled to take theirs. Or maybe it's that when you have children, you realize that everyone is special."

Amy Lowell said, "Youth condemns. Maturity condones." Did you read the Dick Williams autobiography, No More Mr. Nice Guy? *He didn't know from Amy Lowell.*

"I remember his description of Terry Kennedy: 'Kennedy didn't have a mental or physical problem but an equipment problem. He needed a diaper.' People in baseball very often don't understand that when you're writing a book, writing a good book is the most important thing you're doing. They understand that when you're playing or coaching baseball, playing or coaching baseball is the most important thing you're doing, but they can't translate that into book writing, and they don't understand why you wrote something offensive to them, because they don't get the math: Writing something entertaining about Whitey Herzog: 100 points. Avoiding pissing off Whitey Herzog: 1 point.

"A lot of times, when old managers write books, they don't really get it . . . they don't understand the importance of writing an entertaining book. If you look like an ass, you look like an ass; tough shit. They want to write a book, but they want to keep an eye on 'not offending old colleagues,' and an eye on 'maybe I'll get another shot at managing,' and an eye on 'making myself look like a positive person.' It seemed to me that Williams got it, in this sense: He understood that when he was managing, winning was the main thing, but when he was writing a book, writing an entertaining book was the main thing."

Your passion for baseball goes without saying, but your interest in crime stories isn't widely known. Do you ever read crime message boards? Aren't some of those folks slightly off their rockers?

"Forty percent of the people who post to sports chat boards are slightly off their rockers. For crime boards it has to be seventy."

Is there a creepier English phrase than 'crawl space'?

"How about 'donor infection'? Or 'protruding bone fragment'?"

'Flesh-eating bacteria'?

"'Pinstripe dynasty.'"

You win. I wonder if your analytical abilities would have made you a good cop.

"I don't think I'd have been a very good policeman. Detectives have to be able to interrogate a suspect so that they get information while giving out none or only false information. If I were in that situation, I'm certain I'd give out more information than I'd pull in. That does happen in real crime cases sometimes: The interrogator throws the investigation out of whack by giving out more information than he realizes."

How about as a CSI *type?*

"I'd have had to be a forensic scientist. The problem there is a lack of intellectual discipline. In the past forty years, forensics has invented forty-five new fields, and if I had gone into forensics I suspect it would be forty-six. But whether the field I invented would've been used much, I don't know."

I asked Bill what makes a great crime story. He later amended his answer by e-mail.

"There are three or four things that can make a classic crime case:

"1. A durable mystery.

"2. Unusual circumstances, and

"3. Interesting people involved.

"4. An ongoing story, which unfolds after the point at which it begins.

"Crimes are interesting for different reasons. There are very interesting crime cases in which there is no real mystery about what happened—the O. J. Simpson case, for example. The disappointment of *serial* murder cases is that they are virtually never solved by clever police work.

"One which was, resulted in the capture of Albert Fish in New York in the 1930s. Fish had sent a taunting letter to one of his victims. Using very crude forensics, a lot of determination, and some clever reasoning, police were able to track backward on the letter, march toward Fish also on some other approach, and eventually pinpoint him.

"The most fascinating crime case in American history is the Jon-Benét Ramsey murder. Things happened in that case which simply never happen. The basic facts of the case—that a young child is found murdered in her home, with it not being apparent what has happened and her parents claiming to know nothing about it—are EXTREMELY unusual, on many levels. The overwhelming majority of murder victims are adults; this was a child. The overwhelming majority of murdered children are at-risk children who live in poverty, who live in high-crime neighborhoods, and/or who live in abusive homes, often with parents who are drug addicts and/or career criminals.

"Here you have none of that—a bright, attractive child with no observable risk factors, found murdered inside the safety of her own home. Very unusual.

"The beauty-queen aspect and her parents' wealth—the tabloid features of the case—make it somewhat more unusual.

"You have a ransom note and the body both left at the scene of the crime—an extremely unusual combination, if not unprecedented.

"You have perhaps the longest ransom note in the history of the world, about three hundred words.

"You have an extremely unusual—indeed, bizarre—method of killing someone—a garrote . . . actually, there are two almost-simultaneous causes of death, which is quite unusual.

"You have a very large amount of evidence that doesn't lead anywhere.

"Those aside, you have an after-the-fact story which is beyond the bounds of fiction. You have police incompetence on a scale which is inconceivable. I don't know how to explain this. . . . Suppose that there is a 'Police Incompetence Meter' of 1 to 10, in which 1 is 'maybe that wasn't perfect, but those things are going to happen' and 10 is 'I can't believe that a rank amateur, assigned to work as a cop, would do *that*.'

"In normal crime cases you'll always find *something* that wasn't done right, and occasionally, reading crime books, you stumble across a 10. The O. J. case, which is famous for the incompetence of the police, actually *wasn't* badly investigated; there were some little mistakes made and a couple of things that would score at maybe 5 or 6 on a PIM (Police Incompetence Meter), but nothing really unusual.

"In this case you have fifteen, twenty, twenty-five different actions, by different policemen and different police agencies over a long period of time, which are *clearly* tens. Reading about it is bizarre, sort of like being invited to someone's house for a party and discovering that they keep rhinos and polar bears in the bathrooms.

"For the sake of clarity, I am not saying that the Boulder police are (usually) incompetent; they are actually apparently a capable, pretty well-organized outfit which is good at dealing with the kinds of problems that Boulder normally faces. But the chance that you or I will mishandle a situation is proportional to the unusualness of the problem we are confronted with. The usual stuff that we deal with every day . . . we know how to handle that. If you give us an unusual problem that we have to figure out as we go along, there is a good chance we'll screw it up. The Boulder police were confronted, with no warning or preparation of any kind, at a vulnerable moment just after Christmas, with an extremely unusual case. They screwed it up beyond belief. For example, what is this, on a Police Incompetence Meter:

> When you have a crime scene and you have no real idea what has happened, leave one relatively inexperienced cop in charge and allow friends, relatives, and acquaintances to come and go and trample around the crime scene as they please.

"What instructional manual does THAT come out of? Do you think, if you were suddenly put in charge of a police investigation, you would do that?"

> *Ask the relatives and friends of the kidnap victim to search the house top to bottom for anything out of place.*

"If *that* isn't a 10 on the PIM, what would be? But it gets worse from there.

> *There was unidentified DNA found on JonBenét's body and in her underwear. The Boulder police were insisting for years after the fact that this DNA had nothing to do with the case and was of no interest to them.*

"Huh? How incompetent *is* that, exactly? And there are *dozens* of things like this; I can't begin to explain them all. It's mind-bending.

You just can't conceive of a modern police investigation being conducted this badly.

"This then bleeds into the two other very unusual features of the case. First, the tabloid television intrusion into the investigation is unprecedented in modern history. You have dozens and dozens of reporters scurrying around Boulder—a town about the size of Lawrence, more or less—trying to dig up any information they can. Many of these people are unethical. Many of them have generous accounts they can use to try to bribe people to talk.

"Finally, an open war breaks out between the police and the prosecutors, in which they are publicly charging one another with incompetence, malfeasance, and dishonesty. This is unprecedented.

"The war between police and prosecutors and the tabloid intrusion into the investigation actually do have a precedent, which is the Hall/Mills case in New Jersey in the twenties. But they're unprecedented in modern America.

"It's a very, very unusual set of events. But at some point in the future, I believe, the case *will* be solved; we will know what actually happened—at which point it will slide down the list of fascinating crimes. There's a lot of evidence. Once the police stop RESISTING the evidence and start following it, I think there's enough there to find the person(s) responsible.

"I think what maybe drives my interest in the case is the specter of these utterly innocent people, the Ramsey parents, being tortured by the nation's press because the police are, in essence, telling the press that the parents committed the crime. It's a terrible, terrible injustice—in the wake of a horrific crime—and you absolutely can't get people to respond to it on a serious level, because there are a series of things people say to prevent them from actually having to think about what the press and police are doing to these people, in full view of the public. These are:

"1. 'It's just a tabloid story.'

"2. 'I think the parents probably did it anyway.'

"3. 'There are 20,000 murders in this country every year, why focus on this one?'

"4. 'Crimes worse than this one happen every day to poor people, but you never hear about it.'

"Well, there are many other terrible crimes, and I don't mean to diminish the significance of those, either—but there are no crimes worse than this one, and there are no other crimes in which so much of the American public is complicit in compounding the evil consequences."

9

Critical Visions

Before we are forgotten, we will be turned into kitsch.
—Milan Kundera

A self-described class clown in school, young Bill wasn't inclined to write the way his classmates did—or the way his teachers expected. His heroes were the sportswriters who spoke to him in the daily papers. "I wanted to be Jim Murray and to write funny columns about sports like he did," he says. In the acknowledgments of the '84 *Abstract*, he wrote, "I have a feeling that Jim Murray probably hates my work. It doesn't matter if he does. Murray was a man who wrote with wit and intelligence and a great deal of fire. I came to think it must be wonderful to be able to attack a subject with such weapons as words, images, humor, and bald truth."

Bill says, "As much as I loved Jim Murray as a writer, he seemed at times to have an almost pathological dislike of logic. If a position about who should be MVP took more than two lines to explain, he didn't want to hear it." Murray wrote an article in 1957 for *Sports Illustrated* about "phony Hall of Famers." Bill wrote, "By phony Hall of Famers he had in mind people like Ty Cobb—I am not joking—and Rogers Hornsby, who had great statistics but, to hear Murray tell it, never did anything to help a team win a ball game." Bill says, "Murray picked a position on an issue and homed in on it like a laser, logic be damned. I'm the opposite; I start with the issue and dance all around it before I approach a conclusion."

Murray wrote a column for the *Los Angeles Times* for decades. Bill couldn't wait to open the paper three times a week to see what his hero had to say. He remembers lines like this, about a college football player: "Ten thousand football coaches wanted him, ten thousand professors didn't." Bill says, "Jim Murray was able to make almost any subject entertaining by swinging through an unusual mix of figures of speech. From this I learned how to construct a figure of speech, and the value of not letting an article get too linear."

Bill also dedicated the '84 *Abstract* to Leonard Koppett. Koppett was no cheerleader for sabermetrics. In his revised *Thinking Fan's Guide to Baseball*, he wrote, "The Bill James approach, of cloaking totally subjective views (to which he is entirely entitled) in some sort of asserted 'statistical evidence,' is divorced from reality. The game simply isn't played that way, and his judgments are no more nor less accurate than anyone else's."

I asked Bill about the fact that some of the writers and managers he admired were at odds with his point of view. He said, "It never really surprises me that someone can ignore everything that I believe in and still be very successful. For example, Whitey Herzog's simplification of the world was different from mine, but nonetheless, he quite obviously knew what he was doing. So my view was that I could learn something from him, rather than debate with him. His view of the game contained a great deal of truth, whether or not it was the same view as mine."

A mythic monster, sprung from the minds of baseball insiders with axes to grind, has been peddled to baseball fans as "Bill James." Among this illusory creature's nastiest qualities is the belief, as at least one hack has put it, that "spreadsheets are the path to performance." But in the Cleveland Indians comments of the '82 *Abstract*, the real Bill James wrote about what he called "statistical idiocy." That is, "the assertion that nothing is real except that which is measured in statistics." The 1960 trade that sent Rocky Colavito to Detroit for Harvey Kuenn, Bill wrote, "marked the beginning of the moronic conception, the notion that a baseball team is made up of interchangeable parts no more complex than lines of statistics."

Frank Lane made that trade because he had been so successful as a trader in Chicago that he had come to believe more in his own genius than he believed in talent. He thought that he could move players around like APBA cards and turn a contender into a champion because he was smarter than anybody else. It didn't work out because, even if he was smarter than anybody else, it was still the talent which had to go out on the field and win the games, and a bearskin rug stuffed with hamburger is not a bear. He was treating ballplayers like meat, and they played like meat. Genius or not, statistician or not, he was guilty of the same idiocy.

Unfortunately, people conflating Bill James with interpretations and misinterpretations of *Moneyball,* and basing their ideas about his work on what they read in the papers, have given rise to the notion that he doesn't believe in chemistry or character, doesn't think an ace reliever is important, doesn't care about defense, and on and on.

Bill once observed, about press coverage of a great manager, "A fair amount has been written about Billy Martin in the last ten years. If all of the newspaper stories that have been written about Billy Martin were put in a pile in the middle of New Jersey, it would be the best place for them. But *how* does he accomplish his miracles? Did you ever notice how little has been said about that?" The same can be said of a fair percentage of what's written about Bill James.

Typical was a column in the July 9, 2004, *Dallas Morning News* about Toronto, Oakland, and Boston—teams the writer, who shall remain generic, cleverly dubbed "the Moneyball gang." Instead of chasing the Yankees, he asserted, "the Moneyball gang" was chasing its tail. Boston was the biggest flop, the hiring of Bill James a clear sign of misguided thinking. The Red Sox were "a team that would work well in a fantasy league but will struggle to reach the playoffs as a wild card." Struggle they did—and what's the shame in that?—all the way to the World Championship.

Rancor toward Bill and toward *Moneyball* are intertwined, in part because both challenged the establishment, and not in dulcet tones.

Back when he was working on arbitration cases, Bill felt that he was working on the side of right and honor. A player might be asking for a bump from $35,000 to $50,000 from an owner who was, as Bill put it, "of extraordinary wealth and extremely questionable moral worth."

Tal Smith often sat across the arbitration table as GM in Houston, and later as a hired gun for other teams. In a 1989 essay, Bill wrote, "Smith wins more often than he loses, for the simple reason that, like me, he knows that in most cases the only thing that really counts is the figures that are filed. He gets the teams that he works for to file good figures, and that puts him way ahead." That quote is for balance. The fun stuff is this:

> Believe it or not, Tal Smith isn't all that good at presenting an arbitration case; he should be half as good as his reputation. The first two arbitration cases I participated in were both against Tal Smith, when Smith was the general manager of the Astros. We won both cases decisively, but later that year Smith was forced out as Astros GM, and started his business as a consultant. One year later, we viewed with considerable amusement the emergence of Tal Smith as an arbitration genius, as he stormed to (as I recall) seven victories in eight cases in his first year as a consultant, a run of victories that he has since milked for a fortune.
>
> We've faced Smith in arbitration Christ knows how many times since then, and we don't quake at the thought. Tal is boring, pompous, and uses a fixed methodology which makes his presentations predictable in every detail. It's a bullshit methodology to begin with, based on group averages rather than specific comps, and I'm not convinced that anybody buys into it.

Bill wrote those words a decade or so *after* he began doing sabermetrics. Even in 1989, he felt, baseball was still living in the dark ages. "Baseball men have not yet reached the revelation of Sir Francis Bacon, which was in essence that since all men live in darkness, who believes something is not a test of whether it is true or false."

When people are arguing about some baseball-related issue, one
might think that they would be very anxious to know what the
evidence is trying to tell them, and a few people are. But baseball
is an insular world in which there is a great deal of thinly veiled
anti-intellectualism. . . . An assortment of half-wits, nincom-
poops, and Neanderthals like Don Drysdale and Don Zimmer are
not only allowed to pontificate on whatever strikes them, but are
actually solicited and employed to do this, although of course
there are also many intelligent men who occupy similar positions.

Bill now points out, "You've got an outsider telling men who've
lived the game their entire lives that some of what they've always
understood to be true is, in fact, dead wrong. How are they going to
react?" But it wasn't *only* that he said they were wrong, it was the way
he said it: "If God had intended for this to be a logical universe he
would never have entrusted Jim Frey with a baseball team," for example. Bill wrote that Frey's handling of his three catchers in Kansas City
ranked somewhere between "maladroit" and "lunatic."

If you were an insider on the wrong end of Bill's stinger, you might
react like Frey, who told a reporter in 1986: "Take the Bill James book
for example. Here is a guy who is telling you about the war after it's
over. Heck, he's summing up the war after the battles have been fought.
He's not out there trying to figure out what's going on." So much for
looking to the past for clues to the future.

Bill says, "I never pay attention to what is written about me, but if I
do an online chat three or four yahoos will always show up trying to
demean whatever it is I have said, and if anything is credited to me on
the SABR-L discussion, somebody will always write in to make some
snide remark. This is frustrating to me, because I always try to be
polite and helpful to everyone in the field as much as I have time, and
I always wonder what in the hell is really bothering these people. But
on the other hand:

"1. I know that it is human nature to be irritated when someone
expresses an opinion with which we disagree. This is curious, and I

don't really understand why the good Lord made us that way, but that is the way we are.

"2. The notion that I am always polite and helpful to others in the field is probably more self-delusion than substance.

"3. Even if it is true that I try to be polite and helpful to others in the field now, when I was young I was sarcastic and inconsiderate to those more famous than myself, and I can hardly expect others to be better than I was.

"I've still got some bad karma to discharge, I am sure, and I just accept that these people are trying to help me get through that."

Little Joe Ball

Joe Morgan is a sabermetric icon: slugging middle infielder, smart base runner, great fielder, durable, an on-base machine, a *percentage* player, a winner, yet underrated. Public recognition of Morgan's greatness as a player got a lift from the *Abstract*s, and Bill rates Little Joe as the best second baseman of all time.

Morgan is often cited as a perfect player for the system attributed to Billy Beane in *Moneyball*, and he is—if he never bunted or stole a base in his career, he'd still be the best ever. But it's a notion that doesn't sit well with Morgan; in fact, it drives him bats. "I'm not a perfect player in his system. I stole bases, I bunted, I did the little things . . . I am not a perfect player in that system—don't ever accuse me of that," he has said.

It's a failure of analysis on Morgan's part. To the extent that it can be construed as a style of play, "moneyball" is less about what you don't do than about doing the kinds of things that Joe Morgan leaves out of his "I'm not a *Moneyball* player" description.

Bill wrote in 1983:

> For years and years, Joe Morgan was the best ballplayer in the
> National League. In 1972 he hit .292, had an on-base percent-

age of .414, hit 16 homers, stole 58 bases, fielded a league-leading .990 at a key defensive position, and led the league in runs scored with 122. For this performance—Bobby Grich with speed and another 30 points on his batting average—he finished fourth in the league's MVP voting. I will grant you that there were a lot of people having good years. So in 1973 Joe repeated his season and tagged on another 10 home runs and another 12 doubles and another 9 stolen bases and 14 more double plays at second so he could lead the league in that, too. Again, he finished fourth in the MVP voting. So in 1974 he did it all again. He finished eighth in the MVP voting. . . .

Yes, Morgan did win two MVP awards—after he towered over the league like Babe Ruth in a Babe Ruth league. In one season, he hit 27 home runs, averaged .320, drove in 111 runs, drew 114 walks, stole 60 bases, won a Gold Glove award at a key defensive position, led the league in the two most important offensive categories (on-base percentage and slugging percentage), and for good measure threw in league-leading totals in sacrifice flies, stolen-base percentage, and fewest grounded-into-double-plays. Who the hell else are you going to give the award to?

Morgan was a whale of a player, but as an analyst, well, he is what he is. Chris Liss of Rotowire.com says, "Really listen to what he's saying sometime. He says stuff like, 'You've got to score runs. You can't win unless you score runs, but a good pitcher will really try to limit you.' It's all in the tone, though. It's the emphasis on certain syllables that makes it *seem* meaningful."

In the '84 *Abstract*, Bill noted that Joe had told *Sports Illustrated*, "I don't think I've ever had a bad September." Bill teased, "I think we've finally found his weakness: the man has no memory. He has probably had more bad Septembers than any other great player in history." The accompanying chart showed September batting averages of .250, .189, .216, and .233 from '76 through '79.

In the *New Historical Abstract,* Bill explained that the one thing other than speed that can be used on both offense and defense is intelligence. He lays out a method for measuring "Baseball IQ" that points to Joe as the baseball-smartest player of all time. But he also takes a hard swipe at Joe the talking head, in the form of an open letter that reads in part, "This is not to deny that you were a brilliant player, Joe, but you are becoming a self-important little prig."

An awful lot of what's written about Bill's work is suspect. One website, as of 2005, has a review of David Halberstam's *Summer of '49* that claims, "No less an authority than Bill James (the modern guru of baseball statistics and factual writing) has declared it among the best baseball books of the decade." If that were true, it would be a shock to readers of the '91 *Baseball Book,* in which Bill wrote *his* review of Halberstam's book: "*Summer of '49*: Or Was that '50: Wait a Minute, I'm Almost Sure that Was '37: And I Think Maybe that Was *Vince* DiMaggio."

"Welcome to the world of 1949," Bill wrote, "where memory is truth and facts are whatever old ballplayers remember them to be." In a scathing 2,500-word review, he chronicled plenteous errors of fact. "None of these things really bother me," Bill wrote. "If David Halberstam doesn't know where to find a Macmillan *Encyclopedia* or how to use one, that doesn't disqualify him from writing baseball books. What bothers me are the ridiculous characterizations of men and events."

The intriguing question is, is Halberstam this careless with the facts when he writes about the things he usually writes about? There are two possibilities, one frightening and one irritating. It is frightening to think that Halberstam, one of the nation's most respected journalists, is this sloppy in writing about war and politics, yet has still been able to build a reputation simply because nobody has noticed.

What seems more likely is that Halberstam, writing about baseball, just didn't take the subject seriously. He just didn't figure that it mattered whether he got the facts right or not, as long as he was just writing about baseball.

And that, to me as a baseball fan, is just irritating as hell.

Alan Schwarz, in his excellent book *The Numbers Game*, asserted, "Contrary to popular belief, Bill James actually wrote very little about walks and on-base percentage." Bill held the "popular belief" himself. He wrote in the '88 *Abstract*, "God knows I have run the idea that on-base percentage is the key to an offense into the ground." Back in the '80 *Abstract* he wrote, "For some reason, most people totally ignore the 'Walks' category, although one player may reach base eighty times a year more than another because of it." And from the same edition: "The most ignored category is walks."

I guess it depends on what the definition of "very little" is, but Bill's books are littered with references to walks and on-base percentage. You can make a case that he didn't want to advocate walking as *the* way to get on base—he speculated that players who walk a lot might be more prone to slumps—but in the Kansas City team comments of the '85 *Abstract*, he took stock of the progress that had been made in the perception of walks as an offensive weapon.

Where we are right now is that people *know* about walks, and if you ask they mostly agree about their importance—but they forget about them. The sportswriters of this generation have the knowledge of today and the awareness of today, but they still have the habits of twenty years ago. A couple of examples:

1. Tracy Ringolsby, a fine Kansas City sportswriter who reaches a national audience through *The Sporting News* and *Baseball America*, wrote last winter, while comparing Willie Wilson to Rickey Henderson, that the biggest difference between the two was that Henderson had more power. In view of the fact that Henderson walks 106 times per 162 games played and Wilson

walks 32 times, that statement is fairly preposterous. It's quite a bit like saying that Twiggy and Dolly Parton are built about the same except that Twiggy is a half-inch taller. The biggest difference between the two is that Henderson will score an extra twenty runs a year because he's on base so much more.

Bill's second example was that Garry Templeton had been voted the NL Silver Slugger at shortstop in a *Sporting News* poll of sportswriters, over Ozzie Smith, based on a difference of one home run and one point in batting average. Bill pointed out that Ozzie had stolen 35 bases to Templeton's 8 and had a 51/17 walks-to-whiffs ratio, compared to Templeton's 16/81. He also scored and drove in 25 percent more runs but made 50 fewer outs than Templeton.

A classic B-movie cliché is the disembodied brain, alive in a laboratory—an evil, heartless intellect run amok, exerting treacherous mind control. The brain of Bill James has been depicted as unduly influencing the Boston clubhouse. Terry Francona was in no danger of losing his job midway into 2004, they said, "because he has managed the way ownership envisioned when it hired him, adhering to the Bill James method of statistical analysis. . . . Sox ownership remains devoted to sabermetrics, or baseball as dictated by percentages."

Here on earth, the real Bill James doesn't think it's possible to determine the best play in a game situation strictly by numbers. "There are, in every real-life situation," he explains, "thousands of variables, many of which can't be measured reliably." Take the question of whether to bunt . . . what if the third baseman is an erratic thrower with a sore shoulder? That variable could tip the percentages.

Bill has never advocated managing by rote. (In fact, what is touted as "the National League style of play" is often just that, but instead of by percentages, it's by conventional wisdom.) What he has suggested is that it makes no sense for a major league manager to not *know* the percentages. In the San Francisco comments of the '86 *Abstract*, he wrote:

How odd it is that a baseball manager should be at a disadvantage to his fans on issues such as [when to bunt, pinch-hit, send runners, etc.], how completely unnecessary it is for a manager to arrive at the major league level unprepared in this respect, when there is available such a perfect tool to educate a manager in these things. I refer, of course, to table games like APBA and Strat-O-Matic. In many other professions, simulations are much prized as education tools; a major airline would never think of sending a pilot up with lives in his hands unless he had pulled a few dozen planes out of simulated crashes. . . .

Why is it, then, that an inexperienced manager is not simply instructed to manage his team through a thousand or so games of table baseball before he really takes the field, just to get a feel for what works and what doesn't?

Because those games are for *fans*, that's why. We're *professionals*, you know; we don't have anything to learn from these *fans*. . . .

Baseball is something that everybody has an opinion about, and so it develops that to baseball men, the distinction between professional and fan is blinding, obliterating all other distinctions. Professionalism is the sun around which all baseball knowledge must revolve.

I know that if I proposed this table-game theory to any general manager in baseball, I would probably get a lecture on the difference between managing the table game and managing the real team. In the table game, players' levels are fixed; they don't fall into slumps. They don't have pitchers who have the whammy on them, or pitchers that they can tear apart. Pitchers in table games lose their stuff at known and predictable stages of the game; in the real game they may lose it gradually or suddenly. In the table game pitchers can be brought into the game without being warmed up. In the table game, players are not going to quit on you if they don't like the way they're being used.

Of course, all of that is true and much more. The table game teaches only the percentages, not the individual case. But is it an argument against using the table game to teach those things which it can teach? Isn't it a better argument that a major league manager should be so thoroughly grilled in the percentages that he is able to move past that stage, and use his mind to concentrate on the other factors which complicate the real game? Couldn't a general manager say, "Look, I don't want my manager sitting there trying to figure out what the percentages are. I want him to *know* what the percentages are like he was born with them. Then he'll be able to clean his mind out and work on those subtler things that complicate the game on the field." ...

I've seen major league managers who would finish sixth in a good table league. Jim Frey is one of them—a good man, in many ways, but an atrocious chess player. It seems to me an unnecessary price to pay for defending one's professional status. A command of the percentages is not the whole job—but one would think it was one of the prerequisites.

Bill says, "I'm not suggesting that you can slow a baseball game down to the point at which you can study everything as it happens. It's more a question of reorienting your values to focus on what research shows is truly important, rather than on what conventional wisdom tells you is important."

You've probably heard the one about the Catholic priest, the Baptist minister, and the Jewish rabbi having a meeting. The phone rings, the priest answers, and after hanging up he tells the others, "I have good news and bad news. The good news is, that was God. He's going to unite the world under one religion."

What's the bad news? the others ask.

"He was calling from Utah," the priest says.

Jim Baker, the first of Bill's assistants, contends, "In the wake of the Sox winning it all, there was precious little mention of Bill James and his role in their success. Either the media didn't understand the extent to which he contributed, or they did and couldn't bear the thought of it."

Falling into one of those two categories was an eight-page *Vanity Fair* article. It noted in passing that Boston had "even hired Bill James, the prototypical baseball-stat geek who for years had published his own increasingly arcane analyses, as a senior consultant."

They *even* hired Bill James, the *geek* of the *arcane*? Crazy.

In a review of the 2005 book about Tony La Russa, a *Cincinnati Enquirer* staffer took a typical shot at Bill: "La Russa believes in human nature. When it comes to managing a baseball team, he believes in it more than statistics and matchups and on-base percentages and the cold, hard data of Bill James."

For his part, Bill wrote in 1984 that La Russa's strongest point as a manager was "his inventiveness; his hard-working analytical resourcefulness. He's a beautiful manager to watch." Bill says La Russa is a smart guy and a great manager, but La Russa has been a source of what Bill calls "percentage baseball run amuck" in bullpen-usage patterns.

Bill also pointed out that rather than being *in* the flow of the game, as they're portrayed, very active managers try to *control* the flow. If a manager is concerned with maximizing optimal expected outcomes, as he should be, he'll tend to use strategies such as bunting less often. If he's concerned about putting his stamp on the game, he'll tend to ignore the real percentages.

NYU journalism professor Jay Rosen says, "Bill James was originally a press critic. He came to his ideas via philosophical conflict with the sportswriters' tribe. He thought baseball journalists had a firm grasp on the wrong end of the telescope. They were looking at their subject in a way that shrank it to insignificance, compared to the big picture James saw by tinkering with different measures over longer arcs of time. James thought the baseball establishment—which included the press—knew a great many things that were demonstrably wrong. Lore and legend counted for more in the industry than fact and pattern, despite all the time professionals spent studying baseball, talking about it—living it."

Bill wrote in the '84 *Abstract:*

You know the expression about not being able to see the forest for the trees? Let's use that. What are the differences between the way a forest looks when you are inside the forest and the way it looks from the outside?

The first thing is, the insider has a much better view of the details. He knows what the moss looks like, how light it grows around the base of an oak and how thickly it will cling to a sycamore. He knows the smells in the air and the tracks on the ground; he can guess the age of a redbud by peeling off a layer of bark. The outsider doesn't know any of that.

To a person who sees the image of anything as being only the sum of its details, to a person who can conceive of the whole of anything only by remembering this event and that event and piecing them together in a succession of images; such a person is likely to look at the *Baseball Abstract* and say, "What is this? This isn't BASEBALL. This guy James doesn't know anything about the chatter bouncing off the dugout walls, nor about the glint in the eye of a superstar, nor about routines and integral boredom of baseball's lifestyle, with which each player great and small must contend."

No sir, indeed I don't. There will be in this book no new tales about the things that happen on a team flight, no sudden revelations about the way that drugs and sex and money can ruin a championship team. I can't tell you what a locker room smells like, praise the Lord.

But perspective can only be gained when details are lost. A sense of the size of everything and the relationship between everything—this can never be put together from details. For the most essential fact of a forest is this: The forest itself is immensely larger than anything inside of it. That is why, of course, you can't see the forest for the trees; each detail, in proportion to its size and your proximity to it, obscures a thousand or a million other details.

Ben McGrath, in his 2003 *New Yorker* profile of Bill, noted, "Dan Shaughnessy, the dean of *Boston Globe* sportswriters, told me that he's 'dubious' of the James experiment, and that he'd even heard grumbling among the press corps about the possibility of lineups being faxed in daily from Kansas."

Few of Shaughnessy's references to Bill have been insightful or fair. He wrote that it was easy to see Bill's "fingerprints" on the Jeremy Giambi acquisition, as if it were evidence of a great crime. Bill doesn't take credit or avoid blame, but Giambi, who turned out to have a bum shoulder, was simply a calculated risk that didn't pan out.

Bill stays fairly oblivious about all this, and says, "When I joined the team, I had friends, including ex-players, who would tell me, 'Oh, that Boston media. You've really got to be careful with those guys. They'll cut you apart.' But I've never found that to be true. Anyway, as a writer, I'm pretty antagonistic myself, so who am I to complain?"

He goes out of his way to compliment and understand the Boston press corps, and adds, "Would you rather have the New York writers?" Well, no, but sometimes it's close. Nick Cafardo wrote in the *Globe* in June '04: "When the team is losing, the absence of small ball looks bad. You can't help but question the new philosophy, even if Bill James can prove that his theories are best in the long run."

Bill simply says, "I try not to read too much of the team coverage. My idea is always, 'Don't overreact. Back away from the issue as far as you can. Get perspective.' Reading the daily newspapers makes it harder to keep your eye on the big picture, first because you're pulling a lot of details into the subject, and second because the sportswriters many times do overreact, and insist that, if we knew what we were doing, we would overreact, too."

10

What It Was Really About

During the years Bill was in college, Lawrence was a center of social protest, and the civil rights movement was in full effect. "The sixties weren't about long hair, loud music, tie-dyed shirts, drugs, personal hygiene, or even, really, Vietnam," he says. "What it was really about was race."

He touched on race as it relates to baseball several times. In the '81 *Abstract*, for example, he wrote:

> If there is anything in the world that can safely be said about racists, it is that they are mediocre. Nothing characterizes a racist like his mediocrity. Racists are people who can find no rational or apparent basis for believing in their own superiority, and so seek to identify themselves with a superior thing, with a badge that won't come off. The baseball world is not an exception to that. When an organization, whom we will call for illustration the Boston Red Sox, turns over half of its roster without giving up or acquiring a black player then, given the racial mix in the major leagues today, we are entitled to look questioningly at that. But baseball is no different than the outside world; the racists are the mediocrities. If you're looking for racism in baseball, start in the middle of the standings and read down.

In a biographical essay on Dick Allen in the 1990 *Baseball Book*, Bill wrote, "It's so hard to explain, for those who are too young to remember it, what a strange time it was. The whole world was about race then; looking backward, it doesn't seem that there was any other news. At the start of the decade, there had been avowed racists, Ku Klux Klan members, in the United States Senate. By 1965 overt racism was in retreat, and black militancy in ascendance."

Dick Allen is a focal point of any discussion about race and baseball in the sixties and seventies. Allen's dad stranded his mom with nine children in a small Pennsylvania steel town. He was signed by the Phillies in 1960 and sent to the minors. After the '62 season he held out for a raise. The Phillies sent him to be the first black man to play pro ball in Arkansas. He did well on the field, but off the field had a rough time. In 1964, his first full season in Philadelphia, Allen had one of the greatest rookie seasons of all time. His life in baseball was marked by great talent, unmet expectations, controversy, defiance, racism, injuries, and incidents that range from sad to bizarre. Bill wrote:

> I'm not a psychologist, but it seems obvious, in retrospect, that Allen was suffering from clinical depression, which today would probably be recognized and dealt with as a psychological illness. Often a person who is depressed just wants the world to go away and leave him alone. Allen expressed this in irrational ways— hiding in the equipment room, refusing to take batting practice at home. He told a reporter that "I wish they'd shut the gates and let us just play ball with no press and no fans. Like it was in Wampum when I was a kid." But at the time, no one said "This man is depressed. He needs help." They said "This man is acting like a jerk. He needs punishment."

While the 1990 *Baseball Book* portrait is largely sympathetic, Bill wrote, "Justifying his attitudes by the racism of the society, he raised selfishness to an art form." Bill ends with a quote from Allen's autobiography. "I was labeled an outlaw, and after a while that's what I became."

In 1994's *The Politics of Glory,* Bill took up the topic of whether Allen belongs in the Hall of Fame, granting that while the statistics say he probably does, the "other stuff," which is being "forgotten and revised and rewritten out of existence," says no—the other stuff being "that Allen never did anything to help his teams win, and in fact spent his entire career doing everything he possibly could to *keep* his teams from winning."

Bill's view was that Allen, being charming and manipulative, split his teammates into pro- and anti-Allen factions. "It has become fashionable to say that Dick Allen was a victim of the racism of the time," Bill wrote, "and for this reason it is politically incorrect for me even to mention any of this old business."

> Dick Allen *was* a victim of the racism of his time; that part is absolutely true. The Phillies were callous to send him to Little Rock in 1963 with no support network, and the press often treated Allen differently than they would have treated a white player who did the same things. That's all true.
>
> It doesn't have anything to do with the issue. Willie Mays was a victim of the same racism. Jackie Robinson was. Roy Campanella was, Curt Flood was, Bob Gibson was, Hank Aaron was, Ernie Banks was, Monte Irvin was, Lou Brock was, Minnie Minoso was, and Roberto Clemente was. Those are all very different personalities, and they all dealt with racism in different ways. The best of them used the racism of the outside world to bond the team together, us against them, those bad guys out there. Allen directed his anger at the targets nearest him, and by doing so used racism as an explosive to blow his own teams apart.

Craig Wright wrote a rebuttal in the *Baseball Research Journal.** He reported that many of Allen's teammates and managers liked and respected him.

*It can be found online at whitesoxinteractive.com in the WSI Interviews section.

Bill says, "Craig told me he was writing that article. I decided that no matter what he said, I'm not responding. I'd said what I had to say, and that was enough. I'm not at all convinced by Craig's view. When you're writing a biography of somebody, you work on it for days or months where you're accumulating all the facts you can, trying to put them into context and see the patterns. You begin to understand how that person sees the world and why they act the way they do, and you almost always begin to sympathize with them; you almost always begin to like them.

"When I wrote the Dick Allen entry, I worked on it for about two weeks. The first four or five days, I went through that process of getting to see the world in his terms and beginning to identify with him and getting to like him. After about eight days I was less sympathetic, and at the end of the two weeks I was sick to death of him. I'm not saying all the criticisms of him were fair, or that everything written about him was accurate, but my view of him is that he was the most negative, divisive player ever to play in the major leagues, with the exception of Hal Chase."

In a polemic on race in baseball, written for ESPN.com in 2003, the late Ralph Wiley tarred Bill and sabermetrics with the racial-bias brush. He wrote, "It is usually the American-born blacks' records and place that are resented instead of celebrated. For example, it's the stolen base that is denigrated as a weapon by baseball sabermaticians like Bill James, at precisely the time when a Rickey Henderson steals 130 bases in a season. There are sour grapes when a baseball man uses stats to tell you a stolen base isn't important. Any time a baseball manager will give up an out for a base, as with a sac bunt or groundball to the right side, any time a base is so precious, then it goes without saying that the stolen base must be important. Not the CS, the caught stealing, or stats of success rates, but the stolen base itself."

Of course, the fact that a manager will *treat* an out as less precious than a base doesn't mean it *is* less precious. More important, the invidious implication is that sabermetricians weren't making unbiased studies of the value of base stealing. A generous interpretation of

Wiley's point would be that James and his fellows slandered the stolen base *blithely* at the moment that Rickey was setting the record, making sabermetrics a weapon in the arsenal of racism.

Wiley probably didn't intend to single out Bill James, but he used Bill's name as an identifier for those who might not recognize "saber-meticians." Wiley did an online chat soon after, and said, "Writing is like pitching (or hitting). You are not going to always put the ball exactly where you want, but I'll say this. It was still the right velocity. Actually it was a systemic thing James just happened to be part of; *SI* asked him to write a piece about the effect, meaning of the stolen base in 1982, as Rick was stealing 130 bags. James does not care for the stolen base. Or, should I say, the unsuccessful stolen base. So, let's just call it a rather unhappy coincidence. Unhappy because I came with Rick, see? I was a rookie on the beat when he was a rookie in the Show, and I've seen him do some things. I meant no harm to Bill James."

It's hard to argue with "I've seen him do some things," but one of the virtues of sabermetrics is that it tries to strip out the style points and offer a perspective beyond eyeballs. Not everyone wants that per-spective, just as people who've seen the Virgin Mary in a water stain don't want science to diminish what they've seen.

If sabermetrics demystified the value of steals, it also brought the value of walks and power to the fore. As the all-time career leader in walks, runs, and leadoff homers, Rickey Henderson is a sabermetri-cian's dream. Bill says, "Sabermetric analysis is not one percent kinder to white players than it is to black. The assumption that black players have speed and defense but lack the skills that are most respected in sabermetrics is absolutely false. Black players have no tendency what-soever to lack the skills that are most valued in sabermetrics."

Salon.com columnist Allen St. John wrote of Rickey in 2001, "When he burst onto the scene with the Oakland A's in '79 (around the time that Bill James earned a place beside Henry James on my bookshelf), he was the epitome of the postmodern baseball player. His genius was subtle, and to appreciate it took an aficionado's eye—it was the baseball equivalent of touting Tobe Hooper as an auteur. Henderson's batting average may be average, but look at that on-base percentage. Sure he steals bases better than anyone ever, but he'd be a Hall of Famer without a single sack swiped."

Bill wrote often about Rickey over the years. In the 1982 *Abstract*, in the Willie Wilson comment, Bill revealed his true color bias . . . for Royals blue.

> Wilson has taken some really bad raps in the last year or so, a good part of which he brings on himself because he is sometimes rather hostile and rude to the press. But truth is truth, and bad manners on his side do not justify malice and inaccuracy on ours. Wilson was widely blamed for the 1980 World Series defeat although—this is just the facts, men—he reached base more times, stole more bases, and scored more runs in the Series than did the Philadelphia lead-off men. He also played spectacularly well in the field. Peter Gammons wrote, supposedly in defense of Jim Frey, "It wasn't Jim Frey who caused Willie Wilson to walk to first base all season." Gammons is completely off-base, absolutely has no idea of what he is talking about. Wilson isn't Pete Rose, but then neither is anybody else, and he isn't Garry Templeton either. I have never seen Willie Wilson fail to reach first base on any play because of lack of hustle. Wilson's speed focuses so much attention on his running that if he doesn't make a GB6 into a close play it makes the newspapers.
>
> Then too, Wilson happened to make the worst defensive play of his career, Larry Milbourne's home run, on national TV and by playoff time Al Michaels had designated Rickey Henderson as "in a class by himself" among left fielders. Perhaps that was intended the way it came out: a backhanded slap at Wilson. Perhaps Michaels just wasn't thinking as fast as he was talking. In either case, I will offer my humble opinion that, while Henderson is an outstanding outfielder, Wilson is a far better one.

The '82 *Abstract*, with ratings based solely on Bill's statistical methods, showed Henderson to be the best left fielder. Bill called him the greatest leadoff man in baseball, a title that has become virtually a legal addition to Henderson's name.

That was the summer in which Bill wrote the steals-debunking *Sports Illustrated* article Wiley cited. It's a great article, with four or five major writing highlights and at least as many surprising facts. "Picture a vast desert," Bill wrote. "A single tumbleweed blowing across the desert will attract the eye because it's the only thing moving. A runner stealing bases draws attention not because what he's doing is important, but because he is moving." It was a lot of people's first Bill James encounter. While it undoubtedly opened many minds to sabermetrics, it ensured others would be sealed shut.

In the '83 *Abstract* the top left fielders were, in rank order, Dave Winfield, Rickey, Dusty Baker, Rock Raines, and Willie Wilson. Three of those five are among the greatest base thieves in history, yet it was their all-around play that accounted for the rankings. The idea that what distinguished Rickey as a player was his baserunning, and that to call attention to the overvaluation of stolen bases was to devalue him, is an absolute lemon.

In the *Historical Abstract* (written while Rickey was still playing), Bill asserted that Rickey and Raines were harbingers of a new type of lead-off hitter, combining "the speed and base stealing ability of Aparicio with the pesky patience of a Luke Appling." The revised *New Historical* showed Rickey as the fourth best left fielder ever. Bill wrote that "you could find fifty Hall of Famers who, all taken together, don't own as many records, and as many *important* records, as Rickey Henderson."

Sweet Lou Whitaker was one of the two or three best defensive second basemen—and *the* best offensive one—in the American League for about a decade. The '86 *Abstract* player rankings, based in part on a poll of Project Scoresheet scorers, put Whitaker at the top among AL second basemen. "I don't remember seeing any ballots that didn't have him marked '1,'" Bill wrote. "What do you think of him as a Hall of Fame candidate?"

Whitaker's value was never fully appreciated by the mainstream, a circumstance not helped by his icy relationship with the Detroit beat writers. In the 2001 Hall of Fame election, Lou received only fifteen votes, not even enough to put him on future BBWAA ballots.*

Whitaker's double-play partner, Alan Trammell, is still deservedly on the writers' ballots, with vote totals in the seventies for four years running. In the '91 *Baseball Book,* Bill addressed the treatment of Whitaker and Alan Trammell by the Detroit media:

> Black athletes sometimes complain that when a white player does something the press always talks about how hard he works and how smart he is and what great character he shows, but when a black player does the same thing it's just "great natural talent." Perhaps the most appalling example of this is the treatment of Alan Trammell and Lou Whitaker by the Detroit media. You couldn't name two players of more identical accomplishments. Playing side by side for thirteen years (in the majors) they have played almost the same number of games (Trammell leads 1,835–1,827), scored almost the same number of runs (Whitaker leads 1,040–1,009), and driven in almost the same number (Trammell 810–781). They have the same on-base percentage and almost the same slugging percentage. One year one of them will be a little better than the other, and the next year the other one will have the better season.
>
> In spite of this, there is, believe it or not, a widespread belief among the Detroit public that Trammell is a tough, aggressive player who has built himself up to this level by working hard, while Lou is just . . . well, a kind of a shiftless black guy who has a lot of ability but hasn't done much with it. This appalling attitude, as close to overt racism as you can get without ruining your linen, is expressed freely in the Motor City media. Joe Falls, while exalting Trammell, wrote that Whitaker has watched a Hall of Fame career drift away from him, and a couple of radio guys

*He is eligible via the Veterans Committee under the new rules.

stand right behind him, one holding the gasoline and the other the match.

I was in Detroit last spring, doing radio shows. The third time this was put to me, I challenged the caller on it. You know what he said? He said, "Yeah, they have about the same totals now, but when they came up Whitaker was already a .300 hitter. Trammell was a .220 hitter. He's worked hard to become the player he is now." In fact, of course, they were as even when they came into the league as they are now. In their rookie season Whitaker hit .285 with 3 homers, Trammell .268 with 2 homers. Trammell, not Whitaker, was the first one to hit .300 and the first one to drive in or score a hundred runs, which he did in 1980.

Of course there are *individual* differences between them, which contribute to (or more likely justify) the racist preference. Trammell is a visible on-field "leader," a holler guy; Whitaker is quiet, laid back. Sometimes he's a little bit of a space cadet. But the survival of this blatant supremacist stereotype into the 1990s is shocking and unseemly. Lou Whitaker may not be the player you dreamed he would—but who's been better? What American League second baseman would you rather have had these last thirteen years? Give the man credit for what he is.

After the 2001 vote Falls' column in the *Detroit News* was headlined with one of the great buzzwords of New Age hucksterism: "Whitaker Lacked the Aura of a True Hall of Famer." Aura? Is that how we want the voters to evaluate a player's career? And what does the qualifier "true" indicate? Certainly there are inductees who shouldn't be there, but is it aura they lack, or qualifications? Many of the undeserving are there because of aura and little else.

Falls wrote, "I didn't think he'd make it but I never dreamed he would be so completely rejected, and embarrassed. It was pretty bad what happened." According to Falls, Whitaker "could be rude, curt, abrupt and, at times, nasty." He noted Whitaker's "nonchalance," and added, "He did it all easily, almost as if he weren't trying." He also recalled Whitaker's occasional failure to run out ground balls, as well as his requests for days off.

Bill says, "Joe Falls is entitled to his opinion." I try to keep in mind what Bill wrote in the *Guide to Managers* book about former Reds owner Marge Schott. He paraphrases his point: "People are entitled to wrong and stupid opinions; you don't have to beat them out of them." The Schott essay read in part: "We're beating up Marge Schott to prove to ourselves that we're better than she is. But are we, really? Which of us has no bigotry in our soul, no dark pockets of unvented anger? We may be more clever than Marge, more discreet in our bigotry, but I don't really believe that the Lord made any of us tolerant by nature."

On the question of whether Whitaker's bad relationship with the press affected the vote: Falls asserts that because Tigers catcher Lance Parrish—who was well liked by the media—got just nine votes, "that should take care of the belief that the writers judge the players by how they [the writers] are treated." Rob Parker of the *Detroit News* also wrote, "Being cold and distant didn't help [Whitaker's] cause. After all, we are humans, not robots. Still, it's not the reason."

It's hard for me to see how those assurances close the issue, but Bill says, "I think it would be difficult to convict the writers of voting for people that they like, or voting against people that they don't like. The Veterans Committee does that (or did that), but there is little or no evidence the writers ever did. Did the writers like Steve Carlton? I don't think so, and I don't think there is any significant likeability effect in Hall of Fame voting, among the writers."

I would argue that while the writers may not refuse to vote for a player *solely* on likeability, they *had* to elect Carlton no matter how they felt about his personality. It's the specifics of Whitaker's situation—*arguable* Hall of Famer, depreciated by the writers as a player, disregarded by them as a candidate—that inform the question.

There may be a cascade effect. Local writers send out a negative message about a player: *He's shiftless and undeserving; he skates by on raw talent.* Over time, that view becomes common. Maybe it costs the player some postseason-award votes. When it's time to assess his cre-

dentials for the Hall, he can be docked not only for "lacking character," but also for not winning enough honors. All he has left is his statistical record. And if (1) his offensive stats are concentrated in areas
such as OBP and not RBI, (2) much of his contribution is in fielding
(which, for most writers, begins and ends with "How many Gold
Gloves did he win?"), and (3) his record isn't viewed in context, he
gets shafted.

That's *my* suspicion re Whitaker's case. Bill doesn't buy it. He says,
"I suspect Joe Falls plays a role in influencing other opinions, but I
doubt that it is a large role. I don't think that has anything much to do
with Whitaker's low vote total. Whitaker's low total is explained, to
me, by his low number of 100-run, 100-RBI seasons and other Hall of
Fame–type accomplishments. The de facto standards, not the theoretical ideal."

In the '84 *Abstract*, Bill wrote, "One day the whole country is going
to wake up and say, 'Damn, that Lou Whitaker can play ball.'" It's
clear that the wake-up call never came, but Sweet Lou was the type of
player Bill championed, a sabermetric underdog: high secondary average and on-base percentage, despite a so-so batting average; excellent
power for a middle infielder and leadoff hitter of his time; great defense
at a key position; and lacking the obvious appeal of a media favorite.

Bill says, "Whitaker is a really interesting case. I think your observation that the public never did awaken to his skills is essentially right.
On a certain level, this can be attributed to the lack of star-quality
seasons by Whitaker. Lou Whitaker had 351 Win Shares in his career;
Ryne Sandberg had 346—yet Sandberg had seasons of 38 Win Shares,
37, 34, and 33, while Whitaker's career best was 29. (Thirty, as a rule of
thumb, makes you a serious MVP candidate.) Whitaker drove in and
scored more runs than Sandberg did in a career of about the same
length, but Sandberg scored 100 runs seven times and drove in 100
twice, while Whitaker scored 100 only twice and never drove in 100,
or even 90—a 9–2 edge for Sandberg in Hall of Fame–type accomplishments.

"Sandberg won one MVP award and came close to several others;

Whitaker never won, and I don't think he ever came close. Sandberg hit 40 homers one year and 30 another; Whitaker never hit more than 28. Sandberg stole 54 bases in a season, and stole 30 or more five times; Whitaker's career high was 30. Sandberg, of course, won many more Gold Gloves (although Whitaker turned almost 400 more double plays—probably the largest statistical difference between them). Sandberg simply has many more Hall of Fame–type accomplishments."

"A surprising part of this can be traced to the pattern of playing time. Sandberg played 150 games or more eleven times, had 600 or more at-bats nine times. Whitaker played 150 games three times, had 600 at-bats three times. Whitaker had ten seasons in his career of 300 to 500 at-bats; Sandberg had two.

"It is hard to overstate the difference that that makes. If you take any marginal Hall of Famer and recast his career into seasons of 300 to 500 at-bats (with the same career totals), you're going to have a non–Hall of Famer. Kirby Puckett's career hits, home runs, batting average, RBI, on-base percentage, slugging percentage . . . they're all similar to Will Clark's—but Kirby did it in 650 at-bats a year. Kirby had eight seasons of 600 or more at-bats, only one season of 300 to 500; Clark had seven seasons of 300 to 500 at-bats, only one season of 600. That 'concentration' of the stats into fewer seasons makes Kirby's numbers look a lot bigger. It's the same with Steve Carlton and Don Sutton. Their numbers are the same, but Carlton did it in big seasons; Sutton did it in 33 starts a year."

As a rule, Bill tries to stay out of Hall of Fame arguments, his writings on Dick Allen—"If that's a Hall of Famer, I'm a lug nut"— notwithstanding. He wrote in *The Politics of Glory*, "I can't write at length about those subjects without drawing some kind of conclusion." But he tends to restrict his comments to analysis of the de facto standards.

But he does say, "The Hall of Fame argument proceeds from 'star-type' accomplishments—200 hits, 100 RBI, 100 runs scored, .300 batting average, appearing in the All-Star game, hitting homers in the World Series, getting 3,000 hits, leading the league in some offensive category, etc. My analysis is based on 'win impact,' rather than star-type accomplishments.

"If you contrast Whitaker with, let's say, Lou Brock . . . certainly Brock has many more star-type accomplishments than Whitaker does. Brock scored 100 runs seven times (Whitaker twice), had 200 hits three times (Whitaker none), led the league in stolen bases many times, led the league in at-bats, in runs scored twice, in doubles once, in triples once, was an All-Star six times, got 3,000 hits, was in the top ten in MVP voting five or six times. He has 154 points on the Hall of Fame monitor, as opposed to 92 for Whitaker.

"I would still argue that Whitaker was a better player. Whitaker scored 200 fewer runs, but drove in 200 more, which meant that he didn't get to 100 in either category. He had fewer hits but more walks, an on-base percentage twenty points higher overall, but it meant that he didn't get 200 hits in a season. He had fewer stolen bases but more homers. The *balance* was better for Whitaker, but the visual impact was better for Brock.

"Or Ernie Banks . . . I would argue that Whitaker had a better career than Ernie Banks. Banks' numbers are superficially more impressive, but in the one stat most closely tied to wins, on-base percentage, Whitaker is 33 points ahead . . . the same as the difference in career batting average between Willie Mays and Matt Lawton. Big item. Banks played in a better hitting park. Half of his career he was a short-stop, true, but half of it he was a first baseman. If you balance everything, Lou contributed more to his team, over the course of his career."

In a *Sporting News* column, Ken Rosenthal wrote that he supported Sandberg and Trammell for the Hall. "I have difficulty separating them from Whitaker. I didn't vote for Whitaker but regret that he is no longer on the ballot. He at least deserved to remain a candidate for the maximum fifteen years."

Sandberg was elected two years later with 76 percent support.

Rosenthal wrote that Sandberg versus Whitaker was close. He compared Ryno's career OPS of .796 to Sweet Lou's .789. What sets Ryno apart, Rosenthal decided, was that he won nine Gold Gloves to Lou's three, appeared in ten All-Star games to Lou's five, and had three top-five MVP finishes (he won in 1984) to Lou's zero. But there is a devilish circularity to factoring in awards. If a player is undervalued by the writers while active, he won't win the awards that will later be cited by the writers as lacking.

In the *New Historical Abstract*, Sandberg is rated seventh all-time among second basemen. Bobby Grich is twelfth, Whitaker thirteenth, and Willie Randolph seventeenth. So, by Bill's take, we're talking about whether one of the fifteen best second basemen of all time belongs in the Hall. Sandberg got 393 Hall of Fame votes; Grich, 11; Whitaker, 15; Randolph, 5. Their Hall of Fame qualifications are open to debate, but it's safe to say the top second basemen of the seventies and eighties have been underrated, maybe in part because, as Bill wrote of Willie Randolph, their central skills "preferred the shadows." Maybe, too, because there are no fair, systematic standards for the Hall of Fame.

It's curious that the voters were practically unanimous in their opinion of Whitaker, when his credentials compared to Trammell's are so close, but the Hall vote may be too blunt an instrument to use as a yardstick of respect. Bill says, "I think it is reading the vote as more subtle than it is to see a bias. I think that historically, Hall of Fame voters are impressed by a finite range of accomplishments, I think that if you compare Whitaker to the Hall of Fame second basemen *on those* accomplishments, Whitaker ranks very low. If you try to make the vote read any other way, it's my opinion you're probably misreading it."

As a ten-year BBWAA member, Rob Parker is eligible to vote. In a *Detroit News* piece, "Whitaker's Swing and Miss at Hall of Fame Seems Fitting," he noted Whitaker's career statistics in hits, batting average, homers, and RBI, and wrote that "those numbers are good but not great." But he didn't put those numbers in any context, such as good but not great for a top-fielding second baseman of his era—which is clearly untrue. He didn't mention runs scored, although Lou was primarily a top-of-the-order hitter. He left out on-base percentage and fielding numbers. Finally, he held up Joe Morgan for comparison, unintentionally making the point that if Lou Whitaker couldn't be Joe Morgan, he could never meet the expectations set for him.

11

After the *Abstract*

The *Abstract* **days** behind them, Bill collaborated with Susie on a little project they named Isaac, who dropped in May 1988. Near the end of the year, Bill hired Rob Neyer to be his assistant. In spring 1989 they started to work on the first *Baseball Book.* "Bill's instruction was rare," Rob says, "and usually came in the form of pointed memos in response to something I'd written. There was one in particular in which Bill went through an article I'd written about Bill Almon, and he just destroyed virtually every sentence. It hurt a little bit, but I knew that Bill was right in every case, and a lot of his criticisms stuck with me, in a good way.

"He would sometimes ask for help when working on salary arbitration cases, but generally that just involved me collecting numbers. The only specific case I remember—and this is weird, because I worked on a dozen of them—was Rafael Belliard. Bill called me from wherever the hearing was about to be held and asked me to see how many errors Belliard had made playing second base. The answer? Zero! And this was considered a big find. It was stuff like this that really turned me against arbitration, as I realized there must be more to life than trying to get more money for Rafael Belliard."

It was at least a year before Rob was comfortable working for Bill. And for a long time he had the distinct fear that he was about to be fired. He says, "I didn't *think* I'd be fired. Rather, I feared I'd be fired because it didn't often seem that my work was pleasing Bill. I wasn't a great worker. I couldn't really write, and I also wasn't real good at reading Bill's mind, which sometimes seemed to be what he expected.

I was dedicated, I didn't mind spending hours and hours in the library, and I learned to leave Bill alone, which is probably why he kept me around as long as he did.

We rarely argued, but when he was mad at me, he'd leave a note when he went home at six A.M. or whenever. Don't get me wrong; he could be understanding, too. I wasn't particularly organized in those days—more organized than him, but not organized enough—and he was generally patient with me, for some reason."

The first of Bill's new books in the post-*Abstract* era was the 1990 *Baseball Book*. It was divided into three parts. Much of the first, essays on the 1989 season, was written by Bill's friend Mike Kopf. Bill's plan for the book was to put current baseball events into historical perspective. For example, Jim Abbott, a left-handed pitcher who was born without a right hand, was a rookie in 1989. Bill wrote a terrific essay about players who were considered "handicapped" in their own time, such as "One Arm" Daily and "Three Finger" Brown from the 1880s, through to Jim Eisenreich (Tourette's).

The *Baseball Book* was redesigned for 1991. The opening section covered current players with a basic question about each. For example, did Barry Bonds deserve the MVP Award (for which he was an almost unanimous selection)? Bill's answer was yes. He felt that new information, which had become available in the last ten years, played a key role in the voting. Bonds had driven in fewer runs than teammate Bobby Bonilla, but hit .377 with runners in scoring position, neutralizing any argument that Bonilla had been a better run producer "when it counted."

"Why is this man on a roster?" Bill asked about Wayne Tolleson, then a Yankee. "For precisely the same reason that John Sununu is in the White House: because the Boss has the only vote that counts."

In the area of "errata from the previous edition," it was noted that Mike Kopf had written that Heinie Groh "eventually won his battle with the bottle bat to star for the Reds." Someone at the publisher had deleted *bat,* changing a cute reference to the type of stick Groh wielded into a false implication of alcoholism.

Bill wrote an impassioned essay on the reaction of some sports-writers to the fact that the compilers of the 1990 *Baseball Encyclopedia* had the temerity to fix errors in the old stats. "Jerome Holtzman Has a Cow," the piece was diplomatically titled; Holtzman being a *Chicago Tribune* writer. Tracy Ringolsby and Tom Barnidge had rung in, too, as had Seymour Siwoff of the Elias Bureau, who called the changes "a disgrace." Bill used four-plus pages for response to the writers. It included: "Among the three of you, I'll bet I could write everything you know about the subject on one piece of paper, and have room left over for Rachel to cut out a couple of paper dolls and Cher to make a dress for next year's Academy Awards."

The third and final *Baseball Book* was another redesign and the best of the three. Bill wrote up a study of no-hitters—impossible to sum-marize without losing a ton of information—and found that the number-one factor in determining the occurrence of a no-no is the quality of the pitcher. Seems obvious, but some folks imagine other-wise. The aggregate career winning percentage of no-hit pitchers was .550, an amazing statistic if you consider the number of fine pitchers who can't match it. Power pitcher, at home, in a pitcher's park are the next biggest factors, followed by facing a tired team that strikes out a lot. There is no tendency for no-hitters to be thrown against bad teams rather than good ones.

There is much classic Bill James in the '92 *Baseball Book,* including one of the most interesting pieces Bill has written, "Colloquy." He laid out eight ideas for new laws that would benefit the sports fan. The Captive Audience Law, for instance, would require that when more than a thousand people are assembled in a public place, access must be provided for competing vendors. It would open the market, so that the price of a hot dog at the ballpark would be subject to market forces. He covers several possible objections, and points out that most stadiums are public property.

One of his general points is that things tend to be set up to protect the interests of wealthy owners with influence, under the guise of protection of the public interest. The major leagues have a rule against public ownership of sports teams, which protects the people who control the teams. Bill wrote, "For a hundred years, baseball teams have operated as feudal monopolies, owned entirely by the wealthy and operated entirely for the benefit of the wealthy. It has been this way for so long that people have lost the ability to see that it doesn't have to be that way. . . ."

Bill wrapped up his discussion of the eight ideas by writing, "It's easy to think about how the world could be better than it is. What is amazing to me, that being the case, is how much time and energy are devoted to inarticulate battles about the process of change, and how little time is spent thinking about how the world could be better than it is."

In 1994 Bill came out with *The Politics of Glory: How Baseball's Hall of Fame Really Works.* "Baseball went on strike right when the book was supposed to come out," Bill remembers, "and the publicist quit . . . everything possible went wrong. But the book caught a huge break in that *Time* did a two-page article on the Hall that included my picture. I opened the magazine and there it was. It was weird, and it kind of saved the book."

One topic that interested Bill since the early *Abstract* days was, What are the de facto standards of the Hall of Fame? He feels that most Hall of Fame arguments go from cacophony to confusion. "There is some truth in what almost everybody says, but almost everybody will distort the record to advance their own candidate," he wrote. His intent was to serve the discussion, not a particular candidate, but of course he analyzed specific players' credentials. Bill makes compelling cases for Luis Tiant, Vern Stephens, Richie Ashburn, Ken Boyer, Ron Santo, Joe Gordon, and Ted Simmons (with help from Bill Deane), among others.

A common form of Hall of Fame assessment goes, "I saw him play, and he wasn't *that* good." But the Hall of Fame doesn't have a clear standard, and most of us have little ability to gauge how good a player was in historical context. Reading *The New Historical Abstract* brings that into sharp relief; e.g., Darrell Evans as one of the ten best third baseman ever, or Minnie Minoso as one of the ten best left fielders.

Ted Simmons is a perfect example. He received virtually no support in his one year on the BBWAA ballot, yet he ranks as one of the best hitters ever among catchers. To leave him out of the Hall, you have to exact, as Bill put it, "a terrible penalty for his defense." But while opposing teams clearly didn't *respect* his arm, the record shows he threw out enough baserunners to come out ahead of teams that ran against him. The "defensible" knocks against Simmons are based on aura and reputation, not evidence.

Bill opened *Politics of Glory* by describing the origins of the Hall (it was a local museum) and the selection processes—"an afterthought to an accident." Over the years, it suffered from lack of a well-considered, disciplined criteria. Two separate groups were charged with picking new inductees: the baseball writers and the old-timers. At one point in the forties, the writers said, in effect, that Lefty Grove and Jimmie Foxx didn't merit serious consideration. The old-timers went to the other extreme, unwittingly establishing a minimum standard that would include dozens of players in every generation. Bill wrote that the two groups created a gray area so large it could never be made dark.

"Can the Hall be made fair? I think in my heart I've accepted that it's too late," he says. "Writing that book helped me understand that while you'd like to see a fair Hall of Fame, with only the best players inducted, it's not going to happen. Too many mistakes have been made."

The book is still in print as a paperback under the title *Whatever Happened to the Hall of Fame?* "The Hall of Fame initially hated the book," Bill says. "I wrote that the Hall had never thought out the process of how you select the best players, and that there was an immense amount of cronyism involved. I thought this was self-evident; I wondered if I should even bother to write something so obvious. The people at the Hall were not pleased, and I was not popular there for a couple of years. But it was amazing how rapidly that changed. People who were running the Hall at that time retired or moved on, and other people who came in saw that what I'd said was self-evidently true."

The *Player Ratings Book*s were Bill's annual offering to fantasy and Rotisserie leaguers from 1993 through '95. John Sickels came on board as Bill's assistant for the 1994 book. In spring of 1993, fresh off a job delivering pizzas, his wife asked him what he wanted to do for a job. He said, half-joking, "Work for Bill James," The next day his wife came home from her job in a luggage store and said that Bill had come into the store that day and bought a briefcase. She recognized his name on the check and told him her husband would love to work for him. They met for lunch. "I've got another candidate to consider, but I'll call you in a couple of days," Bill said. John recalls, "I wait a week and don't hear from him. I'm thinking it isn't going to happen, but I've got to know, so I call him. He says, " 'Oh, yeah, I've decided to hire you, when can you start?' "

After six weeks Bill called John into his office and said, "I'm not happy with your performance." Bill told John he didn't shave often enough and dressed too sloppily. Huh? From the man who once wrote that Sparky Anderson "really believes he made a winning team out of Pete Rose, Johnny Bench, Joe Morgan, George Foster and Davey Concepcion by teaching them the virtues of shiny shoes and clean upper lips"? Bill acknowledges that he isn't always great at managing his assistants.

John told his wife, "He doesn't like me. We're not getting along." His work was almost entirely data entry at that point, but he took it upon himself to write up comments on a few minor league prospects. He showed them to Bill, and John was soon writing a fair percentage of the comments for the *Player Ratings* books. "Part of being Bill's assistant is reading his mind," he says. "But he was generous and understanding when there was a health crisis in my family. With the possible exception of my father, he's the smartest man I've ever met. He's very curious about things outside baseball. But he can be gruff and awkward with people. And he hates talking on the phone."

I wondered what John's impression of Bill's politics might be. John says, "Bill describes himself as a centrist. I don't necessarily think that's true. If he were designing an ideal political order, he might be a libertarian. But when it comes down to practical politics, he isn't quite a liberal Democrat, but he's definitely not a conservative. I think he agrees with the Democrats more than he agrees with the Republicans, but he has a lot of problems with the way the Democrats go about things. He agrees with their goals, but doesn't always agree with how they go about trying to achieve those goals. He doesn't like George W. Bush very much. Bill is suspicious of any large concentrations of power, be it big government or big business. I think he believes in God, but he doesn't talk about it much, and he has no use for the religious right. The most important thing in his life is his children, and he wants them to grow up to make wise, ethical decisions."

Another hardcover, the *Guide to Baseball Managers* (1870s to the present), came out in 1997. Bill says, "I'll pick up a book I wrote years ago and find lots of stuff I didn't remember. With the *Managers* book, at the time it came out, it sank under the water and made no impact on the public discussion at all. I was reading a section of it a year ago and thought, this is pretty good. It was a surprise to me that it had so little success."

The New Bill James Historical Baseball Abstract (blue cover) was published in 2001. The first part, like in the first *Historical Abstract*, goes decade by decade, adding a section on the Negro Leagues. The second part is Bill's top 100 players at each position. Bill had been at a Royals game with a friend. He asked whether the friend thought Mike Macfarlane might be one of the hundred best catchers ever. The friend claimed he could list two hundred who were better. When he got to about thirty, he started naming guys who were maybe a little better, maybe not. That triggered Bill to do an analysis of the hundred best at each spot. Two years later he finished the revised edition (green cover).

The player ratings in the *New Historical* were based on Win Shares. In 2002 Bill put out a book through STATS Inc., *Win Shares*. About two-thirds of the 700-plus pages are lists of Win Shares by team (year-by-year, 1876–2001), decade, all-time leaders, etc. The first third explains the system, then shifts to "Random Essays," several of which are fascinating.

Bill discusses the fact that independent putouts by catchers (catching pop-ups and tagging out runners) "have declined rather astonishingly over a sustained period of time." He analyzes the differences in fielding stats between Bill Mazeroski and Willie Randolph, finding that the gap between the two isn't wide. In fact, Mazeroski recorded 7.5 percent more assists per inning than Randolph, but *relative to the ground balls of his team,* Randolph recorded *more* assists than Mazeroski. Other essays cover Nap Lajoie's fielding; a comparison of Chuck Klein, 1930, to Carl Yastrzemski, 1967 (Yaz wins); and "Biases in MVP Voting."

Win Shares are essentially "Wins Created." As *runs created* combines a player's stats to formulate an estimation of how many runs he created, Win Shares moves forward from runs to wins. The system is too complex to explain here, but it does two things: 1. It removes illusions of context; players from different eras, leagues, and teams are on equal footing. 2. It lets the contributions of pitchers, hitters, and fielders be stated in the same form. Bill says that the system's initial incarnation wasn't perfect, but Win Shares have made a significant impact on sabermetrics in a short time.

12

Baseball Evolving

Bill says, "In the seventies there was a phase where some scientists thought we were about to enter an ice age. A few years later, everyone was talking about global warming. The first group of scientists was wrong, but that doesn't mean global warming isn't a problem. People have a hard time looking at the science for what it is, rather than coloring it with their prejudices about new knowledge.

"I'm not trying to get people to think like me, any more than a chemist is trying to get consumers to invent plastic. A chemist wants to invent plastic for people to use, and what I've tried to do is create knowledge that can be used whether you have an understanding of sabermetric methods or not."

In baseball circles the question is, How much art to how much science? But even if you take science as far as it can go, there will still be limitless unknowns. Bill says, "We've gone from a cup of knowledge to a barrel, but we're drawing it out of an ocean. The knowledge is useful, but it doesn't eliminate the need for a broader understanding."

One of the army of straw men that are trotted out to discredit the idea of searching for clear and convincing evidence is, "You can't predict everything that happens on a ball field, because of the human element." (People who make that declaration would do well to document when anyone actually said that you could.) Do self-appointed defenders of the human element really think there is so much objectivity in baseball that it needs to be counterbalanced? Or is it like *Inherit the Wind,* hard data and discomforting ideas butting against soft data and cherished beliefs—"Mister, you may conquer the air; but the birds will lose their wonder, and the clouds will smell of gasoline!" Sir, you can grasp the importance of on-base percentage; but players who do the little things but don't get on base will look like a quiet little drain on your efforts.

Two recurring themes in Bill's books are *unintended consequences* and *multiple factors behind change.* For example, you hear people talk about the days of Bob Gibson and Don Drysdale, when pitchers weren't afraid to pitch inside. Romantic notion, but the number of hit batsmen is way *up,* not down. From 1960 to 1969 there were 1,080,332 major league at-bats and 6,993 hit batsmen. From 1998 to 2004 there were a similar number of at-bats (1,167,517) but many more hit batsmen (12,073). Bill says, "Hit batsmen are up because the hitters now are right on top of the plate. Also, pitchers often plunk the next hitter after a home run, and from 1998 to 2004 there were a lot of home runs."

Bill thinks that the rules in place to stop beanball wars have had the unintended consequence of increasing hit batsmen. But it isn't that simple. He says, "I think the increase in hit batsmen is an unintended consequence of the rule against brushbacks. But it is also a consequence, in part, of batting helmets with ear flaps; and, in part, of the use of aluminum bats in amateur baseball, which have created a generation of hitters who drive the outside pitch in the air, which was unusual twenty-five years ago. And probably a consequence of other things as well."

Another example of unintended consequences: The number of innings pitched by left-handers has dropped significantly in the past twenty years. Bill thinks it's in part an effect of using radar guns to measure pitch speed. He says, "Left-handed pitchers, on average, don't throw as hard as right-handers. The use of radar guns, beginning in the 1970s and becoming widespread in the 1980s, increased the emphasis on throwing hard.

"Before, when you didn't *know* exactly how fast a pitcher was throwing, you could put a Mike Caldwell or Geoff Zahn or Randy Jones on the mound; he may have been throwing 82, but you didn't know it. You knew he wasn't a hard thrower, but you didn't have specific data. Now you have one guy throwing 85, the other throwing 89, you tend to favor the guy throwing 89, even though it probably doesn't make any difference to major league hitters whether a pitcher is throwing 85 or 89. This works against finesse pitchers in general, and, since a lot of left-handers are finesse pitchers, it works against left-handers."

The average fastball of a left-handed pitcher is substantially slower than that of a right-hander. Bill says, "In the population as a whole, I would guess that the average arm speed of left-handers is the same as the average arm speed of right-handers. But in the population as a whole, only 8 or 10 percent of the population is left-handed. Among pitchers, it's three times that. Being left-handed is an advantage for pitchers, which means that, in selecting which pitchers move up the ladder to the majors, left-handedness competes with other advantages. Lefties are disproportionately represented, so they are less carefully selected to be hard throwers."

Naturalist Stephen Jay Gould was a huge baseball fan and a sabermetrician in his own right. He and Bill met once in Lawrence when, as Bill says, "Some right-wing nitwits got themselves onto the Kansas state board of education—largely because nobody gives a rat's ass who's on the Kansas state board of education—and were trying to ban references to evolution from state textbooks."

Bill wrote in the '86 *Abstract* about the mistaken belief that Milwaukee County Stadium was a hitter's park:

> The "dispute" isn't a disagreement about the evidence, but a disagreement between people who are looking at the evidence and people who aren't. It's like asking a naturalist why he doesn't do a

complete, once-and-for-all study of the evidence on evolution and creationism. The evidence is already conclusive; it's just that there are people who don't intend to accept it unless the hand of God appears in the sky one afternoon and writes, "ALL RIGHT! I CONFESS! I DID IT BY EVOLUTION! IT TOOK ME YEARS! I'SE JUST KIDDING ABOUT THE SEVEN DAYS! AND BY THE WAY, MILWAUKEE COUNTY STADIUM IS A PITCHER'S PARK . . . BE BACK NEXT MILLENNIUM. LOVE, GOD. P.S. IF YOU DO ANY MORE MOVIES I'D PREFER DEBRA WINGER TO GEORGE BURNS."

Bill remembers telling Gould, "I'm afraid that if I'd had to choose between standing up to the creationists or letting the education budget hang in limbo for another six months, I would have said, 'Hell, it doesn't matter what these guys say, let's just go ahead.'" He says, "I wasn't sure how he'd react, but he understood."

Bill's influence on Major League Baseball is analogous to Charles Darwin's influence on nature. By changing the way we understand it, and changing the terms of the discussion about it, he did much to change the thing itself.

Another way to frame his influence is as the Babe Ruth of baseball analysts. Ruth was a catalyst for great change. Bill quantified Ruth's legacy within the modern game, its post-Ruthian evolution.

In the eyes of many old-schoolers of his time, Ruth was spoiling the game. In the Houston Astros comments of the '83 *Abstract*, Bill noted that Craig Wright had come up with the idea that the Astrodome was "a baseball time machine, jerking the game back to the days before Babe Ruth, before the home run came and forced all who did not choose to lose to adopt it." Bill elucidated:

The Astrodome is the one park in baseball in which you simply cannot play longball successfully, and this takes the game back to the way it was played long, long ago. The bunt, the hit and run, the squeeze play . . . in the absence of more powerful weapons, these subtle plays attain a huge significance. In watching the

1980 NL Championship games, I understood for the first time what the old-timers who felt that Babe Ruth had ruined the game were talking about. One cannot oppose a home-run-hitting offense with a run-at-a-time offense; you'll get beat. Babe Ruth was a cyclone who swept up the precious strategies of the generations before him and scattered them in ruins.

There is also a character parallel between Ruth and Bill. In the *New Historical Abstract*, Bill wrote about Ruth, "Up until 1920, any young hitter who experimented with an uppercut was told to cut it out and swing level, because everybody 'knew' that if you uppercut you would hit a few home runs, but you'd hit twenty times as many fly outs and pop ups. Babe Ruth was 'allowed' to uppercut, and wasn't coached out of it, because 1. he was a pitcher, and 2. it wasn't Ruth's nature to do what he was told." Swap in "an outsider" for "a pitcher" and "Bill's nature" for "Ruth's nature," and you have an apt description of what "allowed" the sabermetrics revolution.

On the other hand, if a premise such as "Babe Ruth changed baseball" or "Bill James changed baseball" gets up a head of steam, it can roll into mythology. I asked Bill what he thought about the idea that Babe Ruth was an agent of change who set the blueprint for modern players and strategies, and that Bill, through research and observation, quantified the evolution, like a baseball Darwin. He demurred, then answered:

The period 1918–1921 is a remarkable vortex of baseball history, a short time frame in which multiple currents came together very suddenly. These include:

1. The gambling scandals
2. The coming of the commissioner system, as a consequence of the gambling scandals
3. The arrival of the two colonels in New York
4. The banning of the spitball, which was attempted before the 1920 season, thus before events one and five
5. The death of Ray Chapman

6. The Federal League lawsuit, which was before the Supreme Court more or less at the same time that the gambling scandal broke

7. The arrival of Branch Rickey in St. Louis (as general manager, or what would later be called general manager)

In addition, two factors from a few years earlier were working to progressively reshape the game. The first modern parks, built from 1909 to 1914 (Forbes, Wrigley, Fenway, Shibe Park), had forced baseball to improve its management, which, until 1915, was done almost entirely by the people still called managers.

Perhaps most important of all, up until about 1915 many of the best players were trapped in the minor leagues—permanently. About 1915, the minor leagues agreed to the agreements which allowed higher leagues to buy players from the lower leagues, not allowing the lower leagues to hold on to star players. This change caused the quality of play in the major leagues to improve rapidly from 1915 to 1930.

So it wasn't that Ruth changed baseball, but that baseball changed for a complex set of reasons, Ruth being a big one. That's true in Bill's case too—he was to the study of baseball what Ruth was to the game on the field, but changes that big don't happen in a vacuum.

Of course there are fundamental differences between the actors onstage and the critics in the seats. But an outsider's ideas can change the inside world, because insiders have to respond to the spread of new knowledge. Just ask Detroit about Ralph Nader. He never designed a car, but his influence on car design was incalculable. Babe Ruth represents the point at which baseball broke from the dead ball era, and the *Abstract* represents the point at which the quantification of that change became part of the process of change.

It's essential to keep in mind that we're talking about baseball at the major league level. "A lot of people interpret major league baseball as an extension of their experience in playing baseball," Bill says.

"They think speed is tremendously important because, in the lower levels of play—high school ball, etc.—speed *is* tremendously important. They assume the pitcher controls when a walk occurs because, in the lower levels, the pitcher's control is so weak you feel relieved when he can just get the damn ball over. People think aggressiveness pays, because, at lower levels, it *does* pay. A lot of things that are true in amateur ball are *not* true in pro ball, and you have to really study the game to straighten those things out. . . . And Babe Ruth is a dividing line in that."

Bill's daughter Rachel e-mailed, "An odd little thing that seemed like Dad: I spoke to him today, and he asked me about my classes. I mentioned that I was reading T. S. Eliot, and I loved 'The Love Song of Alfred J. Prufrock.' Dad proceeded to recite the first two stanzas of the poem. He memorized it one summer when he was young."

Looking back at end points can break your heart. One day you're kissing the one you love, and later it turns out to have been the last time. Along those lines, I used to read poetry, but somewhere along the way I just stopped. Still, I remember one by Raymond Carver about Charles Bukowski that says the people who go to poetry readings come to see if the poet's socks are dirty, and he won't disappoint them.

At the little house-office Bill keeps not far from the James family home, I don't want to know if his socks are dirty, so to speak. But the state of his work space is too kooky not to describe, and I figure he set a precedent for poking gentle fun at personal traits with his *Historical Abstract* essay on 1950s pitcher Don Mossi, "The Man Who Invented Winning Ugly."

> I always kind of identified with Don Mossi. Don Mossi had had two careers as a major league pitcher, one as a reliever and one as a starter, and he was pretty darn good both times. No one who saw him play much remembers that, because Mossi's ears looked

as if they had been borrowed from a much larger species, and reattached without proper supervision. His nose was crooked, his eyes were in the wrong place, and though he was skinny he had no neck to speak of, just a series of chins that melted into his chest. An Adam's apple poked out of the third chin, and there was always a stubble of beard because you can't shave a face like that. He looked like Joe Torre escaped from Devil's Island.

Bill's office circa summer 2004 is the Don Mossi of work spaces. He sits at a desk overflowing with papers, books in varied states of open, a pair of old box PCs, cans of Diet Pepsi (fresh and not). An old twin bed abuts the desk, as does most everything in the room. Boxes piled up inches behind him, printer and mini-fridge in front. There's barely space for me to wheel in a chair. The best thing about the room is the wall that has three items tacked up: a ripped-out article from *Collier's* magazine about Hack Wilson, a generic black-and-white calendar more than a year out of date, and a dirty white flyswatter hanging like a pendulum under the calendar.

"One of my many attempts to get organized," Bill says.

In the outer room, eleven-year-old son Reuben is watching cartoons. In the office, the soothing lilt of *SpongeBob SquarePants* can hardly be heard, due to the cacophony of a landscaping crew grinding a big tree into nonexistence outside the window.

Next to Bill's desk is a modern floor lamp with three clip-type bulbs. It jangles metallically when nudged, and one of the bulb covers is missing, so it does a nice imitation of an interrogation tool. It's got a certain charm, I offer.

"No it doesn't," Bill says. "It's annoying as hell."

I tell him I'll e-mail him in a year and see if it's still there.

"I'm changing offices, and it won't be moving," he says. "But you never know."

I guess we look for personal tics in people who are smarter than we are. It's silly to see Einstein's not knowing his own phone number or not wearing socks as defining characteristics. But if you want to riff on the absentminded-professor motif, Bill mixes frugality and disorganization like a true genius. Rob Neyer says that when he was Bill's assistant, "For bookshelves, he had me buy long planks from the Oskaloosa lumber yard and a big pile of bricks from a Topeka brick seller. Typically, Bill's desk was piled high with books he was in the middle of, materials for whatever the current project was, unopened mail from weeks and months ago, empty cans of Diet Pepsi, and a dozen other things. I bought a second-hand office chair for myself back in 1990 or 1991. Almost immediately, I realized that there was a tiny hole in the leather, and thus a tiny spring kept poking through and putting tiny holes in the seats of my pants. I got around this by making sure I had a towel under me, and kept using the chair. Here's the punchline: I was in Bill's office last summer . . . and the poky green office chair was still there!"

Reuben pops into the office. "I lost a tooth," he reports. "I swallowed it chewing gum."

"Was it a tooth you were supposed to lose?" Bill asks.

It was. Reuben then instigates a wrestling match with his dad. Bill is huge, and Reuben is eleven, so they look like a clip from *Animal Planet*. That makes me think of a story Bill's most recent ex-assistant, Matthew Namee, told me. One day a column of ants came marching up the porch steps and under the front door. Bill broomed them away, but in a minute they were back. After repeating the action a few times, Bill mused, "You'd think the guys in back would notice their buddies keep disappearing."

I'm pondering rigid creatures marching in lockstep when outside a train rolls past, shaking the foundation. This little house in Kansas is a long way from any major league front office. It isn't what you'd expect for a senior baseball operations advisor. But then, Bill elucidated the line between himself and the purveyors of "inside baseball."

In the '84 *Abstract* he wrote, "Inside looks, inside glimpses, inside locker rooms, and inside blimpses; within months we shall have seen the inside of everything that one can get inside of without a doctor's help. . . . This is *outside* baseball. This is a book about what baseball looks like if you step back from it and study it intensely and minutely, but from a distance."

In a sense, the *Abstract*s were a gob of spit in the eye of professionalism—"the curse of professionalism," Bill calls it. He described announcer Milo Hamilton:

Hamilton as a broadcaster is a model of professionalism, fluency, and deportment; he is, in short, as interesting as the Weather Channel, to which I would frequently dial while he was on. Milo's skills would serve him well as a lawyer, an executive, or a broker. He broadcasts baseball games in a tone that would be more appropriate for a man reviewing a loan application. He projects no sense at all that he is enjoying the game or that we ought to be, and I frankly find it difficult to believe that the writers who ripped the Cubs for firing Hamilton actually watch the broadcasts.

"I think the broadcasters of thirty, forty years ago were on the whole better than the broadcasters of today," he says. "They were bolder, more colorful, more interesting. The concept of professionalism, which has damaged our culture in so many ways, has made the broadcasts more predictable." Professionalism is a regular object of Bill's scorn. He wrote in the *New Historical Abstract*:

Now, I don't know where you stand on "professionalism," but I think professionalism ranks with socialism, psychology, and twice-baked potatoes as the worst ideas of the twentieth century. Cops became police officers, but the crime rate soared. Professionalism in law has brought us the O. J. Simpson case in lieu of justice. Professionalism in education has given us teachers who know how to administer sophisticated evaluative instruments, but simply don't have time to deal with the kids who can't read. We would all be far better off if the principle of civilian control of the military was extended to civilian control of the judicial system, civilian control of the schools, civilian control of the police force, and civilian control of the medical profession.

Ah, the doctors. The inevitable defense of professionalism is, "Would you rather be operated on by an amateur surgeon, or a professional?" But the costs of professionalism in medicine, as in every field, far outweigh the benefits. Professionalism in medicine has given us medical miracles for the affluent, but hospitals that will charge you $35 for an aspirin, insurance companies that won't pay for an overnight hospital stay after an appendectomy, and no access to health care for 45 million people. My father was a small town janitor, but when we got sick a doctor came to the house. Doctors are too professional for that now. We work for them.

"I oversimplified, of course," he continued; "there are legitimate benefits to professionalism, as well as things which are sold as 'professionalism' because that sounds better than 'organized selfishness.' A lot of what was contemplated by professionalism has failed or been discarded; a lot of it has been written into the ground rules."

This isn't directly about professionalism, but a comment Bill wrote about "Senator" Steve Garvey in the '83 *Abstract* has a related perspective. Garvey was the model "professional ballplayer" of the seventies. He's as difficult as Pete Rose to truly explain to someone who didn't catch his act, but both were manifestations of the same drives, expressed as opposites in an "every cop is a criminal and all the sinners, saints" sense. Garvey was divorced in 1981. Paternity suits started popping up. He was traded to San Diego.* His hitting declined. His ex-wife later wrote a tell-all book. Bill wrote:

What is it about Senator Garvey that rings so false when you know in your heart that it is probably as genuine as the contented look on the face of a cow and as deeply held as Halloween

*"Steve Garvey's not my Padre!" was a popular bumper sticker.

candy in the hand of a child? I have a cousin who strikes me exactly the same way, and I'll bet you do too; we'll call mine Wally. Wally graduated from high school with highest hosannas and went straight to Harvard, where he met and married a reasonably pretty girl with an awfully sensible head on her, and then he got his master's degree and went to work in corporate America, shinnying rapidly up the ladder of success and making oodles of money and saving it so that his children will never have to worry about who will pay for their next orthodontist's appointment. Wally is an awfully nice man and he has never said an unkind word to me in his life, and he is brilliant, and I avoid him at all costs. There is something about the very sensibleness of his life that seems to any normal person to be almost accusatory, for sometimes I am chubby while he retains an accusing trimness, and sometimes I am underemployed while he rests in accusingly attainable affluence, and sometimes I might neglect to have my teeth looked at for a decade or two because of an irrational fear of dentists while I know without a thought that if Wally had such a fear he would deal with it directly, and if he didn't his wife would spin him around and kick him in the butt and send him on the way to his appointment anyway, so that you would never know the difference.

It does not ring false, perhaps, but hollow, that since the very essence of life is a mystery, life seems unreal without self-doubt, and we must see that self-doubt in others before we can accept that they share our humanity. Garvey never allows the question marks to rise in his eyes or to afflict his performance, and thus he seems . . . what is it that people say about him? A robot? A programmed performer? How can he be a human without doubting himself, without yielding to periods of frustration and futile anger? It is not only Garvey's chin which seems chiseled in granite, but his values, which were given to him in grade school along with the rest of us. But while the rest of us have eroded ours by turning them over and over and examining them in different ways, Garvey seems, impossibly, to have let his stay untested and unworn.

One might think that when this period is in the past Garvey will be humanized somewhat by what the networks refer to as his "mental torment," by his accompanying sub-Garvey seasons. Self-doubt comes directly from pain, as ashes are left by a fire. What is so unnerving about Wally and Steve is to think that they have never lost a year or two out of their lives because they were wondering about something, got their values confused, never sifted through the ashes before. 1981 and 1982 were the years Garvey lost in the fire, and one might hope that he will have the sense not to hide that from us. Welcome, Steve; welcome to the human race.

Bill, Reuben, and I are walking to the office after dinner. Reuben says he recently read a book called *Skinnybones* about a boy who plays baseball badly. Reuben's plot summary ends, "Why would anyone put a baseball cap on their grandma?" which reminds me that James Thurber once said the most profound question he'd ever heard was "How did a seal get in the bedroom?" It comes out that one of Bill's favorite baseball books is *Rhubarb*, about a cat who owns a baseball team, and that there's a song called "Never Hit Your Grandma with a Shovel" (because it makes a bad impression on her mind). I promise Reuben that I'll send the tape of our conversation to him when he's older. "I'm probably laughing at myself in the future," he says.

At the office, watching the Sox on satellite, I've got metaphors and nicknames on the brain. And being in Kansas has me thinking about tornadoes. I ask Bill if he ever saw one in person. He's seen three, in fact, all in the year before he left for college. Bill says, "The first tornado I saw on June eighth, and I can still see it. There's a bright blue sky on the bottom, and the top of that sky is dark black. Hanging down from that black line is this twisting black mass. Now, if you had never heard of 'tornado'—no one had ever explained the concept to you—when you saw it you would have immediately realized it was going to kill you."

David Ortiz is at the plate, and I'm thinking that last line fits Big Papi as seen by an opposing pitcher. Bill notes that when the Sox signed Ortiz, some said his left-handed uppercut wouldn't work at Fenway. "But it turns out, when he pulls the ball he hits it so far, the outfield dimensions don't matter; and when he goes the other way he pops it up and over the wall . . . perfect for Fenway."

Kevin Millar comes up with men on base. He works the count, and Bill says, "He can hit a fastball." Millar bangs the next pitch off the wall. "Yes! Yes! Yes!" hollers Bill.

"You scared me," Reuben says, speaking for both of us.

Aren't there times, I ask Bill, when he can feel what's going to happen before it does?

Bill says, "Particularly with George Brett, sometimes I could just feel when he was locked in, or when he wasn't."

In his formative years as a sabermetrician, Bill was as locked in to major league baseball as any non-insider has ever been—the level of intelligence and the intensity of interest. And he was *really* locked in to George Brett. He wrote in the '83 *Abstract:*

What has happened to George over the last two seasons is unusually simple to explain, and can be traced unmistakably in the records. It all began on October 10, 1980, and no, that is not the date of Dickie Noles' knockdown pitch. That is the date on which, after the nation had just spent three days listening to Billy Martin (working the series for ABC) explain how his pitchers had stopped George in 1980 by a steady diet of breaking balls, Goose Gossage delivered a 98-mph fastball, and George Brett deposited it in the third deck. And it is overstating the case, but not by much, to say that that was the last fastball that George has seen.

Pitchers, basically, like to throw fastballs. Most of them are in the major leagues because they have strong arms and can throw hard. They are proud of the fact that they can throw hard. They like to. When a pitcher throws breaking stuff and changes speeds a lot, the hitters will sit in the dugout and scream at him, essentially, to fight like a man. Challenge the hitters, that's the spirit.

Besides that, the fastball is easier to control than a breaking pitch, and it doesn't put as much strain on the arm.

I have known since 1976 that George Brett was basically a fastball hitter, and so, I suspect, has every pitcher in the American League. But there's knowing something, and then there's *knowing* it. Before 1980, the fact that Brett was a fastball hitter represented a challenge to the pitchers. It didn't dissuade most of them from throwing their fastballs, it simply caused them to try to throw harder. But when Goose loaded up and threw him the best fastball that he had and George said Whoopee, that did it. Billy's bragging about getting George out with slop took on a whole new meaning. Throwing him a fastball was no longer regarded as a challenge, it was regarded as suicidal.

Before 1980, he didn't walk much; since then, because breaking pitches are harder to control, he walks quite a bit. Because he is taking more pitches, he is also striking out a lot more. Through 1980 he was an amazing clutch performer; now, with men on base he gets impatient and lunges at off-speed pitches. Whereas he used to hit a hundred points better in Kansas City, he now does better on the road where the fences are easier to reach if a curve ball hangs.

But watch out, he is adjusting. I think there is a definite limit to how many curve balls you can show the man before he starts rocketing them all over the park, and I think we're pretty close to reaching that limit.

We'll see. There is more to this story than just that, of course; there's a Roger Maris Syndrome involved. I think that the irate locals who portrayed George's contract disaffection as an act of infantile temper were making a more profound point than they realized. George is a man whose masculine family—his father and his brothers—are everything to him. He is a bachelor. In the Herzog years, the Royals were a close team, with a warm, we're-all-in-this-together sort of atmosphere. They're not that way anymore; Howser is a fine manager, but he's just different. I think George misses that terribly. How does he feel when he sees

Jamie Quirk, whom he's been with since the low minors, pushed out of the nest? Like it's time for him to go, too, I suspect. He wants the Royals to tell him that they love him, and instead they tell him it's a business. Sure, he's a spoiled kid, but we're not all too adult to sympathize with those feelings, are we?

You'll notice the phrase "amazing clutch hitter." The question of clutch ability has long been a sabermetric bugaboo. On the facing page of the Brett comment, Bill wrote regarding Mike Schmidt:

> The great difficulty about clutch performance, it seems to me, is that it separates what a player *is* from what he *does*. A lot of people have the same trouble with fielding. This new guy has hit well for us, they will say, but he is a bad fielder, and he can't hit in the clutch. Get it? A subtle linguistic shift, from *has done* to *is*; batting is simply performance, clutch hitting is character. But I don't see it that way, perhaps because statistics are so clumsy at measuring character. In 1982 Mike Schmidt didn't hit well with men on base, and he didn't hit well in the thick of the pennant race. But in 1980 he hit very well in key games, and he might again in 1983. I don't see a conflict, any more than I see a conflict in the 1980 and '82 batting averages of Miguel Dilone or the 1980 and '82 earned run averages of Mike Norris.

In spring 2005 the *Baseball Research Journal* published "Underestimating the Fog," an essay in which Bill wrote, "I have come to realize that a wide range of conclusions in sabermetrics may be unfounded, due to the reliance on a commonly accepted method which *seems*, intuitively, that it ought to work, but which in practice may not actually work at all." He explained that all skills are persistent to some degree, and baseball fans are engaged in a perpetual struggle to figure out what's skill and what's luck. He noted, "Walter Johnson hit .433 one year in about 100 at-bats; the next year he hit .194, and the year after that .348. Just luck."

If a skill can't be measured as persistent, we tend to assume it's not real. On the other hand, as Bill wrote in the '88 *Abstract:* "In general, the most suspect conclusion in any research is the finding of no effect. If you find no effect, that means that either there is no effect, or you looked in the wrong place. To convince people that there is no effect, you have to demonstrate that you looked everywhere that the effect could reasonably be hiding."

Bill revisited eight findings in "Underestimating the Fog." Of course, the focus fell on the most controversial—whether clutch hitting is a reliable skill. Belief in clutch ability has long been an article of faith in baseball. Studies based on comparison offshoots (the suspect method) have led many sabermetricians to conclude that clutch hitting was not "an important or a general phenomenon."

The press loves a mea culpa, real or supposed, and Bill's was covered by the *New York Times*. David Leonhardt wrote that if you believe in clutch, "you belong to the majority party. Call yourself a traditionalist, and know that most managers and players stand with you." Most journalists, too. Leonhardt, stretching the political-party analogy, wrote that Bill James had "announced that he was thinking of switching parties." But he didn't mention these bits from Bill's essay: "I am not writing about clutch hitting, I am talking about the method" and "I am not saying that these conclusions [that clutch hitting isn't a reliable skill, etc.] are false."

Instead, he quoted from an e-mail that said in part, "I was wrong about something, wrong about something important, for a long time." Again, there's a difference between being wrong about method and being wrong about the conclusion. Leonhardt also didn't mention Bill's assertions that clutch ability "should be regarded as an open question" and that sabermetricians "need to find some more affirmative way to study the subject."

Leonhardt wrote, "If it exists, clutchness probably creates only a few extra hits for a batter over the course of a season, despite announcers who claim to see it in every game. So James's old view might have had the rare distinction of being wrong and still being closer to the truth than the other side's argument." That's reasonable, but what was Bill's old view? Did he ever argue that there's no such thing as clutch ability, or just that there's a lot of nonsense put forth in the name of it? In the '80 *Abstract*, he wrote that if you wanted to learn who was a good clutch hitter and who wasn't, all he could suggest was that you use as many different statistical sources as possible, and take a grain of salt with each. "I believe you can find a few players who line up as solid clutch players," he wrote.

> I am not saying that "clutch ability" does not exist; I do believe it is greatly overemphasized, and that the talk about it says more about the prejudices or experiences of the speaker than it does about any player. But to take the passions and prejudices out of the game would be to take the game out of the game, and I certainly would not want to be a part of that.

He wrote something in the '82 *Abstract* that's more or less what was depicted in the *Times* as his revised, moderated view:

> Clutch hitting is supposed to be a whale of a matter, and if there is anything certain about it, it is that if you got a line on it it would turn out to be a goldfish. . . . At the same time, that lies may be told in the name of the Lord is a poor reason to be an atheist, and that exaggerations and rampant sloppiness are common in the name of clutch performance does not mean that there are no clutch situations or that it does not occasionally happen that a team will perform over its head or below par in those situations.

In the first *Historical Abstract* there's a piece about the fact that pinch hitters are rarely successful for more than a season. Gates Brown is as famous a pinch hitter as any, but his 1967–69 batting averages were .154, .462, and .205. Dusty Rhodes became a clutch legend for his 1954 performance, but his career pinch-hitting average was .186. Was he clutch or wasn't he?

Bill's ideas often get lost in translation, because the topics that get people talking stir up emotions and are complicated. Mix in his reticence to respond to things that are written about him, and sometimes the stuff he sends out takes on a life of its own. That's what happened with the closer-by-committee straw man of 2003.

Bill had studied bullpen usage patterns and found that what he called "the Robb Nen pattern"—in which the ace is used mainly in one-inning save situations—was less than optimal. First, using a bullpen ace to protect a two-run lead is less effective than using him when *behind* by one run. Second, each run saved in a tie has eight times the impact of a run saved with a three-run lead. The ultimate inefficient use of your relief ace would be to leave him on the bench in the eighth inning of a tie game you end up losing, then, the next night, bring him in to save a three-run lead.

None of which has anything to do with a bullpen by committee. Bill says, "I was writing about how to get as much as possible out of your ace reliever. That's almost the exact opposite of not deciding who your ace reliever is." In point of fact, he wrote in the '84 *Abstract*, "I like *definition* in a pitching staff."

I'm a little skeptical about group bullpens in principle. Jim Baker has suggested that teams which have great group bullpens in one year often tend to have group collapses the next year. We can't prove that, but it does seem that way. Even if it doesn't, I still don't really like group bullpens. For one thing, if you're counting on three or four relief pitchers, then you have to get work for all of them. That means taking the ball away from the starter whenever he gets into trouble, and I don't like that. . . . For another thing, if you don't have a bullpen ace, things can get awfully confused sometimes; one pitcher gets into a slump and then another and another, and you don't really know who it is that is supposed to get you out of this.

In 2002 the Red Sox had an "established closer" in Ugueth Urbina—
he wasn't an especially good one, but he was priced like one. Instead of
throwing nine million bucks to Urbina, they spent it on Bill Mueller,
Kevin Millar, David Ortiz, Mark Bellhorn . . . each a crucial member
of the 2004 championship lineup. But by letting Urbina walk, the Sox
went into 2003 without a known quantity to anchor the bullpen. As
was clear throughout baseball in 2005, a team can do perfectly well
using the *right* unproven relief ace, but there is a lot of luck involved.
But in early 2003, when Boston's relievers stank up the field, people
blamed the "new system."

Shortly after Bill was hired, before the 2003 season, a couple of articles came out that conflated his ideas about how to use a bullpen ace
with the closer-by-committee concept. Bill says, "After the season
opened and our bullpen was so wretched, it wasn't possible for me to
step forward and try to straighten things out. It would have been seen
as 'I don't want to take responsibility for this.'"

What *really* went wrong was that the Sox tried to save money in the
bullpen and guessed wrong about a couple of pitchers. "We screwed
up," Bill says. "But once things had gone awry, that was another reason
I couldn't step forward and try to straighten it out, because all I would
have been doing is trying to explain *how* we screwed up. What's the
point in that? 'The mistake we made wasn't *this*; the mistake was *that*.'
Who cares? Didn't work; end of story."

"Derek Jeter is so overrated," Reuben says. In the James household,
the Yankees' captain is known as "Dirty Rotten Jeter." I'm as guilty as
anyone of thinking Jeter is overrated, but we may have reached a point
at which he is both overrated and underrated, depending on who does
the rating. It reminds me of what Bill wrote in the '80 *Abstract* about
Reggie Jackson (in Jeter's case, slot in *sabermetrics* for *sportscasters*):

> Jackson has undeniable dramatic skills which, combined with a
> certain amount of being in the right place at the right time,
> served to bring him almost unparalleled recognition. Once he

got the recognition, people began to talk about all the things that he doesn't do, and it became a sort of sportscasters badge of sophistication, you knock Reggie to show the ignorant public how knowledgeable you are about baseball. He emerged as a media paradox, a player who was widely known as being not as good as everybody thought he was. But, while he's not the player of the decade, the fact is that he's a damn fine player.

When the Yankees were ahead of the Sox during the 2004 ALCS, Jeter made an interesting statement on another of those sabermetric bugaboos: momentum. "The Red Sox were supposed to have the momentum coming into the series," he said. "And now that we are ahead, we have the momentum? You can throw all that stuff out the window. I don't believe any of that."

Jeter isn't the only momentum doubter within baseball, but most insiders don't think twice about saying it's a huge factor. One problem with momentum analysis is, streaks happen even when you're flipping a coin, so unless you think a coin picks up momentum, the fact that teams and players go on streaks doesn't prove much. Fold in the fact that some teams and players are better than others, and that there are extended home and road stretches, and the potential for clusters gets bigger.

As with clutch ability, believers consider momentum's existence self-evident. Of course, neither belief nor non-belief qualifies as proof. Polls show that 85 percent of U.S. adults believes in miracles, 75 percent believe in angels, and 50 percent believe in ghosts. Good luck proving any of those don't exist or do, and good luck with momentum, too. "As a small child, I thought that the trees pushed the wind," Bill wrote in "Momentum, Ad Nauseum," in the '88 *Abstract*. He added, "Momentum is one of those superficial concepts that is hard to resist if you don't think it through, but hard to conceive of if you follow it through and try to resolve the problems it creates."

Bill noted that the *Elias Analyst* had concluded that "the conventional wisdom is completely wrong . . . a player is just as likely to hit well in a game that follows a slump as he is following a week of hot hitting," and he added, "I have studied the issue many different ways, trying to isolate something which can be called momentum, and, being unsuccessful, have concluded that that which is called momentum in baseball is not a characteristic of play but a characteristic of the perception of play."

In an e-mail to the Hot Hand in Sports website, Bill wrote that when the Yankees and Sox met in September and the Sox won the first game of that series, people thought that this had to give the Sox momentum for the rest of the series, which they lost, both games. A week later, they played at Fenway, and the Yanks won the first game before the Sox beat them the other two games. In the 2004 ALCS, the Red Sox lost the third game 19-8. "Momentum was everywhere; we couldn't POSSIBLY recover from a beating like that," Bill scoffed. "People just REFUSE to learn."

But in the "Underestimating the Fog" piece, Bill wrote, "The argument against hot streaks is based on the assumption that [comparison offshoot] analysis would detect hot streaks if they existed, rather than on the proven fact. Whether hot streaks exist or do not I do not know—but I think the assumption is false."

In July 2005, again on the Hot Hand site, he published the results of a study of Tony Gwynn and George Brett, writing, "I may have found some fragmentary evidence that hitters—well, two hitters—actually do have non-random clusters in performance."

On questions of momentum *and* clutch, turn to what Bill wrote about the White Sox in the '86 *Abstract*. The 1985 White Sox were amazing in clutch situations, batting .294 for the season with runners in scoring position. They hit better than their overall team average in late innings of close games, when batting averages almost always decline due to the use of relief aces. As a result, they topped their expected runs scored (the technical version of runs created) by "a whopping—a historic even—" sixty-two runs.

"And yet, what were they," Bill wrote. "They were an 85-77 team that should have been 76-86. The 1985 White Sox are the best illustration I have ever seen of how minor is the role that pressure performance plays in steering the fortunes of a ballclub." Clutch performance can make the difference between eighty-eight wins and ninety-two, which can be the difference between first and second. But it takes extraordinary clutch hitting to make an eight- or nine-game difference.

In many ways, the manager who hopes to win the pennant by getting better performances "in the clutch" is like a man who hopes to get rich by making a few well-timed investments in the stock market. "See," the man says, "in the last two months RCVL stock has gone from seventeen to thirty-seven and a quarter. Amalgamated Trench Mouth has gone from four and a quarter to thirteen in just eighteen days since they released their new computer. Now, if I'd just put a second mortgage on my mother-in-law, bought about 30,000 shares of RCVL in February on the margin, and put my IRS refund all into Trench Mouth, well, I'd be on my way to being a wealthy man now." It's literally true; if you can consistently choose the right stock, you can make a fortune in the stock market—and if you can choose exactly the right moment to get exactly the right hit, you can win a pennant.

A few lucky breaks in the stock market can give a young entrepreneur a tremendous impetus; a few investments in the stock market are not unwise. A few well-timed base hits can give a contending team a tremendous lift; everybody needs that now and then.

But millionaires are *not* just guys who got lucky in the stock market, and anybody who thinks they are has got zero chance of joining the club. And good ballteams are *not* just teams that hit in the clutch, and the same goes for any manager who thinks they are.

The point applies to momentum, too. If you think you can win by chasing the hot hand, good luck—you're going to need it.

13

Inner Workings

It's a late summer evening in Susie and Bill's kitchen. There's wine splattered on the counter and the wall. Coordination, thy name is not Bill James. "We had a wonderful old corkscrew," he says, "but it broke, and this new one doesn't work as well." The old cork has crumbled, leading to the big wine splash. "The rubber stoppers have no practical disadvantages on a twelve-dollar bottle of wine," he says, "but people think that if it's not 'authentic,' it must be a step down."

If there's a unified philosophy in preferring the old-school corkscrew design and newfangled stoppers, it's simply *what works*. Whether the subject is the usage patterns of relief aces or how to get wine out of a bottle, Bill tends to focus on what works, whether in practical or artistic terms. Seems simple, but think of Galileo questioning the movements of solar bodies in an age when the powers that be just *knew* that Earth was the center of the universe. Bill wrote in 1989 of baseball's mind-set, "This is a condition of the world and no one but a fool gets angry with the world because it is what it is, but there are profound frustrations in living in a world which awaits the Enlightenment."

Frustration is a powerful driver, at least for a while. We need things to push against. Bill pushed against being poor, dead-end jobs, academia, the army, table-game competitors, the lords of baseball. When he became famous, he pushed against his image and the labels others stuck on him.

In the '83 *Abstract* he noted that Angels manager Gene Mauch "had a beautiful line last fall when somebody asked him if he wouldn't almost have been happier losing than having to face all those questions about what does it feel like after all these years. Gene didn't like that question either, so he snapped, 'Nobody in this room is smart enough to analyze me.'" Bill quipped, "Nobody in the world is smart enough to figure out why Gene Mauch does some of the things he does, including Gene Mauch."

I'm not smart enough to figure out why Bill James does some of the things he does, but there are a couple of lines from his *New Historical Baseball Abstract* comment on Dan Quisenberry that describe their author as well as their subject: "He was, in fact, a gentle man, but he had an edge to him, too. Like a lot of bright people, he was very aware that he was living in a world inhabited by more than a few morons." And "He hated being patronized, and didn't particularly like being analyzed or evaluated."

Bill has had a habit of spreading a radical idea and then, after it works into the fabric of popular discussion, advocating a moderated view. The Red Sox laid down only twelve sacrifice bunts in 2004, a total low enough that you could take it as a strategic statement along the lines of Earl Weaver's comment that you could stuff the sac bunt up someone's ass and leave it there. In his own words, in the eighties Bill was "skeptical about the value of the bunt." If you asked a thousand people what Bill James thinks about the sac bunt, all but about five would say he's agin it. But in his *Baseball Managers* essay "Rolling in the Grass"—the best historical and analytical overview of the sacrifice bunt you'll ever read—he declares that questions of when and how often to bunt remain open.

Or take one-run games. People talk about the "character" it takes to win one-run games. Bill says that they involve a huge amount of luck—and that that may be the only safe statement that can be made about them. But is it safe to leap to the conclusion that there are no identifiable characteristics of teams that win a lot of one-run games? No. Bill's studies indicate that a team can't persistently win more than its share of one-run games, but there may be some persistent tendency for a team to lose more than its share.

Teams that fit the image of "one-run" ballclubs—more bunts, more steals, better pitching, and so on—show a small tendency to fare better in one-run games. But the extent to which this is true is so minor, it's impossible to work backward from the characteristics to predict whether a team will do well or poorly in close games.

Bill throws himself into the ongoing clash between our simplifications and the real world.

For example, in the eighties he wrote that ballplayers are heroes, that that is their job. In the late nineties, he wrote (of Dwight Gooden) that the press has an unfair tendency to hype young athletes as admirable, then tear them apart when they show weakness. I wondered if this might be a change in his thinking, but Bill set me straight, saying, "I don't think it is an evolution of thought, because I still believe both of those things. There is an obvious conflict between them, but I stubbornly believe that there is a sense in which they are each true. It relates, I think, to Jimmy Carter's self-destructive aphorism that life is unfair.

"About Gooden, I think I was commenting on the tendency of journalists to write onto the blank page of the young athlete the virtues they think should be there, whether they are there or not. A fresh-faced, nice-looking young athlete, so long as he doesn't swear or snarl or get a tattoo, will be sold to the public as a paragon of virtue, regardless of his human faults, not because the 'bosses' want this to happen but because that's what the journalists want to believe. It is hard to remember, but this happened even to Rickey Henderson. I vividly remember a Bay Area reporter assuring me in 1981 or 1982 that Rickey was 'almost a black Jack Armstrong.' This is unfair. Rickey and Dwight—and Mark McGwire—turn out to have human failings, then people dump on them because they're not what they never pretended to be."

Bill continues, "At the same time, people are interested in athletes *because* they see them as worthy of admiration, I believe. I don't think that athletics would exist without the admiration of athletes, and I don't think it can survive without the admiration of athletes.

"I suppose it is another Republican/Democrat false dichotomy, that we have here two simple positions, both definitively false. There are two de facto definitions of 'hero'—a paragon of virtue and a person worthy of admiration. There are two positions from which to observe— the position of the journalist and the position of the athlete. I think it is wrong, from the position of the journalist, to expect athletes to be paragons of virtue, simply because they are not, and also because it imposes upon them an unreasonable burden. But I also think that it is foolish, from the position of the athlete, to say, 'I can't be expected to be a hero,' if by 'hero' we mean simply 'worthy of admiration.' It is shortsighted and selfish to say this, because it poisons the pond.

"It's a common problem, of course . . . how does one espouse and defend virtues without arguing for intolerance? I don't have the answer; I don't think anybody does. If your church leader is charged with securities fraud, you give him a hug and offer your support; if he turns out to be BTK, it's a different problem."

Another example comes in the form of two positions Bill has voiced: one about the way evidence is presented to juries, the other about the effects of "babying" pitchers by overly restricting pitch counts—that it reduces their ability to pitch deep into games. On the evidence-presentation issue, Bill feels that the rules restricting relevant information from being presented have had unintended consequences.

He says, "A great deal of what has always fascinated me about criminal cases is that, in this area where the distinguishing of truth from non-truth is *so* critical, the process of sorting out what one is allowed to say is so deeply flawed. There are logical arguments that one is not allowed to make; there are utterly illogical arguments that are permitted.

"The process of sorting out what is allowed in and what is kept out is based on 'fairness' and 'equity' and 'consistency' more than it is based on what could be called 'true relevance.' Legal relevance, as opposed to true relevance, is based on precedents and the opening of doors. Certain issues cannot be raised by the prosecution *unless they are first raised by the defense.*

"It's a pretty bad system, in all honesty; our crime rates are as high as they are, in my opinion, in some measure because our legal system doesn't actually work very well. Much of my interest in crime stories is in thinking this through . . . why it doesn't work well, how it doesn't work well, how it could work better."

He says, for instance, "In Georgia in the 1940s there was a law stating that a person on trial for his life had a right to address the jury directly and make a statement to them. The statement was not under oath—thus, no liability to perjury—and it was not subject to cross-examination.

"Lawyers tend to blanch at the very idea. But I argue that that's actually a very good idea, and that we should adopt this rule. Why?

"A person on trial for his life should have the right to stand before the jury, look them in the eye and tell them whatever he wants to tell them. The court should vigorously defend that right. That leads to a fairer trial.

"But by defending the 'rights' of the accused in an essentially illogical way, we're not doing so. Modern trials are effectively denying the accused person the right to speak on his own behalf."

So, are modern juries less able to make accurate judgments in criminal cases? Are juries today less able to filter out the chaff from the wheat now than they were a hundred years ago?

Bill says, "YES, WE ARE. We *are* less sophisticated about these things than we were a hundred years ago; juries *are* less able to distinguish the wheat from the chaff now than they were a hundred years ago. The exclusion of 'prejudicial information' has backfired on those that it was intended to protect. Modern juries tend to *assume* that a person on trial for murder is a scumbag. Modern juries tend to trust police and prosecutors to an unhealthy extent.

"And one of the key reasons this is true is that, in the modern trial, the defendant is effectively prohibited from arguing that he is a man of good character—even if he is. If he says *anything* suggesting that he is a man of good character, he is inviting the prosecution to bring into the case every lie he has ever told, every time he ever lost his temper, everybody he has ever known who didn't like him for one reason or another.

"And the remedy for this is to discard this imaginary shield, which isn't actually protecting anybody from anything, and instead *control* the amount of prejudicial information that enters the trial. Juries can handle that far better than they can handle being given half the facts."

I wondered if all this connected back to his ideas about pitch counts and the babying of pitchers' arms.

Bill said, "I think the babying of pitchers' arms is done from a desire to avoid injuries to pitchers, in a situation in which it is unclear what does and does not constitute a risk.

"I think it is true, as you mentioned in an e-mail, that I tend to regard systems of thought about many issues as jerrybuilt and often self-contradictory.

"But there is another idea here, which I will try to explain at risk that you will make it more important than it is. The Huns, in the time of Attila, would slash the cheeks of newborn male babies, to make the point that life is tough, and if you're going to succeed you have to be tougher. They were tremendous warriors—better than the Romans of that time—and they placed a great faith in toughness.

"Well, that's crazy, obviously, but the belief that life is tough and successful people don't whine about it is not. We have gotten 'less tough,' as a society, over time, and we don't BELIEVE in toughness. My father's generation . . . my father was born in 1907 . . . those guys were REALLY tough. I remember my father having a plantar's wart in his foot, and he had to have foot surgery to have it removed, which was done with no anesthetic. I remember he told the doctor (but didn't really need to), 'For God's sake, be sure you get it all. Don't worry about hurting me; I'll be alright. Just be sure you get it out of there.'

"That was a very, very central idea to my father, an idea that he expressed every day, in a billion different contexts: that life was tough, and, if you tried to avoid pain, it just got tougher. He believed—everybody in his generation believed, or everybody that I knew, at least—that you take things on and you deal with them, painful or not. I grew up among old farmers, and, whatever else they were, they were REALLY tough.

"That was, at the very best, a mixed blessing. The old farmers didn't collect much art. Toughness competes with sensitivity for elbow room in the hierarchy of values—and, in modern America, all the mainstream victories go to sensitivity.

"I'm not saying that that's a bad thing. We all benefit from sensitivity to the injury we do to others, and I'm not saying we should throw it overboard. But people tend to view sensitivity as a virtue and toughness as a practical necessity, and thus to make illogical accommodations between the two. What I believe is that if toughness is a practical necessity then it must also be a virtue, and should be logically balanced against sensitivity, or wariness, or the possibility of bias, or whatever its antithesis is in this particular situation.

"All successful people understand the value of toughness, and we all teach it to our children. Nobody really wants to tolerate whining or self-pity—yet liberal Americans seem, at times, to advocate for society what they would never tolerate in those they love: ever increasing sensitivity, relentless efforts to avoid pain, and endless complaining about everything that goes wrong.

"And many times, they're right. Many times we *would* and do benefit from being more sensitive—but many times we don't.

"What I was saying in these two cases is:

"1. The desire to avoid injuries is not a sufficient reason to cut back pitcher innings unless one can demonstrate that this has the practical benefit of reducing injuries, and

"2. The desire to avoid prejudicing the jury is not a sufficient reason to block access to relevant facts, unless one can demonstrate that this does in fact lead more reliably to justice.

"These ideas sound more alike than they are. Nobody really understands the world, and the people who value sensitivity are right sometimes; they're wrong sometimes. The people who value toughness are right sometimes; they're wrong sometimes.

"I think that in the long arc of history, the human race becomes kinder, more and more sensitive, and less tough, and I have no doubt that this is a good thing. We should all work to advance this. There are people who work to make childhood less tough, to make children more sensitive to other children. I admire that, and I applaud it. On the issue of crime and society—the real secret of making the justice system work is to make the system kinder. The criminal justice system abuses those within it, making them tougher and tougher. The secret to ending the cycles of violence within our society is more kindness. Everybody who advocates harsher treatment for criminals is, in effect, advocating more crime.

"My father's belief in toughness was an oversimplification of the world. At the same time, there is over-sensitivity to pain, and there is over-sensitivity to risk. I worry about getting too far ahead of the curve. In the real world, there are a million wrong answers to every question."

The writer changes, the writing is permanent. Things he wrote twenty years ago, things he thought ten years ago, don't per se represent his current beliefs. Bill was twenty-seven when he put the first *Abstract* in the mail in 1977, thirty-nine when the last edition hit the stores in 1988. In his fifties now, he says, "There are things I did then that I wouldn't do now; there are things I did then that I couldn't do now. There are things I do now I couldn't have done then."

Advances in computer technology have changed sabermetrics to the extent that air travel changed scouting. Studies that would have taken three months (or been impossible) in 1985 can be done in a week. The new generation of sabermetricians can and should see Bill James as its Bob Dylan, working and inspiring across time, to be judged in relation to historical context.

He nurtured sabermetrics more or less from infancy, then set it loose to become what it would. But for a lot of people, Bill James still *is* sabermetrics, and vice versa. I asked him about this passage from the '87 *Abstract:*

> It is my belief that most people, as they age, become parodies of the things they once believed in. I can't remember the exact quote, but Nathaniel Hawthorne said something to the effect that writers spend the last thirty years of their lives trying to figure out what it was that they did so well when they were younger. In the context of life, confronted with an overwhelming array of options about what we should be and how we should make decisions, we choose to emphasize certain attributes that we find within ourselves. We select a philosophy of life as a man drifting in an infinite ocean selects a direction in which to sail his raft, because we are desperate to escape this bewildering ocean, youth. Life in the ocean becomes so much easier when you know where you are going and that there is land ahead.
>
> But once we reach the land, then we begin to think that we really understand life. We start to feel superior to the young and to the lost at sea, drifting with the currents. We forget that we once could see truth lying at the horizon in every direction. Surrounded by others who have landed on the same earth or rock on which we ourselves found comfort, we begin to think that this is the only land there is, that all who do not sail in our direction are doomed never to escape the sea. We assert our values without respect to the complexity of real-life problems. Old soldiers, espousing patriotism and love of country over all other political virtues, become blind to the faults of their countries. Their courage, no longer demanded from them, withers into bravado. Young people who chose books and learning to help them make sense of the overpowering world become so enamored of the books that they lose interest in the world that those books were supposed to help them understand until, if they are historians, they are writing papers on where Napoleon went to the bathroom and, if they are psychologists, they are running rats through multicolored mazes and, if they are sabermetricians,

they are trying to figure out whether or not strikeout-to-walk ratio is an indicator of growth potential in a rookie.

He told me, "In history there are a surprising number of writers who reach a point of age—mine, or later—and deny their best work. Walt Whitman grew to be embarrassed by *Leaves of Grass*. Tolstoy became a religious nut, and denounced *War and Peace* and *Anna Karenina*. This is actually a fairly common pattern, and I worry about that, too . . . losing touch with my youth to too great an extent."

Picasso said, "Art is a lie that tells the truth." Oscar Wilde said that art should tell "beautiful untrue things." One idea in abstract painting is that so-called imperfection can be artful, inasmuch as it reveals the essence behind the perception. Bill can be sloppy and imperfect, like anyone. The flaws splatter into the art, the art mixes with the science. Some see him as a charlatan using statistics to obfuscate simple truths. I see a contrarian putting the lie to simplification. Saber-metrics tries to connect with the nature of baseball on its own terms, but if everything we do is more or less a lie and more or less art, Bill James has done as much as any writer to help his readers in working that out.

In a world of ideological gulfs, taking a centrist position can feel like fraternizing with the enemy or sitting on a fence. Bill is perpetually trying to reconcile those realities when talking about the culture wars—baseball's and society's. He says, "The problems in baseball come when people insist on acting as if the real world is as simple as the model. And even more so in politics, which are even more complicated."

Bill's intent was not to trash popular statistics or to complicate the discussion, but to cultivate a field of knowledge. In the '84 *Abstract* he urged, "Call up your nearest baseball fan, right now, and ask him this question: How many more runs will you score in an inning when you have the leadoff man on than when you don't? I'll bet he says 28 percent or something. The answer is 242 percent." When you have data that strong, it's hard to ignore actions that go against it.

> Look, I'm trying very hard to make these analyses a factual and nonjudgmental look at what the manager does. But. There has got to be a point, some point, at which some decisions are clearly and objectively dumb. Del Crandall had Spike Owen batting leadoff last year, and I'm not talking about a few games. I mean two-and-a-half, three months. What on earth could have been in the man's head? Spike Owen is a .196 hitter, with a .259 on-base percentage. This is the man that you would choose to be the cornerstone of your offense? Man, that is insane. That is a crime against your ballclub.

In *Win Shares* he discussed one of many player-to-player comparisons that had troubled him over the years: Al Kaline versus Roberto Clemente. Clemente's batting average was twenty points higher, but Kaline drew twice as many walks and hit twice as many home runs. Clemente had ninety-six more base runner kills (Bill's suggestion for renaming outfielder assists) but made twice as many errors. Kaline's home field was no hitter's park, but it was a good home run park. Clemente's home was the inverse. "And so it goes," Bill wrote, "Clemente answers, Kaline answers. Of course, there are millions of fans who 'know' that Clemente was better, because they saw him play, and there are millions who 'know' that Kaline was better for the same reason. I don't want to 'know' that way. I want reasons."

14

Moving the Curve

Bill says, **"A** lot of people credit me with having influence on how baseball people think, but here's an example of how that's not always true. In the seventies, people would say what it takes to win on artificial turf is speed, or that speed is more effective on artificial turf. From the time it was first said, I was doing studies. The studies showed *there's nothing to it.* Speed is no more of an advantage on turf than on grass; except that if you're *very* slow, then it is a disadvantage. But the period from which someone first said that the way to win on turf is with speed, to the point where it was accepted as universal truth, was months. A year later it was hoary wisdom. You could print research for years showing there's nothing to it and have no effect on the discussion whatsoever."

New ideas change the world every day, but in twenty-first-century America there are millions of adults who hold Charles Darwin in contempt, and in baseball Joe Morgan calls Bill James "a joke." The culture wars are about people wanting facts to conform to personal belief. It would be nice to hear a general manager or manager tell it straight: "We realize having strong pitching and a weak offense will put us in a lot of close games mostly decided by luck, but we think the game is more exciting that way, and if we get lucky we'll look like geniuses." Or "We understand that the body of evidence says stealing bases is less important than getting on base in the first place, but we figure our fans want to see unrestrained speed on the base paths, so if our leadoff hitter has a .310 OBP and fifty steals, we'll accept it."

Instead, people predisposed to sacrifice power for "the little things" or on-base percentage for stolen bases will handpick facts to suit what they want to believe. And that's a beautiful thing. *Moneyball* was the best thing to happen to baseball in a long time, because it reinvigorated all the outsider-versus-insider hostilities Bill James set into motion twenty-five years ago.

There's a push-pull between common sense and science, an effect of how hard it is to get the facts straight in a complex world. Always trust common sense, right? Not so fast. The twisty twist is that breaking pitches do curve, but their trajectory is always smooth (unless the pitch is extremely slow, as in a knuckleball). What looks like a late, sudden break—"falling off the table"—really is an optical illusion.

Not long ago I heard a baseball announcer say that some managers like to look at things scientifically, while others go by the flow of the game. That sounds reasonable, but it's a false dichotomy, like "Some people use logic, others instinct." We all use both, and the more we develop both, the better our decision-making. Science and "flow" can seem to be at odds, but the challenge is to balance the science and the art.

You can't believe everything reported as science, but don't put too much faith in conventional wisdom, either. Ever heard of an animal called the aye-aye? It's a good pick for coolest-looking primate on the planet, but local superstition holds that it's an omen of evil—it looks like a devil—so it's on the edge of extinction in its native Madagascar.

Conventional baseball wisdom often makes about as much sense as persecuting a species because it looks spooky. One of Bill's most fervent essays was in defense of the baseball cousins of the aye-aye—the candidates for the Ken Phelps All-Star Team.

See, on the one hand you've got the Henry Cottos, and on the other hand, you've got your Ken Phelpses. If Henry Cotto is a major league ballplayer, I'm an airplane. Cotto is one of those guys who runs well and throws pretty decent, and one year he hit .270-something (in less than 150 at-bats, in Wrigley Field, with a secondary average of .164), so you get guys like Don Zimmer who will rave about this great young prospect and keep trading for him, so he'll get about eight chances to play in the major leagues before they figure out he can't hit. . . .

Ken Phelps has been a major league ballplayer since at least 1980, when he hit .294 with 128 walks and a slugging percentage close to .600 at AAA Omaha, a tough park for a hitter. Through 1985 he had 567 at-bats in the major leagues—one season's worth—with 40 home runs and 92 RBI. The Mariners still didn't want to let him play. See, the problem was that Chuck Cottier, in his day, was a Henry Cotto, a guy who could run and throw, but couldn't play baseball. Most major league managers were those kind of guys. Ken Phelps, on the other hand, can't run particularly well (although he isn't exceptionally slow, either) and doesn't throw well, and if you're that kind of player and want to play major league ball you'd better go 7-for-20 in your first week in the majors, or they'll decide it's time to take another look at Henry Cotto. . . .

Ken Phelpses are just *available*; if you want one, all you have to do is ask. They are players whose real limitations are exaggerated by baseball insiders, players who get stuck with a label—the label of their limits, the label of the things they *can't* do—while those that they can do are overlooked.

Phelps never saw regular playing time during his prime years. The most at-bats he had in a season was 344 in 1986, at age thirty-one, when he slugged .526 with a .406 on-base percentage. He did even better the next year (.548/.410), and in 1988 was traded to the Yankees in the infamous Jay Buhner deal.

Back to the aye-aye . . . it's a type of lemur. Lemurs are primates found only on Madagascar, an island that's been separated from East Africa for about a hundred million years. Isolated from competition, lemurs evolved in diverse ways. One type is as big as a panda, another is small as a mouse.

Correlating to Bill's misgivings about professionalism is his advocacy of diversity over standardization. He says major league baseball—and all sports—would be far better off if they would permit teams to do more to make one park distinctive from another—even making the bases eighty-five feet apart in one park, ninety-five in another.

"Standardization is an evil idea," he says. "'Let's pound everybody flat, so nobody has any unfair advantage.' Diversity enriches us, almost without exception. Who would want to live in a world in which all women looked the same, or all cars were the same, or all TV shows used the same format? People forget that into the 1960s, NBA courts were not all the same size—and the NBA would be a far better game today if they had never standardized the courts. What has happened to the NBA is, the players have gotten too large for the court. If they hadn't standardized the courts, they would have eventually noticed that a larger court makes a better game—a more open, active game. And the same in baseball. We would have a better game, ultimately, if teams were free to experiment with different options. The only reason baseball didn't standardize its park dimensions is that at the time that standardization was a popular idea, they just couldn't. Because of Fenway and a few other parks, baseball *couldn't* standardize its field dimensions in the 1960s—and thus dodged a mistake that they would otherwise quite certainly have made."

It points up a crucial aspect of how Bill thinks, one that takes a little getting used to if you're not in the habit of envisioning radical change. But what often happens is that as policies unfold over time, they have unintended consequences no one wants. Still, it's hard to see how things could be better when you're used to the way things are. If it seems crazy to suggest letting base paths be varying lengths, think hard on the point about park dimensions: If those had been standardized decades ago, it would seem just as crazy to say we should have one park with a thirty-foot wall in left field.

Bill believes that standardization destroys the ability to adapt; for instance, of the high pitching mounds of the sixties, he says, "We 'standardized' those by enforcing the rules, and I'm in favor of enforcing the rules, but suppose that the rules allowed some reasonable variation in the height of the pitching mound? What would have happened is that when the hitting numbers began to explode in the mid-1990s, teams would have pushed their pitching mounds up higher in order to offset the hitting explosion. The game would have adapted naturally to prevent home run hitters from entirely having their own way. Standardization leads to rigidity, and rigidity causes things to break."

These ideas link back to Bill's belief that antitrust exemption is unhealthy for the sport. There might seem to be a contradiction in the deep diversity of the isolated lemurs versus the idea that baseball's isolation chokes diversity. Bill says, "The difference is that baseball's structure restricts adaptation within the isolation. Baseball has to act as a unit. One team can't go to a 180-game schedule consisting of forty doubleheaders with twenty-five open dates on its own; the league has to act. One team cannot go to a twenty-two-man roster by itself; the league has to act. One team can't ban pointless mid-inning pitching changes by itself; the league has to act. By opening the game up, we would free ourselves of the constraint to act in concert with the entire rest of the civilized baseball world . . . a constraint that has no parallel among lemurs in Madagascar."

Bill once said that new information doesn't kill the old myths, it just breeds new ones. It's a complicated world. "There will always be people who are ahead of the curve," he says, "and people who are behind the curve. But knowledge moves the curve." That, for me, is how he changed baseball, by spawning new knowledge about the game like no one since Branch Rickey—"the only real genius baseball ever had," Bill says.

So, how to stay ahead of the curve, or at least not fall too far behind it?

Bill says, "If you look at Earl Weaver when he first reached the majors as a manager, his teams bunted almost an average amount. Over the years, they did it less and less. In part that's because he grew less afraid of being criticized for managing in an atypical way, so his true feelings about strategy came more and more to the fore. But it was also his way of simplifying the world. He had an idea about how to win games, and as he went along, that idea became simpler and simpler. I'm not sure that that process of simplification made him a better manager. He may have been better off at the start of his career, when he had misgivings about being counter-conventional.

"As we age, we get more narrow. I see the same thing with my writing career. I started out with a broad scope, and in some ways the books I wrote later are better books, but as I became more specialized, my ability to reach out to new audiences became more limited. Again, it's the process of becoming more narrow. The same thing happens to a baseball player. When he's twenty years old, he has a very broad range of unfinished skills. As he matures as a player, some of these skills are enhanced, but others drop off, and his skills narrow.

"It's a perfect image of the process—it happens to writers, it happens to managers, it happens to everyone. We rarely pick up new attributes. We develop some of the ones we have, the ones we don't develop atrophy, and we become more narrow. The better part of wisdom is to fight your own narrowing, to try to stay open to ideas that you don't understand and don't agree with. When you embrace your own ideas too warmly, you accelerate the process of becoming irrelevant."

Appendix
A Selection of Essential Ideas

The Defensive Spectrum

The defensive spectrum is a rough guide to the raw abilities needed to learn each defensive position. It runs: DH 1B LF RF 3B CF 2B SS. The catcher is unique, outside of the spectrum. The spectrum has shifted at times through history; for example, third base was a more demanding position than second base in the days of fewer double plays.

The better the organization, the more minor league talent piles up on the shortstop side of the spectrum.

In general, rightward shifts—e.g., moving a third baseman to shortstop—don't work well.

Secondary Average

Secondary average is a measure of the "kickers" to batting average: it's the sum of extra bases on hits, walks, and steals, expressed on a per-at-bat basis. It expresses the fact that a player who hits .240 can be on base more than a player who hits .320 if the .240 hitter is more selective; that the .240 hitter can drive in more runs if he spikes his average with enough power. Secondary average is a much better indicator of offensive ability than batting average.

The Whirlpool (or Plexiglas) Principle (or Effect)

All things in baseball tend to return to their previous form. A team whose record improves one year will tend to decline the following year, and vice versa. In 1980, for example, only five of the twenty-six teams moved in the same direction in which they moved in 1979. It also applies to individual players.

Bill found a way to express not merely the statistical principle of regression to the mean, but also what he called the 70/50 rule. Seventy percent of teams that decline in one year will improve the next; 70 percent of teams that improve will decline; and in all cases the amount of rise or fall is about 50 percent, so that a team twenty games over .500 one year would be ten games over .500 the next. (The percentages are much different for very big or very small improvements and declines.)

"These were not things that I had expected to find," Bill wrote. "Weaned on the notion of 'momentum' since childhood, I had expected a team which won eighty-three games one year and eighty-seven the next to continue to improve, to move on to ninety; instead, they consistently relapsed. Half-expecting to find that the rich grow richer and the poor grow poorer, I found instead that the rich and the poor converged on a common target at an alarming rate of speed."

The Law of Competitive Balance

This is the force that drives the Whirlpool Effect. The separate strategies logically adopted by winners and losers on balance favor the team that is behind. The essence of the difference is how the two groups approach the need for adjustment. Teams that are winning tend to ignore or not notice their weaknesses. Teams that are losing will (and are more free to) make needed changes.

Tim Foli Effect

Almost every year, some player moves from a bad-hitting team to a good-hitting one, and his hitting will markedly improve. He'll usually attribute the improvement to "seeing better pitches" (e.g., the pitchers don't want to walk Tim Foli with Dave Parker coming up). But it often turns out that the gains in the player's stats are made largely or entirely in his new home park. "But what's he going to say?" Bill wrote. "'No, I'm as bad a hitter as ever, it's just that this park makes me look better.'" In cases where the player moves to a *better*-hitting team that plays in a *worse* park for hitters, the player's numbers will often go down.

Bill calls major league equivalencies the most surprising development of his career. What he found, specifically, was that "the chance of a player having a 'break' in his record between the minors and majors was no greater than the chance of his having a break in his record as a major league performer."

He wrote, "Baseball men generally believe that minor league batting statistics are not a reliable indicator of how a player will hit in the major leagues. After studying the issue extensively, I concluded that minor league batting statistics predicted major league performance with the same accuracy as previous major league batting statistics."

MLEs require park adjustments and league adjustments, as you'd expect, plus translations to the majors, but ultimately they show that "good minor league talent is a far better thing to bet on than 'proven' major league talent that isn't good enough to win."

> The basis of jockism is the belief, which journalists for the most part are unwilling to challenge—indeed they have been nauseatingly active in its promotion—that only men who play the game "between the white lines" have meaning and value, that only their opinions count, that only they can understand the game. This absurd presumption, though it separates major leaguers from ordinary men and thus makes them smaller and less significant than they deserve to be, is nonetheless attractive to them because within their own universe it confers a uniqueness and thus a special value. The belief has its counterparts in every profession, in every town, in each junior high school, and in every heart; it goes variously by such names as elitism, cliquishness, racism, and smugness. It is a small step, then, to one further

shrinking and trivialization of their experience: that only that which happens in the *major league* white lines really counts.

The belief that minor league stats don't correlate to major league performance is partly a function of not understanding that the distortions of different parks and leagues can be corrected for, and that most of the instances of a player being a minor league stud and a major league dud, or vice versa, stem from either the team giving up on the player too quickly or the minor league stats being mistranslated.

Bill wrote that the belief that minor league stats aren't meaningful is in virtually all cases a result of misreading, not an absence of meaning. Wade Boggs was often cited as an example of a player who was much better than his minor league numbers indicated, but once the fact that he was in a pitcher's park and a pitcher's league was factored in, his MLEs projected him to be a great major league hitter.

Major leaguer performance can and does fluctuate from year to year, yet who would argue that major league statistics don't mean much because Adrian Beltre hit .240 in 2003 and .334 in 2004? Jerry Mumphrey stole fifty-two bases in fifty-seven tries one year. The rest of his career he was a counterproductive 60 percent base stealer. There's no magic formula in any form of analysis. Even a consistent player will have big season-to-season swings. Colorado batting numbers don't mean the same thing Seattle numbers do; but, again, that doesn't mean major league statistics aren't meaningful.

Bill wrote up his findings in the '85 *Abstract*, but the impact was heavier in some quarters than others. Bill later wrote, "I was asserting something which is directly contrary to the prevailing wisdom of baseball. I felt that it would not be advisable to keep pushing the issue."

A Low K Rate Equals a Short Career

There is a still-prevalent belief in some old-school baseball quarters that strikeouts are not that important. In the late seventies, Dallas Adams and Bill looked into the question of how to spot a rookie pitcher who would last and develop. They found that there is no such thing as a pitcher who has a long career with a low strikeout rate. "If a pitcher's strikeout rate is less than 4.5 per nine innings, you can pretty much write him off as somebody who is going to have a real career," Bill wrote in the *New Historical Abstract*. Not all power pitchers have long careers, of course, just as not all tall people play in the NBA. But just as your chances of playing in the NBA increase with each inch of height, your chances of having a career as a major league pitcher go up with your strikeout rate. Tommy John, Jimmy Key, and Tom Glavine "define exactly how many strikeouts you absolutely have to have to win consistently in the major leagues, if you're left-handed and you do everything well."

More on Clutch Ability . . . Or, Why Talk About Something We Can't Prove Exists?

Bill wrote:

> A friend of mine, whom we will call Beelzebub because he's about to get me in a lot of trouble, makes the following argument:
>
> a. It is stupid to talk about clutch ability if you don't even know whether or not it exists.
> b. No one has ever offered any proof at all that it does exist (or even a definition of exactly what it is, if it does).
> c. People talk about clutch performance constantly, ergo
> d. People
>
> Well, OK, we're stupid. No, no one has proven that clutch ability exists, and no one will ever prove that it doesn't exist. Why? Can you prove that dodo birds are extinct? We only *believe* dodo birds and dinosaurs are extinct; we can't prove it. The subject requires an honest search, and I'll keep looking.

Batters Who Are Willing to Walk with a Man on Base Hit into Fewer Double Plays

Mickey Tettleton, Gene Tenace, Darren Daulton . . . Bill wrote, "A lot of double plays come when a hitter reaches for an outside pitch that he ought to take, and hits a ground ball to shortstop or second base."

Burt Shotton Syndrome

When you replace an intense, detail-focused manager with a low-key type, on a good ballclub, Bill wrote, "the ballclub will very often have a sustained period, a period of a year or more, in which the talent seems to simply gush out of them." Jim Frey following Whitey Herzog in KC, Bob Lemon after Billy Martin in New York, Burt Shotton following Leo Durocher in Brooklyn, and there are others.

The intense guys tend to be teachers, among other things, and if they're too overbearing, they trigger a defense mechanism. "The problem with low-key managers," Bill wrote, "is that most of the time they don't have a very good command of details, nor indeed a very strong command of anything." Eventually the team loses confidence in the low-key manager, at which point it's time to switch to a strategist, a tactician—such as in replacing Shotton with Chuck Dressen, or Frey with Dick Howser.

Miracles Happen in Compressed Leagues

"If anybody offers you 100 odds against the Chicago Cubs winning the National League East in 1984, take him up on it," Bill wrote in the '84 *Abstract.* The Cubs, who had finished next to last in 1983, and the Mets, who'd finished last, came in one-two in 1984. Bill had written that if he had ever seen a dead giveaway setup for a miracle, the Cubs coming into '84 were it. He listed six reasons, among them that miracles usually happen in leagues in which the difference between the best team and the worst is thin (as in the NL East in 2005).

Image Isn't Everything

In the '84 Abstract, Bill wrote of Red Sox manager Ralph Houk, "In Houk's first year as a manager, 1961, he had a tremendously successful season leading off Bobby Richardson. Richardson, frankly, was a horrible leadoff man. He rarely got on base and almost never got into scoring position. Leading off for the 1961 Yankees, playing 162 games and batting 662 times, with 237 home runs coming up behind him, Richardson scored only 80 runs. 80. Eight-zero. Dick Howser scored 28 more runs that year while batting leadoff for the 1961 Kansas City Athletics, who hit 90 home runs and lost 100 games. Plus, Richardson used up a zillion outs while he was not scoring runs."

> And ever since then, Houk has been leading off these terrible lit-tle second basemen who may be good defensively, but who hit .270, have no power at all, and don't walk. It's painful to think how many runs he must have cost his team by this nonsense over the course of the last twenty years. Jerry Remy, the winner of the 1983 Bobby Richardson look-alike contest, had an on-base per-centage of .321 (the league average for all players was .330), reached scoring position under his own power only 32 times, and scored only 73 runs; still he is probably an above-average Houk leadoff man.

The managerial habit of using image to guide lineup selection came up in regard to Cubs first baseman Mark Grace, who hit third despite having a two-hitter's skills, and second baseman Ryne Sand-berg, a made-to-order three-hole hitter slotted second instead. "Why?" Bill wrote. "Images."

Leave a Good Young Player Alone

In the '82 *Abstract,* Bill wrote about the Mets' treatment of Lee Mazz-illi, "They played him in center for three years, moved him to first, benched him to get Kingman in the lineup, and returned him to the outfield. They talk a lot about his throwing arm—'He doesn't throw well enough to play center.' Well, I don't doubt that. What I am saying is that the cost of keeping his throwing arm in center field could not possibly have been as great as the cost of moving him around like he was a nobody."

When the above-mentioned Dave Kingman was in San Francisco, something similar happened. For three years the Giants shifted him from first to third to the outfield. Bill wrote, "First of all, I do not understand how it could take somebody two-and-a-half years to figure out that Dave Kingman was not a third baseman. But the central point I am making is that the Giants lack or lacked the ability to make a decision about what a young player could do and set that young player about the business of learning to do it."

Bill saw the potential of young Cardinals outfielder Andy Van Slyke in 1984:

> The handling of the talented Van Slyke, a young Joe Morgan–type offensive player, has been equally difficult to justify. Whitey has shifted him from position to position, never really giving him a chance to adjust to any job. With his outstanding stolen base percentage, ability to get one base, and power, Van Slyke was one of the Cardinals' best offensive players last year when he hit .244. He created 5.10 runs per 27 outs used, the only Cardinal to do better was Terry Pendleton, in 67 games. If Whitey gives him a job to do and leaves him alone, he's going to be a terrific player.

Traded to Pittsburgh for the 1987 season, Van Slyke *was* great, creating 108 runs (6.94 per 27 outs).

Build a Ball Club out of Ballplayers

From 1975 to 1979, Bill listened to Whitey Herzog's manager's show on the radio every evening during the season. "I always enjoyed turning on the radio about 7:10 each evening to see if Whitey had been thinking about the same things I was thinking about," Bill wrote in the '83 *Abstract*.

> There are things Herzog believes in *a priori*. He believes in building a team that is close-knit. He believes that you can't do any-

thing unless you have players who want to win. He is never afraid to take a chance with an unproven player, if that player has ability and shows desire. He doesn't tell you those things flat out, but they come through plain enough. Those things he would carry with him no matter where he went. But the style of play? The shape of his ball club is the shape of his talent and the shape of his ballpark. Herzog is too smart to believe in building a ball club by trading, or building a ball club from free agency, or building a ball club out of the farm system. He believes in building a ball club out of ballplayers. That's all.

Baseball Statistics Aren't Good at Abstract Relationships

This comes up when we try to understand, for example, clutch performance. How do we know to what extent a good or bad performance "in the clutch" is situation-related, not simply part of the player's overall performance tendencies? Bill wrote, "Baseball statistics are best at counting things, and not terribly good at expressing abstract relationships."

Ideas for Free Agent Signings

1. When you talk yourself into thinking you *need* a player, that's when you overpay for him.
2. Teams underestimate how hard it is to accurately evaluate their needs.
3. Great players are less vulnerable to value fluctuations than ordinary players.
4. It's generally better to forget about trying to fill needs, and simply sign the best player you can afford. "When George signed Reggie," Bill wrote, "some very smart baseball people said: 'What'd he do that for? They've already got left-handed power on that team.'" Same for signing Gossage when they already had a

Cy Young reliever, and Tommy John when they already had left-handed starters. "I'm mostly propounding a theory here, not asserting that the theory has validity," he wrote. "But I think it has some validity."

Baseball Statistics Are Circular

When something happens to the offense, it also happens to the defense, and vice versa. "One way to put it," Bill wrote, "would be that if a suit cost a dollar in 1900 and a gallon of milk cost $1.45 in 1986, that doesn't mean that the suits of 1900 were poorly made or the milk of 1986 is especially delicious. It just means that the cost has changed." If a utility infielder hit .320 in 1930 and a batting champ hit .301 in 1968, that does not mean that the utility infielder was a better hitter, nor does it mean that the pitchers of the sixties were better than the pitchers of the thirties. It means that the cost of a win, in terms of hits, has changed. This is a crucial point when comparing, say, Joe Morgan's stats to Rogers Hornsby's.

You Have to Be Skeptical of All of It

Bill says, "The extent to which you can trust your eyes is limited, but the extent to which you can trust the numbers is limited, too. If you watched Johnny Damon hit, based on his swing and his follow-through and his balance, you would think he couldn't hit—but he can. The visual impression is not contradicted by 'analysis'; it is contradicted by the outcomes. That's pretty common. There are fielders who look bad, but get the job done. There are pitchers who look like they are quick to first base, but who never pick anybody off. There are catchers who look awkward throwing, but who don't give up many stolen bases. But there are pitchers who go 15–11 who aren't really good pitchers. There are hitters who hit .310 but don't help you, there are fielders who field .980 who don't help you. You have to be skeptical of all of it."

What's Fun to Watch?

Bill wrote in 1979 that while the home run is exciting, "a .230 hitter swinging from the heels is not." His daughter Rachel remembers that when she was about ten, the SABR conference was in Kansas City, and her dad was giving a speech. "Because it was just a day trip, he decided to take me with him. I listened carefully when Dad gave his speech, about the pitfalls and failures of modern baseball. At one point, he made a criticism of the emphasis on home run hitting, saying, 'We need young quick guys who can run around the bases, not old fat guys who can hit home runs.' At the end of the speech, there was time for some Q&A, so I raised my hand and said, 'Daddy, you said we shouldn't have old fat guys who hit home runs. But wasn't the greatest player of all time an old fat guy who hit home runs?' All of the attendees burst into laughter, including Dad, and he told me, yes, but when Ruth was young, he was quick and could run the bases."

The Next Willie Mays

When you hear someone say that a young player is the next Willie Mays, keep in mind what Mays did at age twenty-three: 41/110/.345 (.411 OBP/.667 SLG). The next year, he started stealing bases, going 24 for 28. As great a hitter as Albert Pujols is on the same age track, he doesn't have the speed or the glove. Carlos Beltran? By head-to-head comparison at the same ages, there's no comparison. Comparisons to Willie Mays aren't fair to anyone.

Hazards of Aggressive Baserunning

Bill wrote, "An offense is a chain. The value of the chain depends upon its length, how far it will reach. Imagine that this chain is six feet long, but if you stretch out each length of the chain, maybe you can make the chain seven feet long instead of six. But if you stretch a link too hard and it breaks in the middle, then what? Then what you've got is two worthless pieces of three-foot chain."

He doesn't argue that the stolen base can't be a useful part of an offense, especially for the right team in the right park. But, he explains, "On many teams, the impact of having a running threat at first base is negative, not positive. It is very clear that this is true if you start with the facts, rather than the theory. What happens on a lot of teams is, the hitter takes pitches in order to allow the runner to steal and finds himself hitting from behind in the count. It's a bad trade and another way the running game will bite you in the ass if you give it the chance."

If the Context in Which a Decision Was Made Has Changed, Review the Decision

Bill wrote, "The defining characteristic of the Reds' organization under Dick Wagner was inflexibility. The fact that this rigidity was allied to old-line 'disciplinarian' policies is certainly not incidental, but my point is that there have been any number of successful hard-line managers and organizations. If you keep the hard-line policies but get rid of the inflexibility, then you are dealing with a totally different situation. . . .

"Dick Wagner was like a man driving down a road who is stopped and informed that a section of the bridge over the river has collapsed, and who responds to this by saying, 'Goddammit, the county is supposed to maintain that bridge. I pay taxes, I've been driving over that bridge for thirty years, and I feel that I have a right to drive over that bridge.' And so he does."

The DH rule *increases* strategy

Franklin Roosevelt said that necessitous men are not free men . . . must've been a DH man.

In the '84 *Abstract,* Bill presented a chart showing how many times teams scored a certain number of runs in each inning. It revealed that in the American League, there was a sharp division between big-inning teams and the others; a large gap between teams that invest, say, 160 outs a year on first-run strategies and those that invest considerably less than a hundred. In the NL there was no such gap. "Everybody bunts, and everybody runs," Bill wrote.

> I think that this points up something I have written before, which is that the designated hitter rule, far from draining strategy out of the game, simply removes from the game the most trite, predictable, nonstrategic part of it. Strategy exists only in making choices, only in the face of options. The National League game confronts the NL manager with frequent no-option situations, situations in which he *must* bunt or he *must* pinch hit. The American League game allows a true option, and thus true strategy. That is clearly reflected in the fact that the American League has clear groups of big-inning teams and one-run teams, while the National League does not.

You Cannot Win a Pennant by Stealing Bases

Bill wrote in the '83 *Abstract*, "Nobody ever has, nobody ever will. It cannot be done. It is an argument that cannot be won, a position that cannot be defended."

This, of course, doesn't mean a team that steals bases can't win. But comparing head-to-head matchups from 1969 through 1985 of teams with more steals versus teams with higher slugging percentages, batting averages, etc., he found that teams stealing a lot of bases lost consistently to teams holding an advantage in any other offensive category.

Also, teams leading the league in steals had a lower average finish in the division standings than teams leading the league in any other major category. Teams finishing last in the league in steals averaged a higher finish in the standings than those finishing last in any other category except triples. Bill wrote:

One of the things that I like about this study is that it also refutes many of the side issues which are so often used to confuse the issue. People say, for example, that stolen bases are important because they intimidate the opposition. Intimidating the opposition is nice, but winning is more the point of the game. If, in fact, stolen bases had intimidation value that paid off in the win column, then that would cause those teams to finish higher in the standings, would cause the gaps between the teams which have speed and those that do not to grow larger. People say that speed is valuable because it pays off in opposition errors. Well, that's great, but *why don't they win?* People say that speed is important because it enables people to go from first to third on a single, that it is important because it can be used in defense as well as offense. But this method of measuring its importance wouldn't care why it was important, and as such it throws a road block in front of any and all of those arguments.

Crucial to an analysis of the stolen base's impact is seeing that there may be as many negative side effects as positive. An active base runner can distract a hitter as much as he can a pitcher. The batter may see more fastballs with a fast runner on first, but he may also feel the need to take good pitches so the runner can try to steal. Willie McGee, a .300 hitter from '84 through '86, hit just .253 with runners on first base, "a situation in which batting averages usually soar." Bill surmised that this was due to taking pitches to allow Vince Coleman to steal. "Just one of the little hidden advantages of the running game," Bill chided.

Of course there are real positive side-benefits. . . . I think it is certainly true that Willie McGee had an outstanding year in 1985 in part because he was able to take advantage of the tendency of pitchers to throw fastballs with Coleman on first. My point is not that such side-benefits do not exist, but that there is no reasonable basis for the assumption that the sum of them is significantly positive. If it were significantly positive, one would expect that base-stealing teams would be winning teams, and that simply isn't true; many of them are losers.

One team he felt was an exception to the rule: the 1987 Cardinals.

One-run strategies diminish the chances of a big inning, but because the first five runs a team scores will be enough to win most of the time, it's possible that playing for single runs tends to "rearrange runs into more productive groups," Bill wrote. "A team that uses first-run strategies a lot may tend to score five runs in two games rather than zero in one and ten in the next. A problem with the argument in general is that you will have a heck of a time proving that this benefit actually does accrue to the teams which use first-run strategies."

But in the case of the '87 Cardinals, the benefit was there. St. Louis scored fewer than three runs just thirty-three times, while the pitchers did a great job of winning when given three to five runs to work with.

St. Louis was a lightning rod in the debate in the 1980s. Playing in a stadium that drastically reduced home runs, the '85 Cards were "one of the greatest base-stealing forces of all time." This was in large part due to rookie Vince Coleman, on whom people heaped credit for the team's division title. Yet the '85 Cardinals also topped the league in on-base percentage, the importance of which, Bill had written "God knows how many times," is "the one most universal truth about good offenses."

Coleman contributed little in OBP but swiped 110 bases. The rest of the regulars, except for Terry Pendleton, stole their share of bases and *also* posted high OBPs.

Many teams which get as many people on base as the 1985 Cardinals did will score *more* runs—for example, the 1978 Milwaukee Brewers had almost exactly the same number of runners on base as the Cardinals did, yet scored 57 more runs. This is because power is a much more effective way of increasing the percentage of runners who score than is speed. But the Cardinals compensated for their lack of power (and the difficulty of hitting a home run in Busch Stadium) with base stealing, and they did a good job of it.

Bill ran studies to determine roughly how many runs were added to the Cardinals offense by stolen bases, finding that although they would have still led the league in runs, there was a very good chance they wouldn't have won the division. St. Louis didn't win the pennant *because* of the stolen base, but they probably wouldn't have won without it. The '85 Redbirds were an exceptional case. Bill wrote, "There were many examples of base-stealing teams being successful teams prior to 1985. There is one more now. There were many examples of base-stealing teams being unsuccessful teams. There still are. The ratio has changed by one, that's all."

Batting Order Doesn't Matter Much

Baseball fans like to talk about batting orders, but lineup selection isn't nearly as important as most of us are used to thinking. A study printed in *Fortune* in 1985, using a computer model of the Mets, compared a "traditional" batting order, a random order, and one that put the best hitter first and regressed from there. The random order, with Gary Carter batting second and Darryl Strawberry seventh, behind Rafael Santana, came out the best of the three. Not proof, but interesting.

A study by sabermetrician Dick Cramer found that a model of a team consisting of six pitchers and three Babe Ruths performed essentially the same whether the trio of Ruths batted one-two-three (the most logical) or three-six-nine (the least). In the *Guide to Managers*, Bill cited Cramer's results, and reported those of his own study, which confirmed that "it doesn't make much difference what order you put the hitters in."*

---

*General managers may have a different concept of "much difference," considering how much some shell out for a relatively small contribution.

Although you can think of a thousand reasons why batting order *should* matter, the reason it doesn't is that if you move the best hitter to the worst spot, you may wipe out 20 percent of his RBIs, but, as Bill stressed, *"you can't move everybody down in the batting order."* Enough of those RBIs are picked up by the other hitters that, in the final analysis, the team loses about 5 percent of its run production if using an illogical batting order. Bill wrote, "You take any two reasonable batting orders for any team, put them on a computer and play a hundred seasons, and you'll find they score just as many runs one way as they do another."

The simulator that Bill used was of "reasonable sophistication." At the same time, he wrote, "real baseball games remain vastly more complex than our statistical models of them. For that reason, it is possible that in the future more sophisticated models will yield different results."

> But for now this discussion has two groups. On the one hand you have the barroom experts, the traditional sportswriters, the couch potatoes, and the call-in show regulars, all of whom believe that batting orders are important. And then, on the other hand, you have a few of us who have actually studied the issue, and who have been forced to draw the conclusion that it doesn't make much difference what order you put the hitters in, they're going to score just as many runs one way as another. You can believe whoever you want; it's up to you.

The Devil's Theory of Park Effects

Stadium architecture varies, such that there are a range of hitter's parks, pitcher's parks, and neutral parks. A team should be configured to take advantage of its home park. Yet a fascinating phenomenon Bill discovered was that a team playing in a hitter's park, for example, will tend to have weaker hitters and stronger pitching and defense. The reason: The park effect of inflating the hitters' statistics leads the organization to think its offense is strong enough. Meanwhile, the pitchers, being adversely treated by the park, post stats that make them look worse than they are. The team will focus on getting better pitching, neglecting to get better hitters. Of course, this causes the team to lose, but often the cycle will continue, as management blames the wrong guys year after year.

Similarity Scores

Twenty-five years after he first became fascinated with players' similarities to each other, Bill introduced similarity scores for evaluating the "degree of resemblance" between teams or players. He had met an Air Force man who told him about a system for predicting weather by coding detailed information from past weather patterns, isolating the past situation most similar to the present one, and guessing that history would tend to repeat.

Bill wasn't able to immediately adapt the concept to sabermetrics, but in time he did. This is how it works, in a nutshell: Players (or teams) who are identical in all the areas considered are given a baseline score of 1,000. For every difference between the two, in specified categories, a reduction is made. A final score of 500 or lower indicates the two are essentially not similar. A score of 900 or more indicates strong similarity. Similarity scores can also be used to compare a single player's various seasons to each other, as a measure of consistency.

One of the most important uses of similarity scores is in defining control groups. Bill wrote:

> When people state a proposition, they tend to state it in an "other things being equal" form. Other things being equal, a child raised in poverty is more likely to commit a crime than a child raised in wealth. The problem with checking that out is that wealth and poverty create so many secondary characteristics with respect to health, education, and orthodontia that it is nearly impossible to distinguish groups of children which are the same in many important respects if they are different in this one

respect. Other things being equal, a bird could run faster than a man because the relevant muscles are twenty-eight times as strong, but did you ever try to find a bird that had the body weight and general configuration of a person?

In sabermetrics we have the same problem. We can say that other things being equal, a player who plays the outfield is more likely to develop as a hitter than one who plays the middle infield—but the problem is that outfielders and middle infielders are not alike in many ways, and it is difficult to distinguish the degree to which any subsequent development results from the position, rather than (to pick one) the fact that the outfielders were better hitters to start with.

Using similarity scores, it would be possible to hold the other things constant so that this could be studied. It would be possible to define two groups of players who have essentially identical characteristics as hitters and as to age, but one group of outfielders and one of infielders.

Bill wrote, "It is not an exaggeration to say that 90 percent of salary negotiations in baseball are an attempt to define the group of the most similar players." Thus similarity scores can be useful in that respect.

The method can be used for building theoretical models of teams or players, then picking real teams or players who are like the model and studying how they're affected by conditions or events. If, for example, you think a certain type of pitcher might have a rough time in Fenway Park, you can set up a statistical model of that pitcher and identify the real pitchers who are most similar to him, then check how they've done at Fenway.

Talent in Baseball Is Not Normally Distributed

Talent in the general population, when plotted on a graph, looks like a bell-shaped curve, with the largest number of people in the center, and the extremes of high and low at opposing ends.

Sort of. A major problem here is that . . . in most measures of anything you can think of, the measurement itself is closed on one end. If your average time for the hundred yard dash in this group is 17 seconds, it is much more likely that you will have somebody who requires 27 seconds to accomplish the task than it is that you will have somebody who can do the hundred yards in 7 flat. The easiest way to deal with this problem, mathematically speaking, is to round up all of the people in your group who run the hundred in more than 24 seconds and shoot them. If you don't shoot them, then you've got to take a whole lot of math classes, and we don't have time for that here.

In major league baseball, all talent is drawn from the high-talent end of the general population—the right side of the bell. Thus within the pool of pro players, the most common level of talent is the bottom, not the average.

What's crucial to know is that major league talent is *not* in short supply. In fact, *the belief that it is* and *the understanding that it isn't* are what separate good clubs from bad ones. "Poor organizations," Bill wrote, "believe that there is a magic in 'proven' major league talent. . . .

"Players from the far right part of the graph are anything but available; they're precious. But all the same, I would say that if you look at any successful manager, with very few exceptions you'll find a manager who is not afraid to make changes. You'll find a manager who is not afraid to look at a kid who has not proven what he can do in the major leagues, and say, 'This kid can help me.'"

Unsuccessful organizations have good excuses for their timidity; they say things like "minor league batting records don't mean anything" and "young pitchers will break your heart." But what it comes down to is, they have no confidence in their own judgment, their ability to solve a problem. They look at their lineup and when they consider the possibility of making a change, they see themselves as teetering on the brink of an abyss. A Whitey

Herzog, a Billy Martin, a Dick Williams, a Bobby Cox, or an Earl Weaver doesn't see it that way.

More on Closers

Do some clubs knowingly choose a less-able pitcher who has proven he has the "makeup" to finish games? Bill says, "Probably, but maybe more is said about this than is necessary. There is a natural reluctance to put the game into unproven hands, which sometimes leads to less than optimal pitcher usage patterns. You can interpret that as a 'strategy' or as a consequence of a belief system if you want to, but it seems to me that it may be more accurately stated as a natural consequence of the desire to put the ballgame into safe and proven hands. Yes, there are closers who have undeserved success, but then, there are starting pitchers who go 18–7 although they aren't really very good, either, and there are cleanup hitters who drive in 100 runs with .295 on-base percentages, and you can have them, too. I'm not really convinced that there are more 'undeserving saviors' than there are undeserving stars at other positions; it's just that, for some reason, there is more comment about them. I think there is more comment about them because there is something about the role, that you have to be *chosen* for it, you have to be anointed the closer, which triggers debate about your credentials."

Leadership, Character, and Positive Thinking

In the Reggie Jackson comment of the '84 *Abstract,* Bill wrote, "Many athletes truly believe that they are successful at what they do not because God made them strong and fast and agile, but because *they're better people than the rest of us.* And in order to believe that, they must believe that the games themselves are not merely contests of skill and luck, but are tests of *character* and *determination* and *will.* That's where all the bullshit about clutch ability comes from. Clutch ability is that thing that wells up from inside you when the game is on the line, that thing that separates the 'winners' from the 'losers,' that thing which *only an athlete can possess*, and therefore only an athlete can understand."

Bill had had a long conversation with a friend who tried to convince him that character and attitude had nothing to do with winning a pennant, that they didn't even exist.

> He reminded me about the way that Clemente when he came up and Joe Morgan when he came up and Frank Robinson in his early years got labeled "attitude problems." Then, of course, as soon as Clemente learned to hit a curve ball, he was a great human being, and the "attitude" label went away. Did his attitude ever really have anything to do with it?
>
> But *of course* "attitude" is real, and so is "character" and "determination" and "will." Wanting to win a pennant has *everything* to do with winning a pennant. . . .
>
> But if athletes keep debasing those qualities by focusing them on ridiculously small moments in a person's life, if they keep using them to explain every dramatic success and every dismal failure, then they're eventually going to convince the public that they don't exist, at all.

In the Twins comment of the '87 *Abstract,* he wrote that manager Ray Miller was reportedly convinced that attitude is almost as important for a reliever as a major league fastball. "By the end of the year," Bill wrote, "nobody had too much faith in what Ray Miller thought were the attributes of an effective reliever."

From there, maybe it's easy to conclude that Bill James thinks attitude isn't part of being an effective reliever. One journalist, on Octavio Dotel's struggles as the A's closer in 2004, wrote that Dotel "hasn't exactly proven that he's got the closer's mentality," and added: "Sorry, Bill James, but makeup is just as important as strikeout-to-walk ratios for closers."

The elements that go into making any player effective are a balance of health, luck, mentality, and talent. Bill clearly believes mentality is part of the equation. "There are managers who almost never have serious bullpen problems," he wrote, "because they can look at the physical and mental makeup of the pitchers in camp, pick out a horse to ride, and teach him what he needs to know."

In the Braves comment of the '87 *Abstract*, Bill eviscerated Chuck Tanner as "a parody of positive thinking, representing positive thought chopped loose from life or the understanding of life, positive thought rescued from the sea of values and hailed supreme over all others, positive thinking lying on a great pedestal as dead as a beached tuna."

> The problem isn't with the idea that a team will play better if they keep a positive frame of mind. The problem is that that homily is Chuck Tanner's entire concept of how to manage a baseball team. . . . He has no concept of how it is, exactly, that he is going to win, except that he figures if everybody has a good year we'll win.

The issue, then, isn't makeup or chemistry or leadership or attitude, it's the citing of intangibles abstracted from ability and results, as if any of the three stand alone. In the Cleveland comment of the '87 *Abstract*, Bill wrote about Joe Carter:

> Leadership is a hard thing to define and there are people who think I am betraying sabermetrics every time I mention the word, but Carter was a player who gave the opposition *nothing*. If he hit a single and you didn't hustle in after it, he'd take second. If the team was ten runs behind, he'd try twice as hard, his theatrical hustle becoming an unmistakable message to the rest of the team that I'm not giving these bastards anything and you'd better not give them anything, either. They haven't beat us until we quit.

Free Agent Economics

Bill wrote a series of articles for the *Baseball Bulletin* arguing that the value of individual players in terms of wins was being "enormously overstated." While baseball men were saying this or that player was worth an extra ten to twenty wins a season, the evidence showed the variation between an average player and a superstar at the same position was three to five games.

There were at least half a dozen methods that proved it, the most persuasive being that the standard deviation of team wins in a statistical model was "around nine games." Given that a ball club consists of fifteen to eighteen "roles," Bill wrote, "it is irrational to suggest that the impact of a player playing one of those roles could be twice the standard deviation of the whole."

This appeared to finally take root in the minds of baseball owners when Bruce Sutter, baseball's top reliever in 1984, jumped from St. Louis to Atlanta as a free agent. The teams had compiled roughly identical records in '84, but after Sutter left, St. Louis improved by thirty-five games. The Braves, with Sutter, came out fourteen games worse. Bill wrote that this provided the final bullet to the idea that one player could turn a team around.

> What I did *not* foresee at that time were the full economic consequences of the misperception. One of the unwritten laws of economics is that it is impossible, truly impossible, to prevent the values of society from manifesting themselves in dollars and cents. This is, ultimately, the reason why we pay athletes so much money: that it is very important to us to be represented by winning teams. The standard example is cancer research; letters pop up all the time saying that it is absurd for baseball players to make twenty times as much money as cancer researchers. But the hard, unavoidable fact is that we are, as a nation, far more interested in having good baseball teams than we are in finding a cure for cancer.
>
> That pool of money which we pour into athletics makes it inevitable that athletes are going to be better paid than cancer researchers. *Dollars and cents are an incarnation of our values. Economic realities represent not what we should believe, not what*

we like to say that we believe, not what we might choose to believe in a more perfect world, but what our beliefs really are. However much we complain about it, nobody can stop that truth from manifesting itself.

The internal economic structures of baseball determine only one thing: how much of that money will go to the players, and how much the owners will get to keep. Owners, from 1978 to 1983, tried mightily to slow down the amount of money that was going to the players—but they truly believed that a star player could win them an extra ten or twenty games a year. The salaries of players rose to a level that was commensurate with that belief.

But in this way, economics ultimately correct the belief. Baseball men could *say* that a player was worth ten or fifteen or twenty games a year, and they could go on believing that—as long as they didn't have to pay for it. But when they had to begin putting the dollars out to back that up, they were forced to reexamine their belief, and to realize that it was false.

Teams that take heavy free agent losses do suffer a drop in performance over the longer term, and teams that sign multiple free agents gain a small advantage, his studies showed. Nevertheless, he concluded that "free agents have hurt their new teams almost as often as they have helped them. The gain clearly does not justify the expense."

When salaries trend down, collusion among the owners becomes a question. Bill wrote, "I'm not saying that there was no collusion on the part of the owners. I am saying this: *collusion only works when the owners believe it is in the individual, selfish interest of each ballclub to make it work.* Early in the free agent era, the owners *said* that the salaries were too high—but they truly *believed* that they could help their teams by signing players at the prices being asked. Following the fiasco of the 1984 free agent crop, they no longer believe that. Now they actually *believe* that the free agent outlays are not justified by the probable return. That is the difference."

The cycle has repeated often since the mid-eighties. In off-season

2004 there were whispers of collusion. In winter 2005 there was "reverse collusion," as Jim Baker put it. In a BaseballProspectus.com column, he noted that most GMs are bipolar: "As we know, one of the symptoms of a bipolar person acting out is frivolous spending. One such person I saw documented bankrupted herself in about sixty days merely by buying non-stop from the Home Shopping Network. She had so much stuff coming in she did not have time to open all the boxes. They were stacked floor-to-ceiling in her apartment, rising like the towers of a great city built in tribute to her chemical imbalance."

Pirates GM Dave Littlefield has commented, "The formula of one player eating up a significant portion of the payroll just doesn't work." He points to Alex Rodriguez in Texas as the easiest example. It's been countered that A-Rod wasn't the problem, that the market did shift after he signed his deal, but he was one of the best players in the league while with the Rangers.

But another way to see A-Rod in Texas is as a Bugatti Type 41 Royale. The Type 41 may have been the most amazing car ever, but production got under way at the start of the Great Depression, and only four were ever sold. The words "Type 41" are now found in close proximity to "folly" and "hubris" in the chronicles of automotive history. The car was everything it was designed to be—just as A-Rod did what he was supposed to do—but if the plan was to sell a bunch of them and make a fat profit, it didn't work, and who knows what Bugatti could have done with the resources spent on the Type 41.

The trick isn't just to get great play from a given free agent, it's to balance salary versus how many wins one player can create if he fulfills expectations. If the goal is to win, it can still have been a mistake for Texas to devote the lion's share of their payroll to one player, because, among other things, it left them with less margin for error in putting together the rest of the team.

None of which is to argue that signing free agents is a bad idea. Discussing the Angels in the '82 *Abstract*, Bill wrote, "It is so marvelously typical of the organization that having failed to build a winner by the process of free agency they blamed the process of free agency. It's just like somebody going out and making a bunch of stupid trades and then con-cluding from that experience that one cannot build a winner by trading. It is much easier to blame the process than it is to admit to yourself that you have scarcely a clue about what it is that you are trying to do."

The central point—that no one player carries a team, no matter how much it might *look* that way—was made in the *Abstract* recap of the '85 playoffs, in which Bill wrote that George Brett "turned in one of the most brilliant individual performances in the annals of sport" in Game Three versus Toronto, but, without key plays made by other players, "the Royals could very easily have lost that game."

> I think that just shows how false, how truly silly, the idea is that one player "carries" a team, or that one player turns a team around, or that one player is, really, anything except one player. The man put on a one-game show that nobody could sustain, nobody could match, even for a period of two or three games— and yet without the key contributions of five other players, his team would have lost that one game.

Pitchers' Effects on Attendance

One factor cited in free agent signings is that a superstar will increase attendance. The '77 *Abstract* addressed the subject of pitchers as attendance draws. Bill wrote, "This bit of research was triggered by a surprising remark I read from a NY sportswriter, who wrote that Shea Stadium attendance shows no marked increase when Tom Seaver pitches." Bill found that in most cases there was "very little evidence that a good pitcher will draw a good crowd." Seaver, as it happens, *did* outdraw his fellow Mets by about 4,000 per start in 1976. Steve Carl-ton, though, was Philadelphia's fourth-highest draw despite an NL-leading winning percentage (20–7). American League strikeout leader Nolan Ryan was only the fourth-best draw for California, despite a reputation as a crowd magnet.

Bill wrote in the '78 *Abstract* that the 1977 stats showed the same trend, and that if you took the average of all the twenty-game winners, "I doubt that they would beat the average of their teams by 500 a start." That said, he concluded, "I still get the feeling, as I compile these, that the pitcher does play a significant role in boosting attendance." This was due to the fact that "the identity of the pitcher is a *relatively* small determinant of the size of the crowd," compared to such factors as the opponent, day of the week, weather, and time of the season. Thus, an entire season's worth of extra fans for a star pitcher can be "hidden" by one start in cold weather versus a second-division team on a Tuesday, for example. Also, a star pitcher pitches in turn, under all conditions, but a spot starter may make a disproportionate number of starts in double-headers, which are high-attendance games regardless of who pitches.

"Thus," Bill wrote, "we come back to the question, what does a big name pitcher add to the attendance? And I don't know. I started by saying that nobody has ever proved that he means anything, except in a few cases, and I'll stick by that. But he probably does mean something—a thousand a start, perhaps, or half that, but it adds up." Of course, attendance levels have risen since the late seventies, and so have salaries.

Power/Speed Number

A combination of home runs and stolen bases into one number, such that a player who steals thirty bases and hits thirty home runs will have a P/S score of 30.0. Bill called it a freak-show stat, having little analytical value. The formula is 2(HR × SB) / HR + SB. The trick is, you have to do both things well. A player who hits fifty homers and steals ten bases will come out barely half as well as a player who goes 30/30.

Pythagorean Theory

Named for the formula's resemblance to the famous theorem. The ratio between a team's wins and losses will be similar to the relationship between the square of their runs scored and the square of their runs allowed.

The Johnson Effect

Teams that exceed their Pythagorean projection for wins in one season tend to relapse in the next.

Isolated Power

Isolated Power is simply slugging percentage minus batting average.

Slugging percentage is a very meaningful statistic, but it isn't a clear measure of power, because it includes singles. You have to adjust for batting average. Bases per hit isn't reliable either, because a Dave Kingman may come out on top of a Mike Schmidt.

The Computer Is Nothing. . . .

At his introductory New York Mets press conference, Pedro Martinez offered his interpretation of Mets GM Omar Minaya's reasoning, saying, "In my country, they have fighting cocks, and people bet a lot of money on them. What people look at is the heart, the look in the eyes. That's all it takes to bet a lot of money." Pedro further outlined his education platform by referring to Sox management as "computer geeks."

That brought to mind Bill's essay on computers, from the A's comments of the '84 *Abstract*:

> The main thing that you are struck with in the process of learning about a computer is how totally, incredibly stupid it is. The machine simulates intelligence so well that when you accidentally slip through a crack in its simulations and fall to the floor of its true intelligence, you are awed by the depth of the fall. You give it a series of a hundred or a thousand sensible commands, and it executes each of them in turn, and then you press a wrong

key and accidentally give it a command which goes counter to everything that you have been trying to do, and it will execute that command in a millisecond, just as if you had accidentally hit the wrong button on your vacuum cleaner at the end of your cleaning, and it had instantly and to your great surprise sprayed the dirt that you had collected back into the room. And you feel like, "Jeez, machine, you ought to know I didn't mean that. What do you think I've been doing here for the last hour?" And then you realize that that machine has not the foggiest notion of what you are trying to do, any more than your vacuum cleaner does.

The machine, you see, is nothing; it is utterly, truly, totally nothing. And all of the fascination and the speculation about the computer, about "what *it* is going to do" and "how *it* will change things" in baseball and in other areas is completely misguided, because *it* is not going to do anything and *it* is not going to change anything.

We are going to do things with the computer. *You and I* are going to change the world, and we're going to change baseball, and we're going to use the computer to do it. Machines have no capabilities on their own. Your car cannot drive to Cleveland. What machines do is extend *our* capabilities. . . .

I gather, frankly, that some of baseball's computer people are world-class oysters, dogmatic fellows who think they know more about baseball than anybody else on the planet, and consequently have no intention of listening to anyone. The concern that has been expressed to me is that some of these people may be doing us more harm than good.

If that's true, it's unfortunate. But I'm not all that concerned, and let me explain why. There is, you see, no such thing as "computer knowledge" or "computer information" or "computer data." Within a few years, everyone will understand that. The essential characteristics of information are that it is true or it is false, it is significant or it is trivial, it is relevant or it is irrelevant. In the early days of the automobile, people would say that they were going to take an "automobile trip." That lasted about ten years; after that, people went back to taking trips as they had before. They were vacation trips, or they were business trips, or they were trips on personal matters, or they were trips to the coast or they were trips to the mountains. After the novelty wore off people still traveled in automobiles, but they ceased to identify the trip with the machine and returned to identify it with its purpose. People stopped driving to Cleveland just to have someplace to drive. That's what we're going through now with the computer; twenty years from now, the term "computer information" will sound quaint and silly. . . .

I am engaged in a search for understanding. That is my profession. It has nothing to do with computers. Computers are going to have an impact on my life that is similar to the impact that the coming of the automobile age must have had on the professional traveler or adventurer. The car made it easier to get from place to place; the computer will make it easier to deal with information. But knowing how to drive an automobile does not make you an adventurer, and knowing how to run a computer does not make you an analytical student of the game.

Fielding

The summer he was fifteen, Bill was listening to a Cardinals game on the radio. Back then, KMOX had a network of affiliates broadcasting St. Louis games all over the Midwest. The announcer asserted that a part-time first baseman saved his team a hit a game with his glove. Bill reasoned that if a player was saving his team one hit per game on defense, it would have the same value as if he got an extra hit per game. He calculated the outcome of an extra hit per game added to the player's batting average, which showed him as equal to an average-fielding first baseman with a .430 average. The fired-up teen sat down to write a letter to the *Sporting News*. "I got carried away," he says, "showing that this player could not possibly have been saving one hit per game for his team—either that or his team was insane for not playing him." The letter ran for several pages, but he realized no one would pay attention to it, so he put it away and never did anything with it.

A similar idea came up in a different form in the '83 *Abstract* in response to an argument for Ozzie Smith as NL MVP, an argument with a "pristine logical clarity, unpolluted by evidence." The theory Bill blanched at was: Ozzie saved the Cardinals a hundred runs with his defense.

> If Ozzie saved the Cardinals 100 runs, 100 runs as opposed to what? As opposed to not having a shortstop? Then 100 runs seems reasonable; there'd be an awful lot of balls go rolling through that hole if there wasn't anybody there. A hundred runs as opposed to me playing shortstop? Hey, a hundred is conservative. By the time I got through kicking the ball around, it'd be 300.
>
> But with saying that Ozzie is a hundred runs better than another shortstop . . . well, you're going to have real trouble there. The St. Louis Cardinals allowed 609 runs in 1982, which was the lowest total in the National League. If you say that Ozzie was 100 runs better than an average shortstop, then you are saying that the Cardinals would have allowed 100 runs more than they did had they had an average shortstop.

Bill explained that St. Louis as a team was fifty-three runs better than the league average, so the other Cardinals fielders would have had to be minus forty-seven. He went on to show that while one NL team had, in fact, allowed one hundred more runs than the Cardinals, and that team had a bad shortstop, "you still had to conclude that the Cardinals' edge was created not by one advantage, but by many." Bill calculated that Ozzie saved the Cards in the neighborhood of thirty-five runs.

In his March 1976 *Baseball Digest* article "Big League Fielding Statistics *Do* Make Sense!" Bill noted that Bobby Grich had made 199 more plays at second base than Sandy Alomar. Grich's range more than offset

Alomar's higher fielding percentage. The difference in total chances amounted to at least a hundred *hits* saved, so that "a player's performance in the field is in some cases far more important than his hitting."

The gut sense of that importance might be distorted into "Ozzie Smith saved his team a hundred runs." The fuzzy thinking that swaps the reality of a hundred *hits* for the myth of a hundred *runs* might also misinterpret Bill's dismissal of the Ozzie-for-MVP argument as a belief that defense isn't important.*

On the general question of choosing between defense and offense, Bill says, "I don't believe in trying to sort those things by 'we prefer defense' or 'we prefer hitting.' To me, it's a question of 'how much defense?' and 'how much hitting?' A player can't be substandard in either area." So the question isn't one of choosing this over that, but of the relationship of considerations in a specific situation. The crux of the question is that fielding statistics are notoriously unreliable.

New metrics bump against old standbys such as fielding percentage. One is zone rating, which is the percentage of balls fielded by a player in his typical defensive area, as measured by STATS Inc. Bill says, "Zone rating was created by John Dewan, who is a good friend of mine, but when it was originally created he made a series of what seem to me like obvious mistakes, and it was years before he got around to correcting them. John and I used to have huge arguments about zone rating once every two years."

Some sabermetricians calculate fielding as little as 5 or 10 percent of the game, but Bill doesn't agree. "Fielding is certainly more than 10 percent of run prevention," he says, "substantially more. But other people's ideas on this are all over the map."

Fielding is *very* difficult to measure objectively. "Hitting is solid, pitching is liquid, defense is gaseous," Bill says.

"Hitting is firm, well-defined, easy to measure.

*Some people think of Smith as the prototype of a player who offered scant offense but great glove work. Bill swam against the mainstream in harking the Wizard's assets: "a fine percentage base stealer, a good ability to get on base, and the greatest defensive shortstop in the history of the game."

"Pitching is liquid . . . it assumes the shape of whatever form it is poured into. A 15–10 pitcher with a 3.80 ERA on one team is 10–15 with a 5.00 ERA on another team.

"Defense is gaseous. It is damned hard to capture, formless, hard to see."

Season-to-season one-player variations in fielding are also largely underrecognized. Bill says, "I would guess that fielding is more variable, more unpredictable, than hitting. People think of fielding as a constant because, for good reasons, they don't trust fielding stats, and don't monitor them from day to day. Since fielding stats are kind of a cipher, we're not always aware of changes in fielding performance, when, if a player's batting average dropped thirty points, we would certainly be aware of that."

Asked if most analysts overvalue fielding or undervalue it, Bill answers, "The value of defense is a complicated issue on its own terms. Introducing a side issue of 'what most people think it is,' to me, is just a distraction. The distraction becomes relevant when you start looking seriously at who is available, for this reason: Whatever other people undervalue will therefore be under-priced, and can be purchased cheaply."

However you measure fielding, when it comes to errors, people tend to overreact. The reality is that baseball games contain myriad failures: bad pitches and swings at bad pitches, balls the fielder never came close to catching because he got a bad jump on the ball or was in a poor position to begin with.

In the late seventies Bill wrote:

What is an error? It is, without exception, the only major statistic in sports which is a record of what an observer thinks *should have been accomplished.* It's a moral judgment, really, in the peculiar quasi-morality of the locker room.

The concept of fielding chances, meaning plays actually made plus errors, assumes that one "has a play" on a hit baseball in the same way that one "has an opportunity" at the plate. This, of course, is not true. One "has a play" on a baseball field whenever one has the anticipation, the reflexes, and the speed to get to where the play is. If one doesn't have the, in short, talent, to get to the play, then one doesn't have a play and can't be charged with an error. The official scorer doesn't charge anybody with a lack of talent.

Thanks!

Seth Ditchik, Chris Haven, Rachel McCarthy James, Kit Nylen, Clara Platter, Joe Posnanski, Jay Rosen, James Tetreault, and Richard Todd made major contributions to this book.

Nell Boeschenstein was a great friend and advisor.

Dan Simmons helped me almost survive strange times. I owe Patrick Fusco for just about everything.

Gregg Lindskog says, "Don't blame me. I voted for Kodos!"

Jim Baker, Joyce Cochren, Randy Hendricks, Mike Kopf, Matthew Namee, John Sickels, Carol Wells, Mike White, and Fred Zweifel were generous with time and stories.

Bill, Susie, Isaac, and Reuben . . . Now I know why they're called kissing fish.

Charlie Conrad was invaluable; Alison Presley, irreplaceable.

David McCormick is a terrific agent.

Tricia Wygal and Sean Bell-Thomson were there at the beginning.

Josh Cohen got me back on track.

Dan Okrent gave a crucial boost and good Scotch.

Rob Neyer has been a friend to both manuscript and writer.

Bob Nylen is an inspiration and a gentleman.

Cassie Gray was loving under impossible circumstances.

Leota and Richard Gray were supportive, as always.

Is that all there is?

About the Author

Scott Gray is the author of a series of Street & Smith's sports annuals. He lives in Princeton, New Jersey.